P9-EDN-359

BISON
BOOKS

WILD IDEA

Buffalo and Family in a Difficult Land

DAN O'BRIEN

University of Nebraska Press | Lincoln and London

Publication of this volume was assisted
by a grant from the Friends of the
University of Nebraska Press

♾

Library of Congress Cataloging-
in-Publication Data

O'Brien, Dan, 1947–
Wild idea: buffalo and family in a
difficult land / Dan O' Brien.
pages cm

ISBN 978-0-8032-5096-3 (cloth: alk. paper)
ISBN 978-0-8032-8638-8 (epub)
ISBN 978-0-8032-8637-5 (mobi)
ISBN 978-0-8032-8638-2 (pdf).
1. O'Brien, Dan, 1947–. 2. Ranchers—
South Dakota—Biography. 3. Bison
farming—South Dakota—Broken Heart
Ranch. 4. Ranch life—South Dakota—
Broken Heart Ranch. I. Title.

SF.A450273 2014 636'.01092—dc23
[B] 2014007956

Set in Lyon by Renni Johnson.
Designed by N. Putens.

WILD IDEA

Part One

One

SOME SUMMER NIGHTS, WHEN I STEP OUT ONTO MY RANCH house porch, I am met by the immense, roiling waves of color from the northern lights. In other seasons I find coiled rattlesnakes or perhaps a wind so cold that skin will freeze in minutes.

By any economic ciphering, choosing the Great Plains for my home has caused me to slip behind my contemporaries who chose New England, or California, or the hills of Georgia. Still, like loving a drunk, I had little choice. For over forty years the prairies have been my home and I've shared them willingly with all of the species that call them home. It took many years for me to understand that this place is more than a chaotic jumble of species clawing at each other to assert themselves. It is a complex web of life clawing to keep its balance. I love the wind that stokes me as I sit on my front porch, even when it is too cold to endure. It is the wheezing breath of a single, huge, living thing, and I am a part of it.

Between 1972 and 1990 I worked as a biologist, first for the State of South Dakota and then for the Peregrine Fund, based at Cornell University's famous Ornithology Laboratory. I had no formal training in biology so my duties were really the work of a technician, always seasonal, and always in the mountains and plains of the Intermountain West. The focus was on helping to reestablish the endangered peregrine falcon to the cliffs along the Rocky Mountain Front, but my mind always wandered to the entire ecosystem that the birds depended upon—the rolling, untold miles of grass that we call the Great Plains.

The falcons were raised from captive parents, first at Ithaca, New York, then at Fort Collins, Colorado, and finally at Boise, Idaho. My colleagues in the labs hatched the chicks and I picked them up at about one month of age. My job was to get the chicks to one of several dozen release sites then do my best to see that they learned to fly and hunt for themselves. It was wonderful work, freewheeling and physically challenging. I traveled by pickup, horseback, helicopter, and on foot to a different site every day. Almost everyone who helped in the effort to reestablish peregrine falcons was young, but it was more than youthful exuberance that kept us going. We were driven by the conviction that we were doing something of real value. As early soldiers in the environmental struggle that is still searching for definition we sensed that our lives were under siege by immense forces beyond our control.

DDT, used aggressively for decades by agribusiness, is a powerful insecticide that increased crop yields around the world. But it was clear to most of us that the benefits were grossly outweighed by the harm. The toxic chemical quickly spread into the entire food chain and did damage to all sorts of species, from soil microbes to human beings. In 1972 DDT was banned from use in the United States. By then it had nearly wiped out many bird species at the top of the food chain where the poison accumulated. The peregrine falcon, a pinnacle species, was decimated by DDT because it fouled up the falcon's reproductive system. The first people to notice and respond were a small group of falconers who hunted with and kept peregrines in a quasi-captive state. Those of us with an acute interest quickly became involved. In the end it was a massive effort by thousands of people that brought the peregrine back from the brink of extinction.

The peregrine falcon was placed on the endangered species list in 1970 and it stayed there until several hundred nesting pairs had returned to their old haunts. One day in the fall of 1994 I saw four peregrine falcons in one afternoon on the plains east of Colorado Springs, Colorado. I had never seen peregrines in that area before. I was on my way back to my little ranch on the northern edge of South Dakota's Black Hills after a summer of releasing peregrines.

Since April I'd been going strong, and because I was anxious to get home, I wasn't even looking for peregrine falcons. But that day they seemed to be everywhere. During my entire life I had sighted only a few wild peregrine falcons and that afternoon I stumbled across four. It was a sign, and by the time I got home I had made up my mind that my work with the peregrine was finished.

When I got back to my ranch, I sat on my front porch and looked southeast toward where Bear Butte rose up from the prairie floor like a sentinel guarding the Black Hills. The butte looked lonely and the sight of it made me wonder what I would do with my life from that day forward. It would be another five years before the wheels of the U.S. Fish and Wildlife Service worked through the red tape to remove the peregrine falcon from the endangered species list, but it was already clear that the peregrines living on the eastern shoulder of the Rocky Mountains would be with us for at least a few more generations. The immediate crisis had passed.

The sun was going down and putting on a show for anyone who would take the time to watch. The colors in the autumn grasses pulsed with the breeze and the individual blades cast shadows on each other. As the grasses waved, the colors moved from gold to red, and I thought about all the life that depended on that mosaic. I thought about the mammals, from rodents to deer and antelope. I turned my best ear to the breeze and imagined that I could hear the movement of the billions of insects that supplied the baseline protein for the ground nesting birds for which the prairies are famous. The falcons were again preying on those birds and, at least for awhile, all those wheels would continue to turn.

Many other species are endangered or threatened and it occurred to me that I could become involved with protecting the black-footed ferrets, the eagle, swift fox, or any number of insects or grasses. But over the preceding eighteen years I had learned that concentrating on a single species was only treating the symptom of a problem. A compromised ecosystem is almost always the cause of distress for any species. I sat on my porch contemplating the rest of my life and I recalled much of what I had seen while traveling back and forth across the High Plains. Blowing topsoil, stinking feedlots, subsidized crops irrigated with precious water, and all the ancient, nonhuman inhabitants forced to eek out a living on the edges. The stars came up and, because it was autumn, Orion rose in the gap between Bear Butte and the Black Hills. It was one of those magical nights when time seems to slow to the speed of moving constellations.

My thoughts came to buffalo. They have long been an icon of this waning wilderness. During the last half of the nineteenth century, in one of the great human disgraces of all time, we slaughtered all but perhaps a thousand of the world's buffalo—for sport, for a few body parts, and to help in the decimation of the Natives who relied on them. We nearly lost a unique species that thrived only in the center of the North American continent. I thought hard about that as a million stars moved across the sky in front of me. It made me sick to think of the injustice, and before Orion's sword had swiveled to point at Harney Peak, I knew that my future would involve at least an attempt to put things right on the Great Plains and buffalo would be a part of that attempt.

In the nearly twenty years since that decision I have done my best to heal the portion of northern grasslands for which I am most responsible. Many mistakes were made as the result of my own failings, but also because the science of grassland protection and restoration is not well understood, because the vagrancies of climate and weather are not calibrated to match the span of a human life, and because resources on the Great Plains have always been sparse. I got off to a poor start by planting trees and hybrid grasses that were supposed to grow in a dry, harsh land. I signed up for government programs that encouraged such practices. But I should have realized that trees do not belong on the plains. If they could survive on their own they would have been here from the beginning. Trees need constant care, and the ones I planted dwindled and died. The hybrid grasses I planted had been bred to grow in almost any climate, but they had no evolutionary connection to the mammals and birds of the Great Plains and they too didn't survive. Native birds and animals need the native plants they evolved with—the nutritious, hardy, deep-rooted perennials that have been nearly extirpated over the last century.

My effort began with twelve orphan buffalo, which in a few years built to a herd of fifty animals on my little ranch of twelve hundred acres. The beleaguered grasses responded favorably to the massaging of buffalo hooves and everything on the ranch, from the smallest sedges to the people, seemed to strengthen. In the early years of the new century, I lived with my partner, Jill, her daughter, Jilian, and my oldest friend, Erney. We called the place the Broken Heart Ranch—named for the disused cattle brand, a number 3 laid on its face with a V underneath. Jill has always been a chef and restaurateur. Back then she owned the best white tablecloth restaurant within four hundred miles of Rapid City, South Dakota. Erney and I had been pals since 1970. We met when I was a graduate student in literature at the University of South Dakota and Erney worked for the State Highway Department.

Erney and I had come together at a meeting of falconers and instantly became fast friends. I didn't know why he took to me, but I was fascinated by the fact that this self-taught, simple man knew the Latin names for all the birds of prey, the common orchids, many species of cacti, and lots of bromeliads. I didn't even know what a bromeliad was and I will always remember how he explained it to me. We had spent the entire day watching our falcons chase rabbits and pheasants through the woodlots and cornfields of a glorious South Dakota autumn. As the sun slipped to the western horizon we took a few minutes to sit beside a pond and shoot enough migrating mourning doves to make a dinner. Erney has always been materially poor, and since we met he has owned only one fine thing. He earned a meager $285 per month but somehow managed to save up $4,000 to buy a Browning Exhibition Grade superimposed shotgun, complete with gold inlays. The gun came with a laminated wallet-sized certificate of ownership, with the serial number embossed along the bottom. He stroked the gun as if it was a prized show dog. "She's finer than frog hair," Erney said with a wiggle of his wooly eyebrows.

Erney has never been an agile or coordinated man, but he shot the shotgun with a fluid grace that somehow fit the arch of the migrating doves. I marveled at the confidence of his swing and the ease of his follow-through. Erney knew the doves would come from their feeding field to their evening watering hole, so he was careful to position me in the very best place for shooting. But even with the best angle, my score paled in comparison to his. He had a sixth sense for the twists and turns of the dove's flight.

Not only did Erney shoot more doves than I did, he cleaned two doves to my one. Then he cooked them with a couple dozen baby potatoes, a handful of diced carrots and celery, and generous pinches of salt and pepper. I had never seen a Dutch oven used the way they were meant to be used and was mesmerized beside the simmering pot buried in a pile of ruby-red corncob coals. The smell of baking dove breasts in that still evening air mingled with Erney's gentle tutorial. "A bromeliad is a sort of plant that doesn't need to have its roots in dirt. Don't need much moisture." He stirred the coals on the Dutch oven lid, looked up at me, smiled, and again wiggled his shaggy eyebrows. The smell of the doves and the idea of bromeliads were exciting him. "There are hundreds of species. Some of 'em have great flowers—related to the succulents, grow up in the crotches of tropical trees."

I was young and dumb and thought he might be bullshitting me. He nodded his head and smiled again through his unmanicured beard. "You know, those furry looking, orchidy flowers up in the trees in the Tarzan movies." I nodded my head to keep him talking. "Suck water right out of the air. Trap it up there in those trees when it rains, hang on to all sorts of stuff. Trees, telephone wires, Aztec and Mayan ruins. Some of them look a little like weaverbird nests. Cool flowers."

"You've seen these things?"

"Mostly pictures. Sometimes in the flower shops. Don't have any in South Dakota."

"You ever been out of South Dakota?"

"Couple times. Nebraska to work. Went elk hunting in Wyoming, but didn't have the money for a license, so I was the camp cook."

He lifted the lid of the Dutch oven with a stick and sniffed like a bear. "No bromeliads in Wyoming either." He stirred the pot with the same stick. "Grab you a bunch of these Dan'l, they're about as good as it gets. Finest kind."

I was in my midtwenties, Erney in his thirties. I had begun my quest to own a ranch by buying a dilapidated farmhouse on twenty-six acres on a contract for deed. The total price was seventy-two hundred dollars with nothing down and payments of a hundred dollars a month. Erney and I ran an illegal wire from a power pole and a water line from a defunct cistern to the house. We damned near froze to death that first winter, but we stuck it out in that drafty house, along with a jolly band of bird dogs and falcons. When I got my degree I traded up to a 320-acre place on the edge of the Black Hills. That ranch was a move three hundred miles west, where the prairie was still intact. I moved because I thought I might be better able to write.

Erney was a confirmed bachelor who everyone loved despite his questionable personal hygiene and iconoclastic ways. He reminded me of Henry David Thoreau, but a laconic version with the bark still on. To my knowledge he never had a girlfriend, though women have always enjoyed his company. Just before my move to the Black Hills, Erney quit the State Highway Department when they stopped giving him time off in lieu of overtime pay. He went to work for a rancher—the same rancher who had given me summer jobs during graduate school—who would allow him time to fly his falcon and read his books. He had been slightly crippled as a teenager, the result of two construction trucks coming together and breaking his femur, so I wondered how he would do as a ranch hand.

He was never one to be careful and was notorious for disconnecting all the "bullshit safety features" of newfangled equipment. He worked for that rancher for only a couple of years before his gloved thumb got twisted off in the power takeoff of a tractor. The four months of rehabilitation didn't teach him much. When he returned to work at the same ranch, he went right back to disassembling safety equipment.

Though he has never been one to take care of himself, he has always taken care of the people he likes and every animal that enters his sphere. His mind was always full of wisdom about Great Plains wild animals, birds, weather, livestock, and vegetation. He was the product of a life close to the Dakota elements and he had a knack for observation. He spent long nights reading natural histories in poor light as he had smoked unfiltered Camel cigarettes and butted them out by the hundreds into empty coke bottles. He had come up hard, in a house with no indoor plumbing, no television, and no chance for education beyond high school. He was in his early forties when he called me and said the rancher we had worked for was filing for bankruptcy and that he was out of work. I told him that I had plenty of work and a place for him to live, but the farm crisis of the 1980s had caught me too. There wasn't any money to pay him, but that didn't matter to Erney. He showed up with a worn-out Luv truck, four cardboard boxes full of books, a battered trunk of clothes, and thirty dollars in his pocket. The prized shotgun was gone, sold off when the checks from the rancher began to bounce. I only asked him about the shotgun once. I could see it was painful.

I was having trouble scraping up my mortgage payment, so after my summer stints working for South Dakota Game and Fish, I decided to find a winter construction job. Erney moved in to watch the place in 1986 and he has been with me ever since. He got to the ranch just days before I left for California in search of work, where construction was supposed to be going strong. The snow had already begun to gather in the pasture draws and it was cold. We sat in front of the wood burner and talked.

It was a long time before we had buffalo, but I had sold the few beef cows that I'd been raising to help with the land payment. I told Erney we'd find a way to get some more when I got back in the spring. He nodded as he stared into the fire. He knew I was worried about leaving him alone at the end of a two-mile-long driveway. "Don't worry about me," he said. "Even if I drop dead, there's nothing living out here that can eat me."

"That's because nothing but you is dumb enough to stay here in the winter." We looked out the window to where the moon had turned the snow iridescent. Erney shook his head. "Kinda reminds a guy of Doctor Zhivago, without the beautiful women in the fur coats."

He ate mostly rabbits that first winter. He snowshoed after them with a beat-up twenty-two caliber rifle.

It turned out that the construction boom in California had been exaggerated. I ended up in the central valley—Fresno—living with a friend. I scoured the newspaper for work and spread resumes all over town. Nobody called back, so I kept going to construction company offices and filling out applications.

I was down to the last few construction companies in the area and was sitting at a small desk, filling out a standard form in front of a thoroughly disinterested secretary, when a young guy in clean work clothes walked past. He didn't look like any construction boss I knew. He wore soft leather pull-on shoes, his hair was curled at his temples, and he sported a couple rings on each hand. He was heading for his office but he stopped in front of the little desk and glanced at my application. He pointed to the application. "You really from South Dakota?"

I nodded. "Yep."

He reached out and, with one finger, turned the paper so he could read more. "You worked on a ranch."

"Yep."

Then he looked up and appraised my eyes. "You got a driver's license?"

"A driver's license?"

"Yeah, a fricken driver's license."

"I got a license."

He turned on his heels and continued the march to his office. But he spoke over his shoulder. "Can you get to work at 6:30 in the morning?"

"Yep."

"Be here tomorrow."

Over the next few months I got to know the boss of A&B

Construction. His name was Greg and it turned out that the company had a complicated business structure. His brother-in-law, Al, and his sister, Beatrice, owned the company. Greg and Beatrice were Latino so A&B Construction qualified as a minority-owned business. Their bread and butter was some sort of affirmative action program that identified poor families and subsidized the cost of making their houses and apartments more energy efficient. Apparently Al had had some trouble with his contractor's license so he could not work as an owner of the company. Greg's license was good, so he and his sister were the owners of record. Al masqueraded as a foreman of one of the crews, though he, too, wore several rings and was in on all the business decisions.

I had never worked in California construction so I had no idea that licenses were such a problem. Not only were contractor licenses a major consideration, but so were driver's licenses. I figured that out the first day when I showed up for the job. Only a couple guys on our crew had driver's licenses. Most of them had been taken away for felonious activity. We barely had enough drivers to get the crew from one job to the next. Nobody was getting paid much and, from most paychecks, wages were garnished for unpaid fines or child support. But, somehow, these guys had money for cigarettes, beer, and a little cocaine. There were about eight guys on my crew and at least three languages were spoken regularly. We usually had a guy that could communicate with the poor people whose home addresses were printed out on a sheet from the local HUD office. I am not bragging when I say that I got a raise after my first week of work.

In fact, on the second Friday after work, I was called into Greg's office. It had been a good, and I assumed profitable, week. The four crews had upgraded fifty-three low income homes. I had no idea what each home cost the government to upgrade—all we did was caulk the doors and windows, replace broken glass, wrap the water heater with an insulated plastic blanket, change the showerhead to a low-flow model, and blow insulation into the walls and the attic. It didn't cost Greg and Al much and, by the looks of the cars they drove, they were making a lot of money. Whatever the numbers were, after my second week of employment the brothers-in-law were happy. They were "warming up for the weekend" by sniffing on a plastic device they called a bullet. When they tossed it to me, I had no idea how to operate it.

"You're doing good," Al said. He gently took the bullet from my hand and showed me how it worked. "We're going to give you a raise."

"You gave me one last week."

"This is a promotion. We want you to be a foreman for crew three."

"A foreman."

"Yeah, you talk to the people and make sure everything gets done." Greg was smiling broadly and talking fast. "Little different skill set. Little schmoozing. You're the inside guy. More money."

This was a different kind of construction company than I was used to. It all made me a little uncomfortable, but, as far as the business went, I didn't think that they were doing anything illegal. They loved Ronald Reagan and made fun of their employees behind their backs. Still, I was glad to have the job. The pay was pretty good and because I wasn't paying child support or buying copious amounts of booze and cocaine, I was putting money away.

When I got the promotion to "inside man," I began to relish the work. My job was to talk to the people and get them to understand what we were doing. I was usually armed with papers signed by their landlords, who were taking advantage of a government program that improved their property and didn't cost them anything. I didn't speak Spanish, Vietnamese, Chinese, or Arabic, but somehow they understood that we were there to make their homes warmer and save them money on the gas and electric bills. I was never denied entrance.

Once inside, my job was to check for broken glass, adjust the outside doors so they shut tight, wrap the hot water heater, and change the showerhead. I walked through all the rooms of hundreds of poor, urban people and the things I found behind those doors fascinated me. One of the first times I stepped into a kitchen with live pigeons tied to the legs of the kitchen table I tried not to notice. Maybe they were pets. None of my business. But finally I asked one of the guys on my crew. He was a tall, quiet, black guy named Buzz. "What's with the pigeons?" I asked.

"Pigeons?" Buzz had a way of expressing himself by the way he twisted his face and tilted his head.

"Yeah, tied to the table legs."

"Oh. The Slopes do that," he said. "They catch them off the buildings. Take'm home and eat'm."

I was a little dumbfounded. "So, why don't they dress them out like a chicken?"

Buzz looked at me like I was the stupidest person he'd ever met. "No refrigerator," he said. He shook his head. "Pigeon meat spoils, Einstein."

I never experienced a smell that I could identify as spoiled pigeon meat, but I came across some unusual smells in those kitchens and bathrooms. Mostly it was the aroma of herbs and spices that I had never experienced before. A lot of the people were Mexican, some were Indian or Pakistani. There were a lot of Vietnamese, Hmong, and African Americans. Behind every door you encountered different smells. I got used to the garlic, coriander, cardamom, and peppers. The simmering kettles on the stoves could be menudo, pork rinds, curry. In a lot of cases the houses smelled exotic and enticing. But, in far too many, the predominant smell just struck me as urban and very poor. I never came to tolerate the smell of pigeons on the kitchen floor or the fetid smell of carp in the bathtub as I changed the seldom-used showerhead. I came to loathe the smell of cigarette smoke, old clothes, and unflushed toilets.

Late that winter I complained about those smells to Greg and Al. They laughed. Al said that was the smell of money, and I was instantly reminded that an owner of a cattle feedlot had once told me the same thing. After that, my days in the central valley of California were numbered. I put in my time, waiting for my spring falcon job to start, but my mind was on the ranch in South Dakota—where the poverty had a different smell. I dreamed of places where the resources were limited but washed with a clean wind.

It was a month later that my crew and I were working on the home of a pretty, young black girl with three little kids who all followed me from room to cluttered room. I was letting the little boy handle the tools from my toolbelt when I heard Greg's and Al's voices outside, asking Buzz where I was. I met them at the door and they looked worried. "Anybody come around here today?"

"What do you mean?" I looked over their shoulders and saw that they were driving Al's Mercedes.

"Just some creep looking for us."

"No creeps today, so far."

They looked at each other just as we heard the sound of a diesel pickup truck coming from around the corner. They looked toward the truck noise, which made me look that way too. A bright white City of Fresno truck came slowly around the corner. When I looked back, Greg and Al were gone and I was left on the front step to face the building inspector. Suddenly my crew was gone too. I was trapped. The only guy for miles wearing a toolbelt.

The inspector got out of his truck slowly. He put on his white hard hat and took his clipboard off the dashboard of his truck. He took his time walking up the sidewalk and I noticed Greg and Al, two front yards away, peeking over a hedge like a couple of prairie dogs.

I had no trouble playing dumb. The inspector was looking for Greg and Al. He wanted to check things like building permits and contractor's licenses. By the way my crew had disappeared, he might have been curious about green cards and outstanding warrants, too. I stood there and lied like a bed-wetter. "Greg and Al? Haven't seen them." "Mercedes? Must belong to the guy that lives here." I pointed as convincingly as possible into the low-income rented home and shrugged. "I get dispatched from the office." I gave him the telephone number of the bored secretary. He nodded his head with contempt but didn't bother to write down the number. He asked another dozen questions and I went on shrugging. Finally, he gave me his card.

"If you see Greg and Al, have them call me."

I nodded and thought that would be the end of it. But the inspector had one more thing to say. "They're making a shit pot of money," he said and waved his hand at the house, "but this ain't right."

A week later I was in my beat-up pickup truck on my way back to South Dakota. It would be good to get back to the ranch, good to see how Erney was doing. I'd had my fill of the Central Valley of California. I had enough money saved up to make the yearly mortgage payment on the ranch, even though as soon as I made it I would have to start worrying about how I was going to make the next one. But it didn't bother me that, after a winter of work, I was still on the same treadmill. Cruising east on Interstate 80, I thought about Greg and Al hiding behind that hedge, dressed in clean clothes, their hands smooth and decorated with rings, and I wondered what it would be like to operate like that. I started thinking that there must be a gene for business that I just didn't possess.

I quit thinking about my missing gene and drove for a hundred and fifty miles with an empty mind. But, as the mountains changed to grasslands—as the sagebrush and grama grass turned to wheatgrass and green needle grass—the thought of giant herds of buffalo entered my head. That trip back from California took place many years before I made the decision to convert the Broken Heart Ranch into a buffalo ranch, but even then, as I entered their ancient range, I felt their absence.

Killing 99.99 percent of all the buffalo in the world seems like it would have been a big job. You would think that nineteenth-century technology would have been hard pressed to accomplish it in a relatively short period. But it didn't take much time and it didn't cost much money. In purely economic terms I suppose that the horrific buffalo slaughter paid for itself. Even then, before I was seriously considering doing it, I knew that bringing back even a small percentage would cost a whole lot more than it cost to get rid of them all.

Years ago someone sent Jill and me a great cartoon. It was a sketch of a buffalo standing on an endless prairie, holding a cell phone to its ear. There was no indication who the buffalo was talking to, but I like to think that all of American was listening. "I love the convenience," the buffalo was saying, "but the roaming charges are killing me." It costs a lot of money for a buffalo to roam freely, but it may cost us even more to *not* have them roam freely. If you ever see a herd of a few hundred head moving peacefully under a wild, western sky, you will never be the same. Back during the very early days of buffalo on the Broken Heart Ranch, I would often make my way out to where I could see them grazing. I would sit and watch them moving on the land until I had had enough soul-fuel to keep going. But nursing an appreciation for buffalo doesn't pay the bills, let alone the costs of restoration like the planting of native grasses or the resting of pastures needed to regain land health.

Jill and I were starved for cash, but we knew that simply selling our buffalo production would have made us undistinguishable from generations of livestock producers who had exploited the plains. I had seen the wild fear in the eyes of buffalo as they smell a slaughter plant for the first time. I had watched them standing in their own manure, being forced to eat subsidized grain products. Neither Jill nor I wanted anything to do with forcing buffalo through the cattle production model.

Because most buffalo producers come from cattle traditions, they instinctually do what they have done for generations. But buffalo are not cattle. They are evolutionary marvels that have existed for tens of thousands of years with no aid from humans. It is inhumane and wrongheaded to treat them as if they have been selected to endure the stresses of confinement. But it is not the death of buffalo that bothers me. Death is an unalterable fact for all of us. The only choice we have is how it comes.

When we began raising buffalo there was no commercial alternative to putting buffalo into feedlots, but buried in an obscure section of the USDA meat inspection act are a few sentences that allow for field harvest of animals under strict regulations. We knew then that among foodies and health food nuts there was a nascent market for grass-fed red meat—especially buffalo meat. But it was the obscure USDA regulation that opened the door to what would become Wild Idea Buffalo Company.

The Animal Industry Board of South Dakota inspects almost all the buffalo that are slaughtered in the state. The inspections are conducted under the same regulations as USDA rules, and when we called attention to the fact that field harvest was allowed, we were received with scrutiny but cooperation. Field harvest of buffalo had actually been allowed on a very limited basis for years. We would have to work under stringent operating procedures, but it was doable. We could haul the carcasses to a packing plant and have them cut, wrapped, and frozen for a reasonable charge.

So, after a few years of struggling to survive on a buffalo ranch, we stuck a toe into the ocean of commerce and arranged with South Dakota meat inspectors to harvest five prime two-year-old buffalo bulls in the pastures they had known for their entire lives. We found that they showed no perceivable signs of stress and we also discovered that companies like FedEx and UPS could ship the frozen meat to our small list of family and friends with only slightly more effort on our part. There was even less profit in raising and marketing our buffalo this way than there was in loading them into trucks and selling them to strangers, but our consciences were clear.

After cashing those first tiny checks and receiving those positive reviews of the meat, I felt something odd shift inside me. I knew that we were onto something—if we could bring some money back to the ranch, the birds, mammals, insects, and plants would all feel the benefit. But I was bothered by the nagging realization that the sale of a few buffalo bulls would not change much in the wider world. My idea for reinvesting for the benefit of a tiny ranch was much too modest. Deep down I knew that our ranch was meaningless within the scale of the Great Plains. If the entire ecosystem was going to feel the effects of reinvestment of buffalo profits, then buffalo were going to have to experience a meaningful increase in population. Even then I knew that they would have to pay their own way back. What we didn't realize was how high the price would be.

Two

THE FIRST TIME I MET JILL, SHE WAS WORKING THE FRONT end of her new restaurant, The American Pie Bistro. I'd been out of town for a few months and upon my return had heard that The American Pie was a cut above anything that Rapid City had ever experienced. I'd heard the food was great, but no one told me about Jill. She met me at the front door with a menu in her hand and a smile on her face. "Are you here to join Mr. Harlan?" she asked.

Bill Harlan was a reporter for the local newspaper. We'd been friends for decades and I was there to meet him for dinner. Jill gestured to the back of the restaurant and I saw Bill raise his hand to wave. I should have waved back but I was thunderstruck by Jill and stood transfixed by her green eyes and wispy blonde hair. "My, my, my. What do we have here?" I'm sure that I only thought that, but Jill swears I said it out loud.

We agree that I followed her closely to the table and Harlan stood up and greeted me. I had that rare but energized feeling that most of us get when we meet someone we know will play a role in the next act of our lives. Jill was being very nice to me; later she told me it was because she had me mixed up with another of Harlan's friends: the man that wrote restaurant reviews for the newspaper. She was only aiming for a good review in the newspaper.

It was a month later that I met Jilian, Jill's ten-year-old daughter. She sat in the back of the restaurant doing her homework and didn't bother to even look up when I said hello. I had been advised to take it slow with Jilian because, with a divorce brewing, she was having some trouble sorting out her feelings about her father, and, by association, men in general. I was determined to play it cool and give her all the time she wanted. For several weeks I watched her snub Jill's other suitors. She was polite with me and would occasionally offer a smile. But her eyes flashed like her mother's if someone got too close.

I watched her doing her homework and occasionally helping bus a table. I paid close attention to how she reacted to the customers, cooks, and waitresses. I learned that she liked to play basketball and softball. I overheard that she was a pretty good dribbler and a steady hitter. She got good grades. I watched the customers come and go. She liked it when the women would stop and talk to her. She was not as friendly to the men and sometimes she would roll her eyes at the things they said. I learned that she was more likely to argue with her mother if there was a man standing nearby. In public, I kept my distance from both of them.

During the first few months that I knew Jilian I had the idea that I would figure her out just by watching her. I might even have hoped to enlist her to help me get in good with her mother, who I was already desperately in love with. I knew that any relationship I had with Jill would be short-lived if Jilian was not on my side; I didn't want to blow it. So I engaged her only superficially and continued to watch.

As a life-long observer of wild things, I have learned that you have to look closely but never stare. You can remain visible but must blend in with your surroundings. That was my role with Jilian. I approached the situation as if she was a shy avocet standing at the edge of prairie pond, a young coyote that stayed close its den.

It was the middle of the summer before I was invited to a softball game. I was almost fifty years old and I hadn't been to a kid's athletic event since I was playing myself. Jilian and the rest of her team took the field in baggy baseball uniforms and gloves bigger than their heads. "These things can get crazy," Jill said.

I nodded to where the girls were jogging, lackadaisically, out to their positions. There was a smiling young man in an umpire's suit leaning over to brush off home plate. The first batter was waiting just behind him and she had laid the bat down and was adjusting her hair under the enormous batter's helmet. "I think the ump can handle them," I said.

"Oh, not the kids," Jill said. She nodded to the filling stands. "It's the parents." They looked mostly benign—moms in sunhats and dark glasses, little brothers and sisters, a few dads just getting off work. But the energy was building and a couple parents had begun a chant, "Rock 'em, sock 'em, kick 'em in the butt . . ."

When the umpire shouted, "Play ball," a chubby little man with a monk's hairdo and a clipboard under his arm stood up and screamed "Kill 'em!"

I looked at Jill. "Is he on our side?"

She shook her head. "No. His kid plays for the other team. She's a nice little girl but he's an ass."

For the first few innings I didn't see the game as two teams playing each other. It was just eighteen little girls running around, trying to remember what they had been told to do. It was hard to detect the slightest impulse toward competition. The crowd reacted positively to the occasional hit and, if the ball was actually fielded without an error, a modest roar rose from one side of the stands or the other.

The obnoxious chubby guy and his equally chubby wife had a rule book that they referred to and chided the umpire with. In the first few innings they stopped the game twice on fine points that few of us understood. I got the sense that there were some sophisticated strategies playing out on the field among the coaches, the umpire, a few overzealous fans, and the chubby couple with the rule book, all of which was lost on the little girls. They didn't seem to care what the score was and waited patiently as the adults argued the rules. Finally, one of the moms in a floppy straw hat stood up and yelled, "Let the kids play!"

That was in the last inning. There were already two outs with the score at 6–4, with the chubby guy's team ahead. He was standing at the fence behind home plate, showing the book to the umpire, and when he heard the woman yell, he turned around to the crowd with smirk on his face and pointed to the rule book in his hand. Jill groaned. "This is the part he loves," she said.

"He's done this before?

"All the time."

"Let 'em play," another mom shouted.

The affable young umpire looked up into the stands and smiled to the woman who had yelled. He waved away the chubby guy's complaint. "Play ball," he yelled, then turned to the girl, one of Jilian's teammates, who had been waiting for her turn at bat.

The little girl stood with her legs twisted around each other, the bat limp on her shoulder, and her dreamy gaze fixed on the blue sky over center field. The umpire had to touch her shoulder to get her attention. He pushed her gently toward home plate.

The chubby guy let out a theatric groan. Apparently he believed there was a reason to disqualify the batter. He had been roundly overruled and shook the wire behind the umpire to get his attention. "Jesus," I thought, "Who cares?" And just then the dreamy batter connected with a pitch and looped the ball into short right field. Chaos ensued.

By the time she made it to first base, the right fielder and the center fielder had collided and the ball dropped untouched in front of them. The batter advanced to second base. The right fielder recovered and threw to second, but it was already way too late. The ball careened into left field, where it was muffed by a timid girl who recovered in time to overthrow third base and send the batter home for a triple-error in-the-park home run. Jilian's team was suddenly only one run behind and the chubby guy was apoplectic.

He ran back and forth behind home base, waving his rule book and shouting at the umpire. He called out to both coaches and made such a fuss that the game had to stop. Jill and I were right down front where we could see that the man's head was sweating and the ring of hair above his ears was damp. The parents behind us moaned and let out a few more calls of "Let 'em play."

The next batter was the smallest girl on our team. Her batting helmet was way too big for her and she stood in the on-deck circle swinging two bats as if she was ready to smack the ball to Kansas. I had to smile at her chutzpah and I surprised myself by sobering up as I saw Jilian join the little girl in the on-deck circle. The two girls giggled as the small one responded to the umpire's wave and approached the plate. The chubby guy had been overruled again, and now he was shouting. "This game is under protest."

"Sit down," I yelled. Jill squeezed my arm and I looked at her. "Sorry," I whispered.

The little girl dug in and beat on home plate with her bat. She raised the bill of her batting helmet so she could see the pitcher then snarled like a tiny lioness. The first two pitches were a foot over her head. Now the chubby guy's shiny dome was bright red and he hung on the wire like a fat orangutan. We were close enough to know that he was speaking to the pitcher. "The pitcher is his daughter," Jill said.

"Poor child."

"No kidding. Look, she's stressing out."

The third pitch was wild and in the dirt. "Ball three," the umpire called.

"Throw a strike," the chubby guy screamed.

And whoosh—his daughter smoked one across. "Good for her!" Jill said.

But the next pitch was wide and way high. "Ball four!" The umpire pointed to first base. "Take a walk."

The chubby guy screamed at his daughter. "For God's sake, Brandy. Throw strikes." The pitcher wilted and, I swear, I thought she might cry.

I heard Jill gasp at my elbow. "Jilly's up to bat."

"This game is being played under protest." The chubby guy's wife was touching his back and trying to get him to sit down. I felt sorry for her and the daughter who was getting ready to pitch to Jilian. "None of this matters," the guy was yelling. He had the rule book in his hand again, and when I stepped up behind him, he tried to show me the book.

I put my arm around his shoulder. "I don't want to see the damned book," I whispered.

"It was an illegal substitution."

"Doesn't matter," I said. "You need to sit down." His face jerked up to mine but the defiance flagged.

His voice was softer but came through his teeth. "Why do I need to sit down?"

I smiled but squeezed his shoulder a little tighter and we both looked out to where his daughter was digging into the pitcher's mound with the toe of her tennis shoe. Jilly was oblivious to what was happening only a few feet behind her. I kept smiling and, without taking my eyes from the baseball field, I leaned as close to the man as I could and I whispered even lower, "You need to sit down and shut up or I'm going to break your fucking neck."

As his daughter started her windup, he looked up to see if I might be serious. I was amazed at what I'd said but I knew I had to do my best to make him think that I meant it. I continued to look out to the field with a neutral face and we backed to a sitting position on the first row of seats. "Let's just watch," I said.

His daughter threw a strike and Jilian swung but there was no contact. I still had my arm around his shoulder and kept watching as Brandy threw a ball, and then another strike that breezed past Jilly. Then there came a slow looping pitch that Jilly swatted at as if it were a fly. The ball shot up and toward right field. But it didn't go very far and the first baseman backed up, got under it, and caught it for the last out of the game.

"You win," I said, and patted the man on the back.

We didn't bother looking at each other because now there were little girls swirling around us. Win or lose, they all seemed perfectly happy and Jilly actually came up to me and smiled. Jill took my arm as Jilly ran off to say good-bye to her friends. "Did you have a nice chat with that other father?" I had no answer. I could only stand dumbfounded and look out to center field. No one had ever called me a father before.

That softball game was a turning point. From then on Jill and I understood that we were connected. But Jilian wasn't sure. Her real father was still lurking at the periphery of her life and, if he showed up when he was not expected, she was emotional and struck out at whoever was close by. At those times I would try to back away. I would leave their apartment and drive the thirty miles back to the ranch, where Erney sat beside the fire, reading books on natural history or the settling of the Southern Africa veld.

We were eating a lot of buffalo by then. Erney and I liked it even more than the venison and grouse we were used to. But I never realized how good it could be until Jill and Jilian came out to the ranch for the first time. It was Thanksgiving and Jill had volunteered to cook a buffalo roast. In addition to bird dogs, I had a young female peregrine falcon named Harley, who we used to hunt ducks. Since the fall had been warm, there were still open ponds with migrating ducks on nearly every one. Jilian had heard me talking about Harley and I saw that, even though she seldom looked at me, she was listening. When I asked her if she wanted to see Harley chase a duck, she couldn't help herself. She nodded and smiled.

"You go ahead," Jill said. She was examining the buffalo roast. I had lain it out on a baking pan and now she was feeling it with her hands and poking it with a fork. "Go ahead, Jilly. Go with Dan and Erney while I start cooking."

In the pickup, Jilian sat between Erney and me and didn't say much. We didn't drive far, just down the driveway, through a wire gate, and over a little hill to where we were out of sight of a pond that usually had ducks on it. Erney crept to the top of the rise to be sure there were ducks on the pond as I got Harley ready to fly. I didn't want to use Harley as a tool to impress Jilian because both of them deserved more respect than that. But it was difficult. From the shine in Jilian's eyes it was clear that the broad-chested black and brown bird on my left fist had gotten her attention like I had never seen before. She was too shy to blurt out questions but she quietly asked about the green leather hood on Harley's head. I lowered the bird to her level and let her take a close look at the way the hood covered Harley's eyes. "To keep her calm until we let her loose," I said.

Jilian's eyes got wide. "Don't let her loose. She'll run away."

I had to smile. "She won't run away. She's going to fly."

"Fly?"

"Fly," I said. Then I was stricken with the thought that Harley might really fly away. How would I explain that to Jilian? "She's just going to fly around and then she's going to catch a duck."

"She's going to catch a duck?" Jilian's arms were crossed and she was squinting in thought.

Erney had seen ducks and was standing out of their sight on the hill, and pointing upward—our signal for letting the falcon go. "Watch this," I told Jilian. With my teeth and right hand I loosened the braces on the hood. It sat cocked on Harley's head as I pulled the leather jesses from her legs. When she raised her leg to scratch under her chin the brass bell rang shrill and bright as the bells on a reindeer's harness. Jilian jumped back but smiled. When I took off the hood, Jilian's beautiful blue eyes got nearly as big as the falcon's fierce black ones. When Harley raised her wings and took to the air, Jilian gasped.

Harley went high above the pond and, when the twenty or so gadwalls lifted off, she came down like a two-pound drop of heavenly rain. Jilian did not see the falcon bind to the duck or tumble from the sky. Her eyes had been on the rest of the ducks and stayed with them as they circled the pond then headed south, all at warp speed. She stood there on the bank, looking skyward, her arms straight at her sides and her mouth wide open.

When we found Harley, the gadwall was already dead and Harley stood on top of it, as proud as a puppy with a bone. Jilian sat down cross-legged beside the falcon and the duck as the pile of plucked feathers grew. She didn't say a word but watched every move of the feeding falcon. The feather pile shifted with the slight breeze and was beginning to drift over her little tennis shoe when I picked Harley up onto my fist and continued to feed her.

Jilian's face was at Harley's level and her arms were again crossed in deep thought. Erney stood beside Jilian and explained the duck parts as Harley revealed them. Jilian watched closely as the falcon enjoyed her duck dinner. One of the wings fell to the ground and Jilian's eyes followed it down. She stared at it for a few seconds before she spoke. "Could I pick that up?"

"Sure," Erney said.

She went down into a squatting position as little kids do. Her hands were on her knees and she leaned down to look very closely before she reached out and picked up the wing by the last feather. The wing bones and tendons had been stripped clean of meat. Erney was leaning over to inspect it too. "Those are like your finger bones," he said. Jilian was skeptical and looked at him with a squint. "No foolin'," Erney said. He held out his good hand and flexed the fingers. He pointed to the dissected duck wing. "Right there," he touched a bone. "Same as that one right there." He wiggled his index finger in front of her nose.

When Jilian looked up to me, her face was still full of skepticism. She wanted something from me and so I nodded my head. That seemed to satisfy her and she stood up with the duck wing still in her hand. She looked to Harley, who was still chewing on the rest of the duck. Jilian smiled and held the wing up toward her own mouth. She pretended to chew on it and laughed. "Hope Mom's got that buffalo cooked."

There was no Christmas tree at the ranch house but there were all sorts of holiday paraphernalia at Jill's apartment, just up the hill from her restaurant, and I found myself hanging out there just to be near the bustle of it all. There had been some talk about the possibility of Jill and Jilian moving to the ranch. We jabbered about her monthly rent payment and she considered the possibilities of sprucing up the rickety ranch house. Making the place fit for them would take some time and I had my doubts about ever making the ranch anywhere near as homey as her apartment. We both wondered how Jilian might take to such a move.

I had never been much for giving presents, but that Christmas I went out of my way to get Jilian something that she would never forget. She was not yet eleven years old, so Christmas was still exciting to her and she checked the presents under the tree every day when she came home from school. I had wrapped up a small empty, cardboard box and put her name on it, "from Santa." She kept close tabs on the presents piling up under the tree and knew that the one marked Santa was from me. Every day she would pick it up and shake, ever so gently, as if its weightlessness might mean it was fragile. When she held it to her ear and moved it from side to side, then to and fro, her forehead would knit and she would look at me as if she hoped I wasn't tricking her.

On Christmas Eve afternoon, Jill and I went to the pet store and picked out a little blue parakeet. We stashed the bird and a new cage in the laundry room and went about our business of entertaining a few friends with oyster stew and champagne. There were kids around and they all had to shake Jilian's presents and speculate on what was inside. They didn't spend much time guessing the contents of my gift because they all agreed that it was boring.

After the party was over, Jilian went to bed and Jill and I sat on the couch in the glow of the Christmas tree lights and finished a bottle of Champagne. The party had been a masterpiece of hospitality. The salad and oyster stew were perfect. The company had been great. There were twenty candles still burning and the warmth and smells of Christmas enveloped us. Because Jill and Jilian were spending more time at the ranch, Erney and I had set him up in a little cabin seventy yards from the ranch house. I thought about the poorly insulated house I was asking Jill to move into. The wind would be whipping snow over the pastures and the wooly backs of the buffalo. The driveway was likely drifted shut. Everything would be cold and dingy. "Are you sure you want to leave this?" I gestured with my glass to the warm, pleasant room.

Jill snuggled into my shoulder and held up her glass to be clinked by mine. "Yep."

We clinked, and kissed, and settled into each other for another few minutes. "I have to go to bed," Jill said.

I had already learned that when Jill said that, she meant it. She would be asleep in minutes, bed or no bed. Her eyes were already shut. "Jilly will be up at six," she mumbled.

I was up by five o'clock, just to be sure that I would not get caught being Santa Claus. It took a little time to carefully open the empty present under the tree, get the parakeet into the box, and get it rewrapped. I poked a few air holes in the side of the box and got it back under the tree before I made coffee. Jill and I were on cup number two when Jilian came charging up the stairs.

She stood in the Christmas tree lights and smiled with glee. It dawned on me that because I had chosen a different life, I had missed a lot. Jilian walked right to my present and picked it up first. For the thousandth time, she shook it gently. This time it shook back. Her eyes and mouth opened wide. She gasped and held the present out in front of her. She looked to her mother and me for confirmation and tears filled my eyes.

It took more time than I had hoped but when Jill and Jilian finally joined Erney and me at the ranch, it seemed natural. For all Erney's idiosyncrasies, he was a favorite of theirs from the start. It was a bit of an odd group, but we had some things in common: the ranch, good food, animals, and especially the idea of buffalo on a healthy prairie.

I had put all my money and more into building fence and buying buffalo because I felt a strong connection to them and because I knew that having them close would bolster the entire matrix of life on the Broken Heart. I had purchased buffalo in the late 1990s and, with uncanny precision, picked the exact instant when the buffalo market was at its all-time high. Within a year, after building miles of expensive buffalo fence, the price of buffalo began to fall. I had planned to cover the annual mortgage and operating payments with the money from each year's buffalo calf crop. But before the first calves arrived, the market had fallen to its lowest point in memory. I refused to sell the calf crop at that price and the market continued to fall. By the time we realized the depth of the problem, our ranch was fully stocked and buffalo were nearly worthless.

The buffalo market had been a bubble. What seemed like a new and reasonable industry for the Great Plains had turned out to be a hobby breeder's market, powered by speculation that the price of buffalo would continue to soar. No one had considered the price of meat or the fact that even decent prices were not sustainable unless someone began consuming the product. As ranchers of all stripes were trying to build buffalo herds and giving little thought to selling meat, only a few food people were extolling the virtues of buffalo meat as a delicious, healthy, and sustainable source of protein. Jill, of course, was one of the people who knew early on that buffalo meat, when raised free of feedlots, hormones, antibiotics, and stress, was perhaps the best tasting and healthiest red meat in the world. On the other hand, I was sure that because the buffalo had co-evolved with all the other prairie plants and animals that had been misused to the point of near extinction, they were a management key for bringing back all that had made the Great Plains ecosystem thrive.

Meaningful restoration would never work if it depended only on my largesse or the largesse of any single person or group of people. A buffalo-led ecological recovery strategy would require an economic engine more powerful than donations of time and money could deliver. That kind of economic power could only come from the perpetual regeneration of the buffalo themselves. It would have to depend on the sale of the excess protein from the process of rebalancing the ecosystem. It was not enough to try to sell buffalo meat on the merits of health for landscape, or even for humans. Jill was the first to realize that to set this machine in motion, people would have to understand just how wonderful buffalo meat could taste.

She employed her ineffable talent of understanding how flavors mix with each other, how they react to heat, and the importance of balancing sweet and sour, salt and spice, smooth and crunchy. After a very few false starts with fancy sauces, marinades, and the sort of cooking techniques designed to hide the taste of the meat, she came to realize that bringing out the fine, delicate taste through the cooking process was the name of the game. She played with just how best to prepare steaks, roasts, ground, and brisket. Hot and fast? Low and slow? A little black pepper, sea salt, and olive oil?

During our tastings we ate it directly from wooden cutting boards with only a single knife between us. We cooked buffalo in a hundred different and creative ways and found that barbequing, braising, pan-searing, or roasting worked great—as long as it wasn't overdone.

In those days, and to a large extent still, buffalo that had been raised as they had evolved to live was unheard of in the marketplace and only existed for the few that were harvested on ranches or Indian reservations. Virtually all commercial buffalo was, and still is, run through the cattle feedlot model, where they are fed cheap surplus grains and agricultural by-products in an attempt to make them cook and taste like beef. The catch is that when buffalo go through the same process as feedlot beef, the meat affects the human body and the environment in the same way as feedlot beef. In essence, treating buffalo like cattle negated the advantages of raising them in the first place.

Then came an afternoon when the business landscape shifted. I was working on the ranch and Jill was at the restaurant when she got a call from the woman we had hired to handle the calls people left on our answering machine and to ship out the occasional package of Wild Idea Buffalo meat. The woman worked one day a week and, even though it was her day to work, she had a sick child and there was an order that needed to be packed and taken to FedEx for shipment to a friend in Ohio. Jill couldn't get away, so she called me.

I was running behind when I got to Rapid City, but I had to stop by the restaurant to get the inventory list that our employee dropped off on her way to the pediatrician. Jill saw the frustration in my face. "I'm caught up," she said. "It will go faster if I help you."

Five minutes later we stood in the communal cold storage freezer where we rented space. We looked at the two disheveled pallets of buffalo meat and realized that the inventory list would do us no good. The cartons of meat were not organized. We searched until we found what we needed to fill the order and hurried to pack the box in the freezing cold because the FedEx office was about to close for the day.

That kind of inefficiency drove Jill nuts and, as I rushed toward the door with the package under one arm, I looked over my shoulder and saw Jill standing over the jumble of boxes of frozen buffalo meat with her hands on her hips. "This is mostly the cuts that are hard to sell." She was talking to herself.

"FedEx is going to close."

"Go ahead," she said. "Pick me up on the way back." She handed back to me the folder that held a handwritten sheet with the names and addresses of our few customers, but she didn't take her eyes off the pile of buffalo meat.

When I got back, I found her still in the zero-degree freezer. Now she was on her hands and knees with open cartons of buffalo meat spread out in front of her. "I'm marrying these partial boxes," she said.

"Aren't you freezing?"

"Yeah, I'm freezing." But she kept rearranging meat. I had no alternative except to kneel down and help her.

By the time we left, the two dilapidated pallets had been reduced to a single straight and compact one. As we passed through the office of the cold storage facility, Jill told them that we would not be paying the storage fees for two pallets anymore. "Bill us for just the one," she said.

It was nearly dark outside and I suggested we go for something to eat before we headed back to the ranch. I was surprised that Jill turned down the offer of restaurant food. "Let's just go home," she said. "I've got some things that I want to do." By the way she clutched the single Wild Idea folder, I had a pretty good idea what she was up to.

From that point on, she controlled Wild Idea. The inventory sheets were printed out when we harvested an animal. The inventory of cut and packaged meat was reviewed when it came from the processor. The items were organized by cut and the inventory was adjusted as items were shipped out. The customer list was printed too. She made checks after the names when they paid their bills. Soon she was talking to people about a brochure and asking how to go about building a website. I tried to help her but I wasn't much good at it.

My interest was in the land and the grass and, in my naivete, I believed that what Jill was doing would help us progress toward revitalizing the Broken Heart. But still, that internal, nibbling feeling persisted, that twelve hundred acres in the vastness of the Great

Plains was a nearly meaningless victory. I knew that almost every creature that used our little ranch ranged far beyond its borders. The deer and the coyotes made huge circles and might only touch our place for a few days a month. Most of the ground-nesting birds wintered far to the south. The resident birds moved with the weather. The grasses crept to new ground with the seasons. Even the little herd of buffalo, happy as those animals were, would occasionally stand at the fence and stare to the horizon.

I was not interested in creating a private game preserve for myself. I knew the migrant multitudes moved in and out of my narrow domain and I was happy. But I was not satisfied. I spent many long evenings sitting in the rocking chair in front of the wood stove, trying hard to understand how we could better achieve our goal of preserving even a tiny sliver of the nature and spirit of the Great Plains. Eventually I came to the disheartening conclusion that such a plan had to equal the scope of the landscape.

Nobody knows how many protected acres is enough to ease the Great Plains ecosystem back from the abyss of industrial agriculture. But one thing is sure: while it is true that a small operator with a good heart can help set the tenor of the debate and the action to come, it takes an outfit with the ability to amass huge pieces of land to actually do something significant. To date, only government agencies, large conservation organizations, and very wealthy capitalists have the wherewithal to affect the future of the Great Plains. I had no access to, and little faith in, any of those entities.

On the Great Plains dreams come cheap, and that old wood-burning stove in the Broken Heart's ranch house fostered them as easily as warmth on a February night. I read every book that I could find that even touched on the problem of prairie revitalization. On the kitchen floor I laid out maps of government land where buffalo were raised. I looked at present-day agricultural land-use maps and the distribution of public lands on the Great Plains. I studied the grazing management ideas of large-scale buffalo ranchers and the grazing rules for government-controlled land. I learned about the National Grasslands system, an odd-duck division of the U.S. Forest

Service that manages nearly treeless expanses of grasslands that are perfect buffalo country. When I overlaid the historic buffalo range map with a transparency of these existing National Grasslands, the darkest spot on the map was an area along the Cheyenne River in South Dakota that bordered both Badlands National Park and the Pine Ridge Indian Reservation. It included private land and parts of the Buffalo Gap National Grassland. The fact that this area was named Buffalo Gap seemed a sort of omen and suddenly the answer seemed obvious: the first step had to be a bigger ranch and a real buffalo meat business.

The four of us living on that little ranch had a dream. We also had a practical, short-term problem. Our herd was growing faster than the Broken Heart could accommodate them or Wild Idea could sell them. Though Jill was expending a lot of energy, Wild Idea was little more than a hobby, and something had to give.

I was sitting with Erney in his little cabin, lamenting our situation. "I don't know what we're going to do," I said.

Erney shrugged. "Oh Dan'l, things aren't so bad."

"Jesus, Erney, we're all going to end up in the poorhouse."

He waived away my whining. "Heck Dan'l, this ain't no big crisis. We can eat our way out of this one."

I stood up and exhaled before I walked out into the wind. "Well Ern," I said, "I sure hope you're hungry."

When I mentioned Erney's solution to the problem, Jill shook her head. "We can't eat fifty buffalo and two pallets of hearts, livers, soup bones, and shanks." she said.

"What's a shank?"

"It's osso bucco from now on," she said. "We need to start a real business. We need to organize our inventory and get some information out there."

"Oh, God. I was afraid of something like this."

"Tell yourself that you are doing it for all the birds that nest on this ranch. Think about the grasses that need more buffalo." she said.

Even though I understood what she was saying, I was reluctant. The idea of taking in more money than I spent was foreign to my natural sensibilities. Neither my family nor I have ever been extravagant. In fact, we're known for being cheap. But there is a big difference between being cheap and knowing how to make money. I always underestimate the costs and overestimate the income—sometimes by a lot. So the idea of getting serious about a buffalo meat business scared the hell out of me.

I haven't missed many meals, but I've worried a lot about that. I haven't fallen into a deep financial hole but I have always been a break even sort of guy, living in a break even landscape. For forty years my most obvious income stream has come from agriculture on the Great Plains. I have only recently begun to understand the irony in the statement of one of my neighbors with whom I have engaged in many ranching schemes. For decades we have planned at his kitchen table the purchase of livestock, equipment, and animal feed. We have done deals up to six figures without any paperwork, without any problems, and often without any profit. Once we'd get our plan figured out, my neighbor would invariably looked over his coffee cup with a hopeful gleam in his eyes and say, "I sure hope we break even on this deal 'cause I need the money." I knew the comment was supposed to be funny and I always laughed with him. But it never seemed like an unreasonable goal.

Three

THE LAKOTA PEOPLE HAVE A CREATION MYTH THAT MAKES more sense to me than the stories of any mainstream religion. Instead of Adam and Eve finding themselves in the Garden of Eden or the Sons of Burr lifting Earth from the sea, the Lakota people figure it all started at Wind Cave, in the center of the Black Hills.

In the early seventies, when Erney and I worked together on the same ranch, a Lakota guy named Rocke Afraid of Hawk came to work there too. I had just graduated with a master's degree from the English Department at the University of South Dakota and Rocke had temporarily escaped from the Cheyenne River Reservation with his new, pregnant wife, Pam, and a friend named LeRoy. The unemployment rate on the Cheyenne River Reservation can hit 90 percent, so I guess they were simply looking for work. Rocke and LeRoy were good to work with. They were quiet and preferred to let someone else take responsibility for a job. We put up a lot of corn silage and stored it in a huge silo near the house where the Afraid of Hawks lived. The smell of it kept Pam sick most of the time and that made all of us feel bad for her. Rocke, LeRoy, Erney, and I spent long days fixing fence and baling hay. We got along well and I drank a few beers with Rocke after work. Erney was not a drinker. He would hold up his hand and say, "Go ahead, boys. I drank my share when I was a teenager."

A couple of times we tried gathering at Rocke's house, but we quickly learned that, once they got started drinking, Rocke and LeRoy didn't know when to quit. But Erney and I got along fine with

Rocke when we were outside and working. He was a keen observer of what was happening on the prairie and saw meaning in everything. A fog would bring rain in six weeks. An owl on a fence post meant someone close would die. Erney had fallen away from the Catholic Church and was skeptical of anything that smacked of superstition. "If there are a bunch of cars at Rocke's house," Erney said, "that means Rocke won't be at work in the morning."

There were often cars at Rocke's house. It was usually visitors from the reservation and Rocke, LeRoy, and the visitors were constantly drinking too much. About sundown everyone would start to drink and by ten o'clock personalities began to change. Rocke would change with the rest of them. The same guy who was observant, funny, and thoughtful when he was outside with a purpose turned into a staring, mumbling antagonist when he wasn't. Sometimes he showed up at work in the mornings but lots of times he wasn't worth much until noon. By quitting time he was back to himself and we would renew our conversation about the birds and animals that he considered his relatives. He called them all "four-leggeds," and when I would point out that birds only had two legs, he would smile and shrug. "You white guys are always into counting," he'd say. "You are all accountants at heart." Then he would laugh and punch my shoulder. "Josh," he said. It was a way to say that he was only kidding. He knew damned well that I was not an accountant.

Erney wasn't sure about this bunch of Indians who showed up for work only when they felt like it. Erney is what South Dakotans call a Bohemian. His parents were Czechoslovakian and his father died when he was an infant. There were seven kids in the family and his mother raised them mostly with the money they earned by plucking ducks, geese, and pheasants for out-of-state hunters in the autumn and plucking chickens for the local grocery store the rest of the year. The whole family spent most winter nights in a little house with no indoor plumbing, listening to the radio and stripping the down away from the feather shafts to stuff pillows and comforters. Erney had been raised with no more creature comforts than any reservation kid, but starting at age sixteen he'd been getting up at five o'clock to get to work and he resented those who didn't. We were not quite old enough to realize that Rocke had an alcohol problem.

I cut him slack because I felt he could teach me a lot about living on the Great Plains. I liked him and thought he liked me. So I was surprised to fine that, on a day when he didn't show up for work and I went to get him, Rocke was gone without a word. Pam, LeRoy, and all the friends from the reservation were gone too. What had often been a crowded parking lot was empty, except for a junk car jacked up on cement blocks with the wheels gone. Erney and I pushed open the door of the house and looked in. It was a complete mess: dirty dishes piled in the sink and on all the counter space, spoiled food, and lots of empty beer bottles. The putrid silage smell hung heavy throughout the house. Erney only shrugged. Had he been the sort of guy who spoke disparagingly about people, it would have been the perfect time to make a cruel comment. But Erney has never been that kind of guy. He only shrugged. "Guess they had to go," he said.

I didn't see Rocke for thirty-five years and, by the time he reappeared, Wild Idea Buffalo Company had come to the first of many junctures where we had to decide whether or not to grow. To that point we had been operating under an agreement with the South Dakota meat inspection authorities, who allowed us to harvest animals in their home pastures. The inspector rode with our shooter to insure humane treatment and safe handling. There was some skepticism at first, but once they saw how calm the buffalo were, compared to being forced into trucks and then into a slaughter plant, there was no question that we were on to something. An expert marksman drove a pickup through the herd with the inspector in the passenger seat. When an animal of the appropriate age and sex presented itself, the marksman moved the pickup to where he could get a perfect shot at very close range. This was not hunting, it was a harvest, and as long at the animal could be transported to a processing plant, then eviscerated, skinned, and cooled within two hours, all the USDA standards for animal slaughter and handling were met.

These procedures worked, and about the time Wild Idea needed an additional source of buffalo to meet demand, a group of Native

American buffalo managers came to us and asked us to come to the reservations to harvest their buffalo the same way. Tom Fredrick from the Rosebud Reservation, Ron Brownotter from Standing Rock, and Ed Iron Cloud from Pine Ridge said that they had been watching Wild Idea Buffalo Company and that they liked the way we treated buffalo. Tom put it succinctly: "We hate to see people screwing with them like they're cattle or something." He shrugged his big round shoulders and smiled. "I mean, they're our relatives, right?" It reminded me of Rocke Afraid of Hawk and I mentioned his name.

Tom smiled. "Rocke's back up on the Rez. He's a kind of medicine man. A real buffalo supporter. He'd be all in favor of you guys coming out to harvest buffalo."

We were flattered and excited to have access to reservation buffalo because they were exactly the kind of buffalo that we were raising—real grass-fed animals that hadn't been overworked in corrals or given antibiotics and hormones. We welcomed a chance to encourage that kind of management elsewhere. But we couldn't do what these Native guys were asking. There was some hesitation from the state inspectors because in a lot of ways the reservations are sovereign nations. There is no tribal meat inspection on the reservations and some even dispute the State of South Dakota's authority there. In fact, few areas exist where state government and tribal governments cooperate. But all of that was moot because the two-hour time limit, from bullet to cooler, disqualified almost all reservation buffalo. The reservations were simply too far away from processing plants.

We couldn't help the tribes but their request gnawed at us. If Wild Idea's mission was to facilitate species diversity by encouraging the restoration and management of nearly wild, truly grass-fed, and free-roaming buffalo, this was a golden opportunity. There are about thirteen million acres of reservation land on the northern Great Plains. To a large extent these lands are still in native pasture and their suite of wild animals is still mostly intact. They are populated with people who have a special relationship with buffalo. Whether by culture-driven design or by benign neglect, reservation lands represent perhaps the greatest reservoir of easily savable grassland in the country—perhaps in the world. Jill and I had worked on and around reservations all our adult lives. We had lots of Native friends. Jill's nieces and nephews are enrolled members of the Sisseton-Wahpeton Tribe. The difficulties associated with working on reservations are well known and daunting: lack of capital, organization, expertise, and the will to excel in modern society are great. But we felt challenged to figure out a way to help and spending half a day on the Internet turned up a possibility.

There was a guy in Washington State by the name of Bruce Dunlop, who had worked with a farmers cooperative from the San Juan Islands on a quest to take back the slaughter of their hogs, lambs, and beef from the clutches of industrial meatpacking. His solution was a mobile harvester, and it seemed to me that such a trailer might solve our problem, too.

Bruce had a farm on Lopez Island that produced an array of organic meats, vegetables, and fruits. He also manufactured a limited amount of ready-to-eat products. Jams and syrups were his specialty and, as I talked to him on the telephone about our need for a mobile buffalo harvester, it came out that he hadn't always been a farmer. He was a biologist and chemical engineer who had made a career in San Francisco as a researcher, developing biological pesticides. I got the sense that he had become disenchanted with developing bugs that would eat pests that were eating farm crops. He took a leave of absence and sailed his twenty-seven-foot sailboat to Alaska and back to Gig Harbor, Washington. I imagine that somewhere along the route, as he sailed silently among the islands between Anchorage and Portland, he got to comparing his corporate city job with the intimacy of water, wind, and the solitude of the fir-covered shores. He ended up buying Lopez Island Farm, a postage-stamp-sized but fertile place in need of a loving hand.

He never really went back to San Francisco. In time, he volunteered to work with the Island Grown Farmer's Cooperative—a group of small, boutique farmers who were scattered around the islands and had a problem similar to ours. They needed to harvest their animals economically, humanely, safely, and under scrupulous meat inspection that would allow them to sell their products. The farms were not nearly as far apart as we were from the Native American buffalo pastures, but they were on different islands connected only by a system of ferryboats. The cooperative attached itself to the Lopez Community Land Trust and set about traversing the inscrutable mountain of regulations required to design and build a mobile harvester acceptable under the U.S. Animal Inspection Act. It didn't take long before Bruce, the volunteer, became Bruce, the ramrod. As I talked to him on the phone that first time, I knew we needed someone like him who had actually made a living as a project manager. I had built buildings and fences around the ranch, but most of them weren't even straight. I had almost no experience dealing with a federal bureaucracy like the USDA. Bruce had already figured out most of the hard stuff, and I knew that Jill and I needed to get out to the San Juan Islands to pick his brain.

The San Juan Islands of Washington's Puget Sound and the northern Great Plains are as different as two landscapes can be. The islands have far more water than land, and from the start it felt like we were on a different planet. The farms are small but fertile. A big herd of cattle is a dozen. A pasture is three acres. The people are loggers or boatmen of one sort or the other. They eat a lot of vegetables and fish.

Jill would have liked to eat in three different restaurants every day of our three-day stay in the Northwest. But there were budget considerations, so we drove straight north from SeaTac to the ferry terminal at Anacortes, Washington, where we found a world more like a movie set than anything we were accustomed to. In western South Dakota few people own raincoats and I have never seen an umbrella in any home. On that afternoon in Anacortes, most people wore slickers, rain hats, and yellow boots. I expected Gene Kelly to come dancing out from a side street.

The sky was a gyrfalcon gray and the air was thick as a sauna's, but it was a chilly fifty degrees. The damp air penetrated through the skin, and even though it had been zero degrees when we left

Rapid City, it seemed colder in Anacortes and I couldn't keep my teeth from chattering. We stayed at a long, nautical-looking motel and ate across the street at the Captain's Table, where we got our first taste of fresh seafood. It's difficult to get this kind of food in the center of the nation, so we savored the oysters, clams, and halibut.

The bartender assured us that the next day would be sixty degrees with intermittent sunshine. The first car ferry left for Lopez Island at 6:20 in the morning and we planned to be first in line. The idea of driving a bunch of cars onto a boat didn't seem right to either of us. We figured that if we were the first ones on, we'd be the first ones off. As we walked along the wharf on our way back to the motel from the Captain's Table, a light mist angled across the streetlight beams and the smell of the ocean lay thick on everything. "Definitely not Kansas," I said.

Jill shook her head as if she was shaking off the dampness. "Thank God," she said. She was silent for a minute and I knew she was thinking about the feedlots of Kansas. "I don't know if I want to see lambs and pigs get killed," she said.

I had visited several slaughter plants and watched enough buffalo being slaughtered to know that they were too wild to be benignly subjected to a process developed for domestic livestock. The smell of death, the slamming of steel gates, and the rough voices of workmen were too much for them. They fought every step of the way into the plants and onto the kill floors. I had told Jill about it, and though she had been raised on a dairy farm in South Dakota, her experience had been on a truly balanced family farm. "Well, that's why we're here—to find a good way to do what we have to do."

We were standing in the motel parking lot. I put my arm around her waist and she looked up. "I miss the stars," she said.

"Hard to tell which direction is which, isn't it?"

"Hard to say which way is up."

Our internal clocks were still set on Mountain Time, so we were drinking our morning coffee at a diner by five o'clock local time. It gave us the chance to watch Anacortes wake up and go to work.

By the time we were in our rented car, idling behind the ferry gate, people were beginning to move along the wharf. Diesel engines were coughing from the bottoms of boats and the ferry crew was hustling to get ready to load cars for the first trip of the day.

When the gate opened to let us on, the sky had begun to lighten and the tree-lined shores of distant islands came into focus. The bartender had been right: still some clouds but sunshine was slipping through. The line of cars and trucks behind us was impossibly long. Jill's voice was strained. "They're never going to get all these cars and trucks onto this boat." Our car was the first on board and an orange-vested ferry worker pointed us to the very front of the boat. He waived us tight against the curb and right up against the front doors. "Is there water on the other side of those doors?"

"I don't know," I said.

"We should get out of here," Jill said. "Go up on deck or something."

We found a place at the top railing and watched silently as the traffic moved onto the car deck below. When the portable parking lot below us settled down, the ferry's big diesel engines torqued up and the ship began to push a huge wake in front of us. I gripped the rail like it was the saddle horn on a bucking horse.

The ferry leveled out and the engine noise was swallowed by the sea. The San Juan Islands separated from each other in the morning light and the water birds turned up above us, just as they have been doing since long before there were ferryboats below. Suddenly the watery world began to make sense. The whole ferry system was just another way humans have devised to move things around. A lot of the parking space on the car deck was taken up with panel trucks and trucks with all sorts of trailers. They were bringing things to the communities and farms on the islands. It occurred to me that this was everyday stuff for the people who rode with us. One of the trailers below might be the mobile harvest machine that we had come to see.

At first I was awed by the different landscape, so unlike the plains. But the soggy world of tree-shrouded islands that stretched to the horizon somehow reminded me of the vastness of the plains.

Soon we were settling into the ferry dock at Lopez Island, and when we pulled off of the ferry and back onto dry land the surrounding fertility was overwhelming. Vegetation grew on everything. The ground, the trees, the fence posts—everything looked like a buffalo might be able to eat it. We drove around the whole island, killing a little time until we were supposed to show up at Bruce Dunlop's Lopez Island Farm, where the mobile harvester would be working that day.

Lopez Island is half the size of many South Dakota ranches, but it is many times more fertile and the trees and curving roads make it a warren of human agricultural activity. These are small farms that raise real farm crops and almost no commodities. Unlike the Great Plains, they are close to population centers and able to grow vegetables, fruits, and high-quality specialty meats like lamb, pork, veal, and fine beef. Lopez Island Farm was easy to find and the small sign in front proclaimed the farm's specialties: "fruits, syrups, and sauces. Honest meat."

Unlike the defiant and lonely ranch house on the Broken Heart Ranch, the farm buildings of Lopez Island Farm were moist and folded lovingly into a succulent, nurturing landscape that seemed in proportion to the human presence. Though we were three thousand miles from New England, it was as if all of America's middle could be reduced to the rough rawhide it would take to stitch the coasts together.

We were sensitive to being viewed as people from America's "fly over" country. But there was no need to dread condescension because Bruce possesses the broad and accepting view of a scientist. He is a small man with a wide smile and an easy-to-spot curiosity that lets everyone know he is actually interested in you. He was just coming out of a small pen near an old but elegant barn. A half-dozen lambs were crowding around him as he closed the gate.

"Hey," he said, and shook both of our hands. Then, with raised eyebrows, "Buffalo?" he asked. He turned quickly to Jill to say, "Restaurant? Boy, you guys are gluttons for punishment." He smiled conspiratorially. "Don't worry. You're among friends. We've only got a few minutes until the boys show up, but let me give you a quick tour of the monkey that's on *my* back."

In front of the farm buildings was a small retail shop with a tiny processing area where Bruce built his ready-to-eat specialty products. There was also a glass-topped freezer with packages of grass-fed pork and lamb. Bruce tapped the top of the freezer with pride. "Slaughtered with the mobile unit. Cut and wrapped over on the mainland in the co-op's little plant." He tapped the simple cash register with similar pride. "The heart of the farm," he said.

Just as we stepped out of the retail room a one-ton truck pulling a long white trailer turned into the driveway. It was one of the trucks that had come with us on the ferry and the driver waved to Bruce. A Chevy sedan was following right behind the mobile harvester. "That's the inspector," Bruce said. We were hustling back to the barn and lamb pen. "We're going to slaughter these lambs and those hogs." He pointed to a pen of huge pigs. Bruce rushed off to help set up the harvest trailer and I looked to see how Jill was handling the idea of slaughtering these animals.

I caught her eye and was surprised to see more deep interest than concern. She was looking into the hog pen and waved me over. "Look at these guys," she said. "Look how smart they are." Neither of us had ever been around hogs except to drive by a feedlot full of them and hold our noses as we sped up. Jill didn't even allow bacon in our house. But the pen of hogs fascinated us. We watched them in silence and were intrigued at how they interacted with each other. They had huge snouts and little beady eyes but they were not as sinister as I had expected. They were actually playful with each other and with the water trough lid. They'd flip the metal top up with their snouts and then run a lap around the pen just for the fun of it. We were laughing at their antics when Bruce stepped up beside us. "What are you laughing at?" he asked.

"These hogs," Jill said. "We never had hogs on the farm."

Bruce was smiling too. "Oh, they're characters."

"What are you feeding them?"

"Mostly just grass." He pointed to the pasture just outside the pen.

"They graze out there. Only come in here for water." Just then a hog rattled the lid of the watering trough as if he was trying to be funny. He got us laughing again, and when things settled down, Bruce asked if we noticed anything unusual about the hogs.

We looked at each other. "Everything about them is unusual," Jill said.

Bruce smiled the way we had already come to expect. "Yeah, but there is something else." We shrugged in unison.

"They don't smell," Bruce said with glee.

Jill's eyes went wide. "They don't smell," she said as she looked back into the pen. "They don't smell," she repeated to herself.

"They're not dirty," Bruce said. "They keep themselves really clean if you give them a chance." The inspector called for Bruce to come sign a paper of some sort, so we were left alone again. Jill was still looking into the pen.

"They don't smell," she said, then looked at me as if for an explanation. This was not the way I had described the slaughter plants I had visited. We were standing in a tidy farmyard. The animals were clean and calm, just in from the green pastures they had known their entire lives. There was almost no sign of industrial agriculture, just the hum of the generator in the mobile harvester and the gentle banter of a farmer, a butcher, and a USDA inspector.

The butcher was a quiet Canadian who came gently to the lambs with a bolt gun that stunned them without trauma. They simply went limp in his hands and were winched into the trailer, where they were skinned and eviscerated in short order. The inspector checked the internal organs to make sure the carcasses were healthy and the butcher sprayed them down with a vinegar wash that served as a last antibacterial step before the carcasses were rolled, on the overhead rail, into the cooler at the front of the trailer. The work proceeded methodically—lambs and hogs into the back of the trailer, entrails, hides, hooves, and head out the side door and into a compost pit. Pure, healthy sides of red meat moved into the cooler.

When the harvester pulled away from Dunlop's farm, it left only a small, temporary stain on the portion of grass where the nitrogen-rich blood had been returned to the land as fertilizer. Commerce chugged along without unhealthy side effects to animals, land, or the bodies and souls of humans. It was what we had hoped to find in the islands of Puget Sound, and what we hoped to bring back to the Great Plains.

"It's a huge pain in the butt," Bruce said, as we sipped his apple cider and talked about the possibility of getting a mobile harvester for our infant buffalo business. "The regulations will drive you crazy, getting good help is tough, the equipment is expensive to operate, and just the trailer costs a couple hundred thousand dollars to build.

I almost spit my cider across the porch. "A couple hundred thousand dollars?"

"Maybe more," Bruce said. "We'd have to winterize it, wouldn't we?"

"Yea, South Dakota has winter."

It was clear to see that Bruce's engineering side was coming to the surface. He smelled a challenge. "How cold's it get?"

"Twenty below."

"Below? Below what?"

"Zero."

"Well then, let's say a quarter of a million."

"No way," I said. Jill put her hand on my thigh to quiet me.

"You need to start a 501c3."

"What's that?"

"A nonprofit. Qualify you for grants and tax-free gifts."

I was discouraged, but Jill's hand began to pat my leg. "So how do you start a nonprofit?" I asked.

"Another huge pain in the ass," Bruce said. "But it's possible. What you're doing is good stuff. You'd qualify."

"A quarter of a million?"

Bruce shrugged. "The cost of a combine. Most wheat farms have half a dozen pieces of equipment that cost that much." Jill was still patting my leg and when I looked at her, I could see that she had an idea.

But she didn't say anything until we had bought a jar of apple chutney, three jars of marionberry chipotle sauce, a box of apple cider syrup, and twenty pounds of Bruce Dunlop's free-range bacon. She waited until we were sitting in a white tablecloth restaurant in Seattle to tell me her idea.

The restaurant was Lola, and Jill was beside herself with excitement. This dinner was a treat, and Jill read every word of the menu. She asked the waiter a hundred questions and they talked about wine until I nearly died of thirst. Jill pumped him for information on each dish. "Let her think about it," I told the poor guy. "I'll have a Crown Royal on the rocks while she's rereading the wine list." By the time the waiter returned, Jill was ready to order. "I'll have either the Black Cod or the Goat Kleftiko."

"Go with the Goat, but try the Favaskordalia spread," the waiter said. They exchanged conspiratorial smiles.

"Let me think about it," Jill said.

I waited until the bottle of sauvignon blanc came and let the waiter pour me a glass. They talked about the menu again. "How about the Tzatziki spread," Jill said. I knew Jill was leaning toward the goat but wanted to assert herself when it came to the sauce. It was the most expensive thing on the menu but she sent the waiter away with only an appetizer order—mussels in an anise and white wine sauce. It was something we like to do—order an appetizer and a bottle of wine, and then see what we feel like for an entree. We held the wine glasses up and touched delicately to get the best chime possible. The wine was really good—dry and fruity. I had to smile. "So, what's your idea?"

"Should I get the goat for an entree?"

"Like I have a say in that one."

"And a bottle of Torres Salmos Priorar with the meal? It's Spanish. Got to go with goat."

"What's your idea?"

"So I was talking to Pam Borglum about Jim selling his restaurant at Sylvan Lake." Borglum is a name strongly associated with the Black Hills and particularly Mount Rushmore. Pam and Jim are friends of ours. Jim is a man of means who is engaged in business and all sorts of art—painting, music, sculpture. One of the things the Borglums dabble in is the food business. "We were talking about the restaurant business and she said something about Jim having to reinvest some money in food-processing equipment."

I leaned across the table and plucked a mussel from the central plate. "Some tax deal?" I sucked the mussel from its shell.

"Beyond me," she said.

"You're thinking he could make a donation to a nonprofit?"

"Maybe. If it's tax deductible."

Neither of us had any idea what we were talking about. But we kept talking as we shared Jill's Goat Favaskordalia and my Dungeness crab. We enjoyed a glass of grappa for a nightcap, and by the time we went to bed we had a name for our nonexistent nonprofit corporation: Sustainable Harvest Alliance. We talked about it all the next day as we made our way home on the airplane. Once we were back in Rapid City, I found a pro-bono lawyer who was willing to draw up some incorporation papers. I talked to an IRS agent about a 501c3 designation before I finally got the nerve to call Jim Borglum.

Jim is younger than me and a very kind and calm man. He's a bird-dog guy. He knows all our dogs—Hank, Tootsie, Trixy, and Al. The first time I saw how Jim touched them I knew I would like him very much. But I couldn't imagine anyone taking kindly to a request for $250,000. I almost chickened out, but I kept thinking about those Native guys out on the reservation—how they loved the buffalo, and how they had no good way to market them so no way to make a living from them. The IRS agent had agreed that Sustainable Harvest Alliance had a benevolent, environmental, and cultural mission, so when Jim came on the phone I just blurted it all out in one run-on sentence. "Pam said you had some money to reinvest and I have this idea to help some Lakota people by harvesting their buffalo in a culturally appropriate way and to do that we'd need to buy this really cool machine that costs a lot of money and the IRS agent says it qualifies as a 501c3 and I thought maybe you could give us a quarter of a million dollars."

There was silence on the line. Then Jim spoke tentatively. "Dan? Is that you?"

"Yeah. Hi, Jim."

"501c3?"

"That's what the agent said."

"For harvesting Native buffalo?"

"And other buffalo, too."

"You know I'm interested in good food and I'm always looking for way to help out. Would this be a good thing to do?" He was actually thinking about what I had said.

"It would be a damned good thing to do."

"Well, I can't just give you the money."

My heart stopped. "Oh God, of course not. I'm sorry . . ."

"I'd have to talk to my tax accountant first, but if he says it'll work, I'm in."

I was dumbfounded. I mumbled "thank you," hung up, and sat staring at the phone. An oppressive sense of responsibility settled down on me. I was a grown man who had known many people in Jim Borglum's situation. Some I had liked and some I had not. That awkward telephone conversation marked the first time that such a person had come to the aid of Wild Idea. It would not be the last.

A mutual friend brought Rocke Afraid of Hawk and me back together. Shane Brown was the first buffalo butcher that Jill and I hired. He was a Cheyenne River tribal member and he insisted that if we were going to harvest buffalo we needed to pay proper respect to the animals. He said that we couldn't be like other slaughter plants—that this was very serious stuff. "We need to burn some sage. We need to thank the grandfathers. We need ceremonies," he said. "We need Afraid of Hawk."

"You know Rocke too?"

"He's my buddy," Shane said. "Fishin' buddies. We do walleye ceremonies up on the Missouri."

"Rocke does walleye ceremonies?"

"Oh, you bet. Rocke's a ceremonial technician."

I never thought that I would see Rocke alive again and, when he showed up to bless one of our first field harvests, I told him that. He smiled his crooked smile and said that he figured the same thing about me. Of course a lot had changed since we were twenty-something ranch hands together. My hair was completely gone and his hair had grown gray-black and thick down the middle of his back. His tough life showed in his face; it was weathered and wrinkled like the photographs of the survivors of the Battle of the Little Big Horn. He had pretty much quit drinking but the devilish twinkle was still in his eyes. He was even quieter and his eyes could go completely calm. When they did, it looked like he was thinking, contemplating the horizon. After he had gotten sober, Rocke Afraid of Hawk had become a medicine man. Erney shrugged and said it made about as much sense as Glen Beck becoming a Mormon.

When I first saw him after our separation, Rocke was standing in knee-high grass beside the Wild Idea butchers and the South Dakota meat inspector, holding a small drum in one hand. He was dressed in rumpled clothes with a porcupine quill medallion around his neck and an eagle feather in his hair. We embraced in an immense, windy field with a herd of buffalo standing in the distance and the misty blue outline of the Black Hills along the horizon to the west. Rocke laughed and looked hard at me to see if he could recognize the kid he had known. "You look okay," he said.

"You look better than you did," I said. "Josh!" And we both laughed.

Then Rocke turned to face the dark line of buffalo a half-mile downwind. He began tapping the drum and, in his native Lakota language, began to sing to the buffalo. Like so many other elements of Lakota life, the mournful rhythmic chant of the music matches the landscape perfectly. It sent shivers to the back of my neck but was somehow reassuring. Knowing Rocke the way I did, I could hear a difficult life mixed with the sound of moving grasses, the birds, and the changing seasons. I understood none of the words, but the buffalo seemed to know exactly what Rocke was saying. The distant black lumps turned and began, very slowly, to wander toward us.

Rocke sang until the buffalo encircled our little band of people. Shane lit the sweetgrass bundle and Rocke wafted the smoke over us all. He blessed the rifle with the sweetgrass smoke and the buffalo pressed in even closer. After the chosen buffalo was down and the tobacco offering had been made to the six directions, Shane and Cliff Allen winched it into the new Sustainable Harvest Alliance mobile harvester to begin the skinning process. Rocke touched my shoulder and turned me away. We faced the Black Hills and Rocke told me his version of the Lakota creation story.

"It started there," he said, as he pointed to the Black Hills. "You know—Wind Cave."

"Sure," I said. Wind Cave is a huge cavern that moans with a strange wind that seems to come from inside the earth.

"Well, it wasn't always a National Park. That is where we used to *live*." He has a way of stressing the words that carry the most meaning. He gestured in all directions to include all the people and the buffalo that were still standing close. "We lived deep in a hole in the *earth*." He was staring off to the Black Hills, but then turned back to me and held my eyes like the Ancient Mariner. "Darker'n the inside of a tomcat," he said. "So dark we would bump our heads on the roof of the cave. But the people and the buffalo lived down there like *brothers* and *sisters* 'cause it was safe there inside of Mother Earth." He paused and squinted as if he was remembering back to what it was like to live in blackness. It took a moment for him to come back to the story.

"Now the buffalo," he moved his hand across the curious audience of buffalo who seemed to be listening just like I was, "they are *brave*, and one day they walked out onto the prairie and started to eat the grass. But the people—that's us—they are not so brave and so they stayed in the hole. Just dark. Nothing to eat but *dirt*." Rocke shook his head in disgust.

"Well, the next thing you know, the buffalo come back in and start telling the people how great it is outside on the prairie—how there is *sunshine*, and *wind*, and lots of *grass* to *eat*. But the people are still scared, and they tell the buffalo brothers that they can't eat grass.

They don't have no warm clothes. They are just going to stay in the hole." He shrugged and shook his head. Then he looked straight at me. "But the buffalo wanted their brothers and sisters to come out and enjoy the prairie with them, so they made a *deal.* If the people come out of the hole to live with the buffalo, the buffalo will take *care* of them. They're going to give the people everything they will need to make teepees to stay warm. Going to give the people all kinds of tools from their bones. Clothes. Drums." Rocke slapped the drum that he still held in his hand. "And plenty to *eat.*" He pointed to the mobile harvester, where Shane and Cliff were skinning the buffalo that had just been shot. "Buffalo promised to give us everything we need to *survive.*"

Rocke had been looking right at me, but now he paused and let his eyes move around the scene—fifty buffalo milling around two old men talking. Then Rocke's eyes were back on mine. "You know what the buffalo asked for, for takin' care of the people?"

I shook my head.

"*Love,*" Rocke said, and nodded his head once. "*Respect.* That's the *deal.* The buffalo give us everything we need to be rich." He nodded his head again. "Simple deal." Then he shook his head. "But when you white guys came, you blew it. No love, no respect, and now we are poor." He took a good grip on his worn blue workshirt and pulled it away from his body to show me that he owned very little. "Simple deal," he said.

Later that day, Rocke and I were riding in my pickup and he told me how glad he was that I was helping the buffalo. I had never thought of it quite that way but this was a grand compliment coming from Rocke. The day was warm and the light coming through the windshield made us squint and relax. The time seemed right to ask him, "How are you really doing?"

He was looking straight ahead, across the rolling Cheyenne River breaks, with a soft smile on his lips. The smile was something new, like nothing I had ever seen on Rocke's face. When I had known him thirty years before, his expression was flinty and his eyes changed quickly with anger or a joke. You never knew which was coming. He had been a handsome young man—no doubt part of what had made his early life so hectic and dysfunctional. Now he looked old and haggard, but good. "I am doing all right," he said. "I work with the children up to Takini School. Do some ceremonies, the Sun Dance. Giveaways. Live out by Red Scaffold. Don't have no car that works."

We rolled on for another mile or so, and we both looked out at the undulating landscape. After another minute Rocke continued: "I went back to the Rez and started working with some of the buffalo up there." There was another comfortable pause. "That's what *healed* me," he said. "They helped me and I'm trying to hold up my end of things." Now he smiled broadly and showed a sliver of his teeth. "I love and respect them," he said. "That's the *deal*."

Then he went silent again, but I knew there was more to come. In another minute it came. "But I am a poor man." He pulled on his old workshirt again. "What can I do to really help the buffalo?" He looked at me and the old crooked smile came back to the wrinkled lips.

In a lot of ways Rocke Afraid of Hawk and I are very different. We come from different worlds. I have had many more chances to succeed in the world of western materialism. I was lucky enough to have a family that encouraged me. But in many other ways we are very much alike. Perhaps the most important thing that we share is something common to a great many people: we see how complicated and hard the world has become and, when we are not paralyzed by that knowledge, we want to do something to help make things right. But caring enough to do something is a kind of hell. I wanted to nurture the Great Plains back to health but I knew that our little Broken Heart Ranch was not big enough to be meaningful within the grand scale of the Great Plains. Influencing enough land to matter was likely beyond my capabilities, and falling short might drive me crazy. I was like the guy I met at the Just Foods Co-op in Northfield, Minnesota.

He was stocking shelves in the vegetable department. It was in the days just after Jill and I had decided to try to seriously sell our buffalo meat. I was doing my annual teaching pilgrimage from the hinterlands to the ivory towers of Carleton College, and I had wandered down to the co-op to see what it was all about. I had never been inside a food co-op and I was curious to know what drove the people who worked there. The vegetable guy had been one of the founding members and he knew a lot about food, the food industry, and how tough it was to compete with factory farms. He was an older hippy-type that barely raised his head to look at me as he stocked the lettuce, green beans, squash, and rutabagas. He wore his graying hair in a ponytail with a hairnet. "The big food companies just do everything as cheaply as they can," he said.

"That's kind of the idea, isn't it?" I'd been thinking a lot about business lately and I was sincere in what I said, but he looked up at me with deep exasperation in his gray eyes.

"Your view of business is the standard party line: markets will work everything out." My comment had touched a nerve. "That idea only works if you add in *all* the costs." He had a rutabaga in his hand and tossed it up and down like a pitcher contemplating a fastball. "At the top of Monsanto's list of crimes, misdemeanors, sins, and oversights is the accounting error of grabbing profits while pushing the costs down the line."

"Like to the next generation."

"Like to the next generation. Bull's-eye." He was still tossing the rutabaga up and down. "Now take this humble vegetable. It was grown about six miles from here. No pesticides, herbicides to worry about cleaning up. No water stolen from some imperiled fish." He stopped tossing the rutabaga, held it in front of his eyes like Hamlet considering the skull of Yorick. "This is a rutabaga that comes with no IOUs. It is what it appears to be: a simple rutabaga. No future medical bills attached. No animals, plants, or microbes have been abused in its production. The world has not changed because it has come to be." He tossed it into the air one more time, caught it neatly, and placed it on the growing pyramid of rutabagas.

The vegetable guy may have been trying to be funny, but I'm not completely sure. Certainly he was very serious about his work. He told me that he had been in the sustainability business since the early seventies, when he dropped out of college to join a commune in New Hampshire. "Been at it a long time," he told me. "Composting, biological controls, organic, free range, local, polycultures, CSAs, farmer's markets." He waved his free hand to indicate there were a lot more labels that he just couldn't think of right then. "You name it, I've been there."

His eyes went wistful and his arms stopped moving. "Started off working with Cesar Chavez. I ran the mimeograph machine." He gently picked up another rutabaga and I knew that he was thinking back over the years since he had first peeled himself away from the direction that American agriculture was heading. We both stood there thinking back to *Silent Spring*, *The Population Bomb*, and *The Naked Ape*. I wondered how he thought of himself and the choices he'd made. "Are you doing any good?" I asked. He went dreamy again, and it took a moment for him to come back to our conversation.

When his eyes finally found mine, they could not quite latch on. "I don't know," he said. There was a tiny shake of his head. "It depends on the day. If I stay in this store and keep my head down. If I don't look up from the people who come in here to shop or to sell their products, I can feel like something is happening. But I don't dare look up at the rest of the world." His voice was trailing off. "Keep my head down," he said. I could tell that I was losing him again. He went back to stocking vegetables. "One foot in front of the other," he whispered. But he wasn't talking to me.

The vegetable guy was someone who desperately wanted to be of use. He had burned himself out trying, but he was someone I couldn't help but look up to. I went back to the apartment that I was renting and continued to think about the vegetable guy until my teaching job was finished.

It takes about eight hours to drive from Northfield, Minnesota, to the Broken Heart Ranch. Interstate 90 across the southern half of Minnesota and the center of South Dakota runs right through the heart of the old tallgrass and mixed-grass prairies. As I crossed the ocean of grass, the idea that by selling wild-raised buffalo meat, a person could generate enough capital to restore that land would not leave me. On the surface it sounded like a Rube Goldberg plan for a perpetual-motion machine. I hadn't yet told Jill that the Broken Heart was not nearly large enough for a good test, but, with that lone exception, I could not punch a hole in the idea.

Before I got to the Missouri River I realized that some of the motivators behind the buffalo meat business were the same as those that had driven the vegetable guy to where he was in life. From that point on, the trip that I had always loved was shaded with melancholy. There was the sense that the irrepressible machinery of tragedy had been switched on. I admired the vegetable guy, but I didn't want his life.

Part Two

Four

I DON'T BELIEVE IN FATE, BUT SOMETIMES WEIRD COINcidences crop up that make you wonder. Like the time I got home from Minnesota, after I'd spent many months coming to the conclusion that our little ranch was too small to have much impact on the health of the Great Plains, when a message was waiting for me from a friend who wanted me to partner with him in buying a larger ranch. "Down on the Cheyenne River," he said, when I called him back. "They call it the JD Ranch. About eight thousand acres with a good-sized permit to graze on the National Grassland. I can only handle about six thousand acres and I don't want the hassle of dealing with a government permit."

I pretended that I had no interest whatsoever, but as soon as we hung up I went to the maps that I had been studying for years. I ran my finger down the Cheyenne River, around the southern edge of the Black Hills, then up the east side until it touched the Buffalo Gap National Grassland. The ranch that my friend was dealing on had to be close to where my finger stopped—within the big red circle I had drawn on the map when the idea of large-scale buffalo was new in my mind. It was the kind of coincidence that could not be ignored.

Jill and I took a drive down that way and had a look at the ranch. It was about seventy-five miles between the Broken Heart and the ranch that we were already calling the Cheyenne River Ranch. All the way down we talked about buffalo. At that time we had a tiny corporation to worry about: Wild Idea Buffalo Company. Jill had Wild

Idea Buffalo Company by the horns. She was learning a lot about advertising, processing, shipping, customer income statements, and all the rest of it. She was driven by the idea that buffalo meat was healthy and seemed to like all the details that made it a business. I was more than willing to cede all those details to her. What interested me was figuring out how Wild Idea Buffalo Company could mesh with the land that the buffalo needed and the fact that the land, too, needed the buffalo to be healthy. We drove down the Interstate to Rapid City, then took Highway 44 to the southeast, toward the Pine Ridge Reservation. Fifteen miles out of Rapid we took a county road to the south. After seventeen miles of curvy gravel, we topped out on the endless river breaks above the Cheyenne River. We looked through the windshield of the pickup, over the river bottom and onto Badlands National Park ten miles off in the blue distance. There were no buildings, no roads, not even fences as far as we could see. For a full minute we just stared.

"You can see the curvature of the earth." I said. "We must be parked on the deeded part of the ranch." I pointed out to the endless grassy draws, buttes, and dry water courses. "That must be the Forest Service permit that goes with it.

"We're parked on the ranch?"

"It's got to be around here someplace," I said.

Jill nodded. "Yeah," she said, "someplace."

From where we sat, there were no signs of ranch buildings, but we could see cottonwood trees snaking along the river until they disappeared in both directions. We knew that the ranch buildings were near the river, so we assumed we were close. Even on the civilized side of the river there was no sign of human habitation, save a few strands of rusty barbed wire hung on leaning cedar posts. We were high above the river, where the tops of the bluffs are large flats that had once supported native grasses but for the last hundred years had been used for dryland farming. It was clear that the farming had never been very successful. Without even rolling the window down I could see signs of wind erosion and the tell-tale presence of invasive species of old-world plants.

Situated on the opposite side of the river is a massive portion of the Buffalo Gap National Grassland. If we were where we thought we were, we were looking at what is called the Indian Creek and Corral Draw grazing allotments, both of which were attached to the ranch that was for sale. It was part of the over seventy thousand acres that had been proposed as the first Grasslands Wilderness Area. It literally took an act of Congress to achieve this designation but even without official designation the area had come to be called the Indian Creek Wilderness Area. The 110-square mile area was already being managed as a wilderness, so motorized vehicles were limited to official use only. If Jill and I were ever to explore beyond the river, we would have to either walk or ride a horse.

Using a hand-drawn sketch as our guide, we figured that the ranch house was below us, just over the lip of the bluff and out of sight. Jill was especially interested in seeing the house, but no one was expecting us. We hadn't told anyone we were coming to look at the ranch because it seemed like a crazy pipedream. Neither of us could think of a way that we could swing such a deal, but still, our curiosity drove us to wind our way down a hillside track toward the river.

The path meandered down the bluff, through a spring that welled up in the pickup tracks and created a thicket of willow and ash trees. I was sure we were at the wrong place, but Jill was ready for an adventure, and said that she "had a feeling." Fifty yards past the spring we saw the corner of a metal building, and when we made the gentle turn—bam, there we were in a grove of huge, ancient cottonwoods. We coasted to a halt between the white metal machine shop and the cedar-sided house.

We had gotten too close. We didn't want to get caught looking the property over, but as I hurried to get the pickup turned around Jill was appraising what she saw. "It's nice," she said, as she continued to look over her shoulder. "It needs some work," she said to herself. "But I know just what I would do." I had my head down and was backing up the hill as fast as the poor road would allow.

We drove in silence back toward Rapid City, but I was paying attention. The occupied dwelling nearest to the ranch house was a couple of miles away by marginal roads. The closest real store was over forty miles away; it was easy to imagine that getting to that store in the winter could be a Herculean task. There was a two-room schoolhouse and a volunteer fire hall six miles back in the direction of the Black Hills. As we drove past them, we both wondered what sort of people lived here. We were fortunate to have great neighbors at the Broken Heart, and one of the big unknowns about even dreaming of moving to this remote area was the community we would be moving into. There are welcoming communities on the Great Plains, but there are also insular communities of government haters and Darwin deniers. We did not want to find ourselves in the middle of a community of people who, when presented with new ideas, would expand their chests, jut out their chins, and raise their voices like baboons confronted by a helicopter.

The makeup of the community would mean a lot for both Wild Idea and Jilian, who would be a freshman in high school the following fall. She had begun to notice boys, but her world still revolved around basketball. Jill and I tried to make it to every game, and occasionally Jilian's father showed up. He and Jill were arguing over unpaid child support and bills for his clothes purchases that still came to our address. Sadly, I think his appearances at Jilian's games had more to do with tormenting Jill than they did with a real interest in his daughter.

He was a gum chewer and swaggered into school gymnasiums like a 1950s movie hoodlum. It was comical, but the effect on Jilian was profound. He had been a semi-famous athlete at the high school that Jilian planned to attend and she wanted to please him so much that it made me wince. Early on I realized my role in the situation: to be passive and nonjudgmental. I will forever mark a day in the winter of 2001 as the day when that changed and my feelings for Jilian soared to a higher level.

It was an away basketball game at a small gymnasium in the ranching community of Buffalo in Harding County, South Dakota. The town of Buffalo was a ninety-minute drive from the Broken Heart, and Jill and I were surprised to see that Jilian's father had made the trip from Rapid City. He was sitting in the first row of the bleachers, chewing his gum and instructing Jilian as if he had not been absent from her life for the preceding six weeks.

I loved to watch Jilian bring the ball down the court, and on that day in Buffalo she was particularly good. It was a close game and near the end she was dribbling against a full-court press. She had escaped the collapsing of the defenders twice, but on the third attempt she was cornered at midcourt by three tough ranch girls. She made the mistake of stopping her dribble and had to revert to desperately swinging the ball to keep it from being taken away. It was a melee of arms and elbows, and Jilian was doing well until she suddenly dropped hard to the floor. Jill and I were the first ones there but through the blood it was obvious that her nose was broken. I was on my knees, holding Jilian's chin up and trying to reassure her that she would be all right. But the tears were coming fast and she was hyperventilating. Jill's hand was on my shoulder and, when I felt it tighten, I looked up to see Jilian's father striding across the gym floor. He knelt down on the other side of Jilian, cracked his gum, and told her, "Quiet down, you're all right."

When he reached out his hands, as if to hold her head, I pushed them away and our eyes met over the crying child. I don't think Jilian had any idea of the drama playing out above her, but Jill did. She took advantage of that moment to move Jilian away and I only bothered to glare for one more second before I took Jilian's other arm to help her to our pickup.

Jill's voice brought me back to the present. "What are you smiling about?" I was driving a different pickup but still thinking about Jilian and basketball.

"Nothing. Just thinking that if we moved down to that ranch, Jilian wouldn't get to play basketball in Rapid City."

"I suppose she'd have to go to school out here someplace. Maybe Hermosa or New Underwood," Jill said.

We were only half engaged in the conversation, and I spoke what was going through both of our minds. "She has a lot of friends that she's close to."

It was a long, quiet drive back to the Broken Heart. It settled on us that we were simply not in a situation where we could sanely consider buying half of the JB Ranch. By the time we arrived home that night we agreed that between the lack of funds, concern for Jilian, and uncertainty about giving up our community for an unknown, there was no way we could commit to this bigger ranch. We tried to stop thinking about it.

But it was clear to me that this was the perfect next step in achieving necessary scale in the buffalo business, so I went to a realtor and asked how much we could get for the Broken Heart. He asked some questions and did some figuring on a piece of legal paper. When he pushed the paper across the desk at me, the number that was circled was big enough for a down payment on the new ranch. Of course, the mortgage would continue and the payment would increase, but not too much. "How long would it take to find a buyer?"

"Hard to say. Maybe a year."

When I went to ask Erney what he thought about a bigger ranch, he was a quarter-mile from the house, fixing a corral plank that had fallen off a fence post. The plank had probably been nailed to the posts for eighty years and had finally rotted out around the nail holes. "Looks like we need a new plank," I said.

Erney had a piece of rusty wire in his hand and was trying to thread it through a rotten nail hole. "No need to get extravagant," he said. "Hold that board up there for me, will ya?" I picked up the loose end of the plank that was still hanging by one rusty, old, square nail.

"What would you think about trading this ranch in on a bigger one?" He got the wire through the nail hole and wrapped one end around the post. "Why don't you just put a couple more nails in that?" I asked.

It was a hot day and his forehead was damp with sweat. He looked up at me like I was crazy. "I don't have any nails."

"Well, we could go back to the shop and get a hammer and some nails." He considered the suggestion so stupid that he didn't even look up. He was busy bringing the loose end of the wire around to the other side of the post.

"Break off a piece of that plank and hand it to me." The plank was split where I was holding it. I broke off a ten-inch piece and handed it to him. "Perfect," he said. He began wedging the piece of plank into a crack on the back side of the post. "Why would you want a bigger ranch?" he said.

"You know. All that stuff we talked about—how the birds and animals evolved with buffalo and how some of them are pretty much gone and if they're going to come back they need more room?"

"You mean you want more land to fly the falcons," he said. He was twisting the ends of the wire together with the sliver of wood. "You want more sharp-tailed grouse, more room to run the bird dogs."

He was right: falcons, grouse, and bird dogs were big drivers of my thinking. But I went for a more sophisticated way of saying it. "Species diversity and landscape scale," I said.

"Right." He stood back from his work. "Grab that rock and bash that chunk of wood in when I hold up the plank." He pointed to a smooth rock at my feet.

I climbed though the fence and got into a position where I could drive the stake further into the post. He lifted the plank up to where he wanted it and I gave it a good smack. "Well," he said, "I've spent my whole life trying to get out of work and here you are, wanting to pay big money for more." He shook his head. "Give 'er one more shot," he said.

I hit it again and the stake broke off but the wire held. "Just right," Erney said.

I looked at the post. "I'd say it was a little rough."

"It's a corral, Dan'l. It ain't a piano."

"Don't you think it would be good to have enough space so the deer and the grouse wouldn't have to leave our ranch?"

"Is it your job to protect the world?"

"Well, no. But I've got to do something."

He wasn't looking at me. He was admiring his repaired corral plank. "Yea," he said. "Ain't that a pisser." He reached out and shook the plank. It was surprisingly solid. "I just figured you had enough to do." He gave the plank another shake. "That ought to hold 'til we get a rope." He was beaming with pride.

Erney had a point. Jill was spending twelve hours a day at her restaurant and I was still working at any odd job I could find. Low-wage stuff, traveling too much. Between the two of us Erney and I barely got the ranch chores done. But my drive to expand was great. I once heard a land-hungry rancher defend himself by declaring that he didn't want to own the whole world. "I just want to own the ranches that touch mine!" he said.

In the end I knew I wasn't an empire builder, but I did want to construct a template for how other land managers might advance the cause of a healthy Great Plains ecosystem. In a way I envied the empire builders and the greedy capitalists who had made the job of rebalancing the Great Plains so difficult. Their job had been easier than mine because there was an easy way to measure their success: the more land you own or the more money you have in the bank, the more successful you are. Sustainability is a lot harder to measure. There are few models that show you how it is done and the cost of failure is huge. The threat of failure made me hesitate.

I continued to talk with Erney. He knew that I was a bit of a dreamer and I knew that his sometimes cynical attitude was a kind of defense mechanism. He hated the destruction of the Great Plain ecosystem as much as I did. It was the immensity of the problem that stymied him. This was not just a playful, academic debate. If we were going to move, I needed Erney to be with me. His participation was vital.

One night, as we sat talking in his cluttered cabin, he let me know that he had been thinking about my dream. The cabin was so small and cluttered that the television had to be mounted on the wall next to the door. Since Erney's eyes had begun to weaken and he was too bull-headed to go to an optometrist, he didn't read as much as he used to. *The Andy Griffith Show* chattered behind our conversation. "I think we're going to do it, Ern. If things come together we might have a big old ranch to take care of."

"What were those stables that Hercules had to clean out?"

"King Augeas's."

"That's it," he said. "Decades of cattle shit. That's what you're buying."

"He got them cleaned, didn't he?"

"He changed the course of a river, Dan'l."

He was pretending to watch Andy and Barney, but I knew he was thinking about what he had just said. I didn't make a sound, and finally he began to squirm in his chair.

"On the other hand," he said, "the Lord hates a coward."

"Are you getting religion?"

"Oh, no. I had enough of that when I was a kid. I was just saying that it would be nice to see a couple hundred head of buffalo moving around like they used to do back when Christ was a corporal."

"Well, you'd help me, wouldn't you?"

It took him a long time to answer, but I knew what he was going to say. "Sure I would. But you know as well as I do that I ain't much good." He held up his right hand and wiggled the stump of his thumb. "You'd need more help than me."

Then something else happened that made me wonder if fate wasn't at work—Gervase Hittle, my sixty-five-year-old professor from graduate school showed up at the Broken Heart. He had taken early retirement from the University of South Dakota a few years after I graduated and had been drifting since. He knocked around at the University of Iowa in Iowa City, then in his childhood hometown of Lawton, Oklahoma. It took Gervase ten years to figure out that, although he was fed up with working in higher education, he wasn't ready to retire. He'd been a marine in Korea and a professor of comparative literature, specializing in French literature. His dissertation had been a translation of Alphonse Lamartine, but late on the second night after he showed up at the Broken Heart, after several glasses of whiskey, he confessed that he had always wanted to be a cowboy.

If it took a year for us to sell the Broken Heart, and if I could get the bank to go along with forwarding that money toward the purchase of the Cheyenne River Ranch, all I needed was someone to watch the new place for a year. And there was Gervase, sitting across the table from me with a whiskey in his hand.

I was not surprised. Gervase and I had known each other since the fall of 1971 when he returned from a postdoctoral fellowship in Black literature at Stanford. From the very beginning he seemed more interested in horses and hunting with falcons than with the subjective case of French verbs. He had a way of philosophizing about blue-collar life in a way that was part romance, part nostalgia, and part bullshit. He fancied himself an artisan craftsman but in truth he was simply stuck in the past. His tools were museum-quality hand saws and planes, screw drivers with handmade wooden handles, brace and bits from the nineteenth century. Gervase was not an efficient twenty-first-century laborer, but he was an early riser and not afraid of work. He had some training in horsemanship and an old stock-saddle that may have been the first one ever made. He was a U.S. Marines trained rifleman and we needed a good marksman for when the SHA harvest trailer was finished.

We sat at the kitchen table of the Broken Heart ranch house with a bottle of Crown Royal between us and I imagined him taking care of the ranch on the Cheyenne River while we found a buyer for the smaller Broken Heart. He was no spring chicken and his experience as a ranch hand was limited. But he had a lot of heart. On another visit a few years prior to that time we had sat at the same table on a hot summer day and watched the heat waves rise from the pasture just to the east of the house. I was reading intermittently but Gervase was antsy. Just outside the window, two horses stood butt to nose under the only tree in sight. They swatted flies with their tails, and a third horse lay flat on the ground thirty yards away. These were three hard-to-catch renegades but Gervase wanted very much to go for a ride. I was not interested in riding and I did not want to put forth the effort I knew it would take to capture and saddle those horses. But Gervase has always had an abundance of energy and that day he was persistent.

"I'll catch 'em," he said. "No problem."

"It's not worth it," I said.

He laughed. "They don't look too wild." All three of them had their eyes closed and the only sign of life was the slow flicking tails of the two that were standing. The prone horse was a bay, which was actually the flightiest of the three. He lay on his side—flat as a fish— and looked like he had been dead for a week. The only indication that he was more than twelve hundred pounds of roadside carrion was the red halter that I had left on him because he was so hard to catch.

"They're wilder than you think," I said.

Gervase is a small, wiry, cliché of an ex-marine. He takes great pride in his horsemanship and manhood and is easily offended. He scoffed at my comment. "I think I can handle those three."

"Well, hell," I said, "go on out there and grab that bay. You might be able to sneak up on him."

Five minutes later I was surprised to see Gervase in a sort of ninja crouch, slithering under the bottom fence wire like a coyote. Suddenly what was going on outside was more interesting than the book I was reading. 'What the hell," I thought, "is he going to do?"

The scene was framed by the window—two horses standing under a tree, each with one eye open, a small man tiptoeing toward their prone friend, who was deep in horsey dreamland. I had enough time to wonder what the bay was dreaming about. I thought it might be the image of a spring meadow—dark green with new, tasty grass emerging in every direction, a cool breeze teasing his mane. Whatever he was dreaming as Gervase lowered his stance and moved closer, it exploded into the nightmare of a puma's leap. I couldn't believe how fast Gervase moved. He jumped at the bay from the right side of my vision and the horse was on his feet and wild-eyed in a split second. I saw Gervase's hand close on the halter and then, just like in a Roadrunner cartoon, the horse was gone in a blur and all I saw were Gervase's boots flying horizontal and out of the picture frame. "My God!" I said out loud, then leaned close enough to the window to catch the last glimpse of Gervase, one arm stretched out like superman flying alongside a running stallion. They were gone in a sparrow's heartbeat, and when I looked, the other two horses were looking back at me with their jaws as slack as mine.

A year later, as we sat at that same table, I was wondering if it was possible that Gervase could take care of the new ranch while Jill and I worked at selling the Broken Heart. I'd known the guy for thirty years and I knew that he had almost no knowledge of how a ranch works. But sometimes tenacity trumps knowledge, and my thoughts went back to the day he caught the bay. It hadn't been the most orthodox way of catching a horse, but twenty minutes after they had disappeared Gervase came back over the hill, leading the bay back to the corral. The smile on his face was the same smile the Crown Royal had given him. I poured him another shot. "Gervase," I said, "I might have a proposition for you."

We closed the deal on the Cheyenne River Ranch in the early spring of 2002. My brother, Scott, has always been handy with building things, running equipment, wiring, plumbing, and generally figuring things out, so he was in the habit of coming out to the Broken Heart, where there were lots of things that needed fixing. When he heard that we were trading for a larger ranch, he left his semi-retirement home in Florida and came out to help for a month. He had only been at the Broken Heart a few hours when Jill and I loaded him into the pickup and we drove down to the Cheyenne River Ranch. To give Scott an overview of what we had committed to, we drove out to the bluff that we had found the first day we had seen the place.

I had learned a little more about the surrounding country by then. We got out of the pickup and walked to the edge of the western river break. I pointed out toward the rough Badlands breaks. In the mid-nineteenth century those dry washes were invaded by paleontologists searching for the fossilized bones of ancient animals. It is ironic that one of the first waves of white men to find value in this land were men determined to establish the science of evolution. Fossils from the Badlands traveled the world to be examined by the best scientific minds of the age. It tickled me to think that Darwin himself might well have pondered fossils from the area. I like to think that he might have scrapped a bit of Badlands dust onto his oak laboratory table as he imagined how the flipper he was looking at might have been the precursor foreleg of a different species. He would undoubtedly shake his head in disbelief if he could hear what misinterpretations his theory had suffered in this land of fossils.

From our vantage point I was able to show Scott and Jill what remained of the shack that Adolph Fiesler had inhabited in the early twentieth century. Two weeks before, I'd ridden down to the shack and could barely imagine living there. It was little more than a line camp—a place where old-time cowboys passed a day or two when they were checking cattle or fixing fence. But Adolf had lived there for decades. He was exiled to the Cheyenne River because he had fallen in love with Kitty Daugherty. He'd been cowboying for her father, John, who was a big rancher and strict father. When John saw what was happening between Adolph and Kitty, he sent Adolph to watch a distant bunch of cows for the winter. Adolph ended up living in the shack beside the Cheyenne River for the rest of his life. He never found another woman and I suppose that shack began to feel like home. They say that home is where the heart is, but that day on the river above Adolph Fiesler's shack, it occurred to me that, more often, home is where you get stuck.

The country all around us had a short but frenetic human history. Humans were a rare species in the Badlands and Cheyenne River breaks until the mid 1700s, when the Lakota Sioux from the east, suddenly made very mobile by the acquisition of horses from the Arikaras, burst onto the great buffalo prairies. The land in front of us was the stage for both the genesis and the last act of the unequaled horse culture of the Lakota Sioux. For about two hundred years they moved freely through this land and only gave into the European onslaught when it landed on their very doorstep in the form of thousands of homesteaders supported by a modern army.

The land we stood upon was once at the center of the Lakota Sioux Country. Before the 1851 Indian Claims Commission made an attempt to divide and settle the Crows, Cheyennes, Blackfoots, Arikaras, Pawnees, and Lakotas, the horse Indians of the Northern Great Plains traveled at will. The Claims Commission drew a line around western South Dakota and large portions of North Dakota, Nebraska, Montana, and Wyoming and called the tract Sioux Country. Seventeen years later, after Red Cloud's successful defense of the Powder River country from illegal white encroachment, Sioux Country was trimmed slightly and became the Great Sioux Reservation. Nine years later the reservation was trimmed again, to exclude all of Wyoming and Montana, and nearly all of North Dakota, Nebraska, and the gold-rich Black Hills of South Dakota. The Lakotas were told to leave the Powder River Country of Wyoming and Montana and report to their assigned reservations or face military action. Their refusal resulted in the Custer Battle at the Little Big Horn River on June 25, 1876, a hundred and fifty miles from where we stood that day. The 269 members of Custer's 7th Calvary died in the battle and, as a result, the Lakotas were forced back to the reservation. Thirteen years later, the reservation was again reduced, to five smaller units divided roughly along the lines of leadership.

Across the Cheyenne River and touching our new ranch was the portion of land that was assigned to the Oglala Sioux—the people of Red Cloud and Crazy Horse. It started off with the name Red Cloud Agency, but soon it was known as the Pine Ridge Reservation. By then the reservation was surrounded by acquisitive cattlemen and homesteaders and, although federal law prohibited both whites and Oglalas from crossing the river, raids were not uncommon. Eventually a few more miles of reservation were peeled away, and in the late 1880s, whites were forced to hang on the edge of Pine Ridge, biding their time until an excuse could be found to take a larger bite of Oglala land. Their chance came when a fanatic, messianic, wave of hope swept the reservations in 1890. The idea was that if the Lakota people wore shirts painted with images of their deceased ancestors and danced in praise of an oddly Christian-like god, the good times would come again—the buffalo would return. The day my brother came to see the ranch, it struck me hard that 130 years before, people had likely danced on that very ground in the hope that buffalo would again graze those slopes.

I pointed to Stronghold Table, where the Ghost Dancers had taken refuge, and swung my arm to the southeast, where two hundred of them had been massacred in the valley of Wounded Knee Creek. We were sitting on a blanket that Jill had spread out on the land. We looked out to the folded hills that by some odd Anglo alchemy of ownership had passed to us. "We don't own it," I said. "We just get to live here and make mortgage payments for awhile."

Our reverie was broken by the discreet popping of a Champagne cork. It was Jill, up to her usual catering tricks. Scott smiled. "Might as well celebrate anyway," he said.

"We got lots to celebrate," I said, and looked to Jill. We raised our glasses. "We're getting married," I said.

"Married?" Scott was dumbfounded. He shot down his Champagne and stretched his glass out to Jill for a refill. "I'll be damned."

By the time we were ready to move to the Cheyenne River, Jilian was no longer a little girl. Already I had begun looking back over our earlier years with nostalgia. Sometimes in the middle of my day I would find myself, immobile and staring back into thin air as if I could see her at age eleven, twelve, thirteen. Those were years of a special relationship that had touched me in a way that took me by surprise. She followed me around when I worked on the ranch, especially in the autumn when we started hunting with the dogs and the falcons. She was tough and could stand a lot more cold and wind than her slight, boyish frame and pigtails would lead you to think. If I spoke she listened, and, though I knew a lot about how responsibility settles on the shoulders of middle-aged men, I had not been prepared for what I felt for Jilian.

I had always prided myself in my ability to get around and to see things on the open prairie. But in those years, when Jilian was growing into womanhood, I found myself losing track of wide-running bird dogs and high-flying falcons. I found myself turning to Jilian. Her blue eyes would be focused on the treeless distance and she would point with a gloved finger, or sometimes with only a raised chin, to where the dog coursed or the falcon careened at the horizon. If we lost a falcon, I would stand where we lost her and swing the lure in hopes that she would return while Jilian ran for the pickup. She could easily run a mile and be counted on to thread the pickup back over barren hills and through soggy draws to where she had left me. I had to admit that I was not the man I had once been, but together we could do it all.

Since I had known Lucas, Jill's son, he had lived mostly with his father. By the time the Broken Heart was sold and we were ready to move down to the Cheyenne River Ranch, he was in the navy. But when he was home, our life was like the family that I hadn't experienced since I was a child—kids and friends came and went, screen doors slammed, food was cooked and consumed by the bucketful. The kid's chores were occasionally left undone and somehow I didn't mind finishing them.

Jill and I look back at those last years at the Broken Heart Ranch as days of innocence. We were working hard but hadn't yet taken on the extra layer of debt and attention that the new ranch and a growing business demanded. Those years were good years for Jilian, too. She and her friends had the run of the place. One afternoon when they asked me if "cow tipping" was a real thing, I couldn't help myself. "Sure," I said. "Cows sleep standing up."

"Yeah," Samantha said, "but can you sneak up on them?"

I was pretty sure that sneaking up on a sleeping cow was impossible, but I didn't let on. "Of course you can," I said. "You have to be real quiet, but they're sound sleepers."

"And you can tip them over?" Jilian asked. She had her arms crossed over her chest and one eyebrow was elevated.

It was hard to keep a straight face. I turned my back and concentrated on sorting nuts and bolts into their proper drawers. "It's easy," I said.

I could feel them looking at each other—weighing the chances that I was telling the truth. "Can you do it with buffalo?"

"No," I spoke with certainty. "No, buffalo are light sleepers."

You could feel the wheels turning in their fifteen-year-old heads. "Mumm," Sam said.

"Where could we find some cows?" Jilian asked.

I willed a straight face and slowly turned to them. "It's got to be pitch dark," I said.

"Yeah, but who's got some cows?"

I waved for them to follow me. We walked from the workshop to the top of the hill that overlooked the Whitewood Creek valley. I pointed to a group of Angus cattle out on the flat, three-quarters of a mile from where we stood,. "Whose are those?" Jilian asked.

"They're Steve and Norma's."

"Mister and Misses Bestgen's?"

"Yep."

"They're a long way out there," Sam said.

"Yeah," I said, "and you'd have to drive out there in the dark."

"How many gates?" Jilian asked.

"Just two." I pointed them out. "You'd have to be real quiet and walk the last quarter-mile." I went back to the shop and, when I peeked back at them, they had their heads together and took turns pointing out to the cows.

As soon as they finished dinner they began rummaging through the mud room for flashlights and extra clothes. "What are they doing?" Jill asked.

"I think they're planning to do a little cow tipping."

Jill's eyes were full of disapproval. She had been raised on a dairy farm and I knew what was coming. "Whose cows?"

"Steve's."

"I'm sure he would not be happy to hear that you are instigating harassment of his livestock."

The girls went on with their preparations and I leaned to whisper in Jill's ear. "They won't get within a hundred yards of them," I said. "But I'll call Steve and let him know there might be some strange lights in his pasture."

There was no moon and the stars were obscured with a rare general cloudiness. We made Sam and Jilian wait until the sun was long gone. "Dark as the inside of a cat," I said to Jilian. "Now, be real quiet and don't turn those flashlights on unless the cows start running." Jilian was in the driver's seat. The engine was idling and she sat with her eyes barely over the steering wheel. One elbow hung out of the window, like a safari guide's.

"You think they'll start running?"

"Probably not until you get the first few tipped over." They both looked straight ahead and nodded, as if that made perfect sense.

"You know where you're going?" I touched Jilian's shoulder and she nodded. "Right in the corner of the pasture there, by the duck pond. Turn your lights off there and sneak up on 'em."

She nodded again. "Sneak up on 'em," she said.

"Sneak up on 'em," Sam said.

"And when you push them—push hard." They didn't look up at me, but both heads nodded.

Jill and I watched from the top of the hill. The pickup lights moved down the hill like a dingy on the ocean. The engine sound faded almost instantly and the night was still and very dark. "Are you sure about this?" Jill asked.

"They'll be lucky to get to the first gate."

"I don't know. They seemed determined."

The lights moved slowly through the blackness and our depth perception began to fail us. It was difficult to know where they were, but they were headed in the right direction. When the tiny red embers of break lights came on, it was as if the dingy flashed a pair of flares. "They made it to the first gate," I said. "Another quarter-mile and they set out on foot."

"You're cruel," Jill said with a laugh.

The distant lights did not move for several minutes so we suspected the girls were struggling with the gatepost. Jill held her breath, but when the lights began moving again she exhaled and clicked her tongue. "Isn't there a ditch down there?"

The lights dipped out of sight, then rolled to the sky. "Right there," I said.

"They made it?"

"They did."

The clouds moved away to expose one star. It was bright white and Jill pointed up to it. She smiled and I could just make out her face. We moved closer to each other until our shoulders touched. "They're still going," Jill said.

Now they were a long way out. "Should be getting close to the second gate." And just then the break lights came on again and the headlights blinked off. "That herd of cows should be a couple hundred yards straight ahead of them."

There was a tiny wink of light. "Must be crawling under the fence."

We waited for what seemed like a long time. It was easy to imagine them sneaking through the grass toward ink-black blobs on the ridgeline. Then two flashlight beams waved erratically and we thought we heard a faint teenage squeal. The lights went all over the sky until they lined out for where the truck was parked. But then an odd thing happened: the lights went out again.

We watched for five full minutes and I was about to go for the other pickup when the flashlights came on again—this time further out into the pasture. Now the kids were a good mile away and the lights again flashed wildly before they went black again. This time we waited ten minutes, and when the flashes came on again, they were far to the south. "They're following the cows," I said.

"You have to go get them," Jill said. "They'll get lost out there."

"They'll be alright." I tried to sound confident. "But what are they doing?"

"They're cow tipping."

This went on for forty-five minutes, and just when I had decided to head out in the other truck and run the girls down, the flashlights, now nearly two miles away, drew together and started back toward us. We waited another half hour until the pickup lights came on and headed in our direction. When Jilian and Sam came into the house they were both splattered with mud, and their hair was tangled and falling into their faces. They had been sweating and Jilian's shirt was torn. Jill and I did not let on that we had been watching. Jill looked up from her book. "So how'd it go?"

The girl's were exhausted and stood frustrated, with their hands on their hips.

"We need fresh cows,' Jilian said.

"And tamer ones," Sam said.

They grew up fast. It was only a year later that Jill found an envelope of photographs on Jilian's dresser. She handed them to me and let her shoulders slump while I thumbed through them. I recognized the home of one of Jilian's friends and I knew what I was looking at. The week before we had given Jilian permission to sleep over at a friend's house. We were told that the parents were home but from the photo's contents it was clear they were not. I leafed through pictures of the darling little girls that I had watched growing up. Everyone had been a cute, bright kid, but in the pictures everyone was smiling stupidly and obviously drunk on their asses. There were several photos of a table filled with empty beer cans. There was a repulsive picture of an unrecognizable girl with her head in the toilet.

I calmly put the pictures back into the envelope. "Look at the bright side," I said. "There weren't any pictures of boys."

Jill nodded and smiled but she was worried. "There will be," she said.

I wrapped Jill up in my arms and we rocked back and forth. "She's too young," Jill said.

"Yeah," I said. "She seems young."

"We have to slow her down." We were still rocking back and forth.

"I suppose we do."

And that is what we did. Grounded for two weeks. No parties, no friends. Basketball practice and school only. That was it. Jilian took it with blazing eyes and a granite chin. She didn't say much during those two weeks of punishment. But when she did speak she said the thing that hurt me the most. "I'm going to move in with Dad."

Five

JILIAN WAS GONE FOR ONLY A COUPLE OF MONTHS, BUT it was still too long. Jill and I worried about her and made a special effort to go to all her sports events and have her out to the ranch on the weekends. Even though she wasn't happy with her father she was reluctant to submit to our discipline and, in the end, it took an emissary from France to bring her home.

Years before, when Jill and I were on a book tour in France, a fellow falconer befriended us and showed us the ancient tradition of falconry as practiced in France. Henri Desmond is an agricultural solicitor in France, so he has great connections for places to hunt with his falcons. He had taken us to a series of elegant farms north of Paris and we watched his peregrine falcons chase partridges over grain fields that had been hunted long before the United States was a country. I was impressed with the quality of the falconry, Jill was impressed with the food, and we were both impressed by Henri's English setters.

They were fortunate dogs. Henri's brother had a grouse moor in Scotland and the dogs did double duty in the wheat fields of Flanders and in the heather of Scotland. We drank some good wine and sampled wild boar for the first time. But the thing that I could not forget was the sight of those tall blue belton setters working the partridges. They ran every bit as wide as our American dogs and they held their points for long periods of time, while the falcons took their time getting into position for the flush and stoop. The setters' hair was long and silky, and after the hunt, when we were feeding Henri's falcons and sipping brandy, they hung around genteelly, like just a couple more dignified members of the hunting party. Henri called their demeanor "Nobility created from centuries of enlightened breeding." I thought that might be a little self-congratulatory, but I sure did like those dogs.

We offered to host Henri's sons on a summer of experiencing the American West. the two boys came during separate summers—one to do some North American hunting and the other to help build buffalo fence. In the fall following the second visit we got a call from Henri. "There is a litter of puppies," he said. "You must have one."

Just before Labor Day we drove to Minneapolis to pick up the puppy at the airport. He had been quarantined in England, and then shipped direct to Minneapolis. He was a gorgeous, three-month-old male setter, but he had not traveled well. He emerged from the shipping crate with a deep sad look on his face and vomit from one end to the other. "He's a wimp," I said.

"He has a delicate, French stomach," Jill said as she hugged him, puke and all.

It turned out that he was neither a wimp nor did he have a delicate stomach. Once we got him washed up and walked around the airport grounds for half an hour, he jumped up into the pickup like he had been born on a ranch. He pushed Jill into the middle seat and hung his head out the window like a blue heeler. By the time we got to the South Dakota line, his name had evolved from Henri, to Henry, and finally to Hank. The first time Jilian saw him, she was out at the Broken Heart for the weekend. It took a single afternoon for them to bond for life.

Like all good dogs, Hank wanted to be with people. But he was not needy and could amuse himself for hours around a corral full of horses, other dogs, grasshoppers, songbirds, or mice. It took a few months until his curiosity matured to include the sharp-tailed grouse of the Great Plains. When it did, he discovered his heritage and the main purpose of life. Until then, he focused on charming us with his intelligent dark eyes, gentle affection, and mostly elegant manners.

Jilian happened to be out at the ranch one day when Jill came back from Rapid City with a pickup load of groceries. She was catering a party for some of Rapid City's elites and was doing some of the preparations at home. Though her menus always included special ingredients that were hard to find, the one bright spot in her shopping trip that day had been the discovery of crusty French-style baguettes that were new to the stores in our area, and she was planning to use them for bruschetta.

It took a half-dozen trips back and forth to the truck to get all the grocery sacks into the house and, as Jill, Jilian, and I worked, Hank sat in the front yard watching our progress. Catering is a high-pressure job and, on occasions like this, being preoccupied with thinking through the steps of the cooking, arranging transportation, and hiring of wait staff, Jill can lose her sense of humor. Jilian and I needed to get away, so we went out to see Erney in his cabin. It was the time of year when the caddis flies hatched on the high Black Hills lakes and the fly shop had called with a desperate plea for more elk hair caddis imitations. Erney was never a fast tier, but when we pushed his door open, he was moving at full speed.

His cabin was always a mess, but that day we saw wind rows of elk hair and feather clippings on all the horizontal surfaces. A young falcon stood on a tall perch in the middle of the room, the TV blared, and Erney sat slumped over his fly-tying desk. It is difficult to tie flies without a right thumb, but Erney had learned to use his left hand and developed a way of holding things between the index and middle finger of his right. He was surprisingly efficient. His tying desk was set up in front of the dirty little window that faced our house. The light that could penetrate the dust came through the glass and settled on his work. Jilian moved close to him and stood, leaning forward and studying the movements of Erney's hands. Her fingers fidgeted under her chin, and when Erney said, "Okay," she would smile, reach out with her little index finger, and hold the thread against the hook shank while Erney completed a knot with his massive, maimed hands. "Perfect," Erney would say. "We're going to put you on full time!" Jilian beamed like the little girl I had feared was lost.

When Erney looked up and out the window, he shook his head. "What's your mom doing?"

"Carrying in groceries."

"No. She's playing with Hank."

We crowded around the window to see Jill on her hands and knees in the frontyard. She was crawling toward Hank, who was ten feet away with his front legs stretched out in front of him and his butt in the air.

"He's got something in his mouth," I said.

"Are they playing fetch?" Jilian asked.

We leaned closer to the dirty glass. "Oh, my God!" I said. "He's got a baguette!"

We burst from Erney's cabin door but I caught Jilian's arm. "Go easy," I said. "If we lose that baguette, it's a seventy-five-mile round trip to get another one."

Now Jill's butt was in the air too. But when she advanced on hands and knees, Hank jumped up and ran a playful circle around her. The baguette stuck out a foot on each side of his mouth, and once he was behind Jill, he crouched down and waited for Jill to crawl around and face him. His silky, white tail was wagging like crazy. "I need that goddamned baguette," Jill hissed through her smiling teeth.

When Jilian got down on her knees, Hank knew the jig was up. He stood perfectly still, the first sign of the rock solid points for which he would become famous. Jill crept in while Jilian talked him down. Then—snatch. Jill was inspecting the baguette for damages and Hank jumped on Jilian. They rolled in the grass and Jill stood up with the prize in hand.

There were a couple of canine punctures, but the bread was not soggy. Jill shrugged, brushed off the baguette, and said, "They'll never know the difference."

I'm not much help when Jill is cooking. But I can do dishes as long as I leave the crystal to her. That night we talked while I scrubbed pans and she sliced, diced, simmered, and braised. She told me that Jilly had had a fight with her father, who was actually living with his parents, Jilian's grandparents. There was something about a window screen that had been removed. One thing had led to the next and there had been some pushing. I put down the scrub pad I was applying to a stubborn pot and actually considered driving into Rapid City right that minute. Jill laid down her paring knife and came to my side. She leaned over and kissed my cheek and we went back to work.

Just before bed we descended the stairs to look in on Jilian. Her bed was in the corner of the basement. We had partitioned it off from the furnace and storage area. The walls were not finished but Jill and Jilian had secured glow-in-the-dark stars to the ceiling. Below the big dipper, Hank and Jilian were curled up together. They had no idea we were there.

"They feel safe," I said.

Jill nodded. "She so needs something to love."

"She's staying here," I said.

"Yeah, she's staying here. And she's coming with us to the Cheyenne River."

About that time we received a call from a man I didn't know who introduced himself as Joe Ricketts. I got the immediate impression that I should know who he was. He told me that he had read some of my books and wanted to talk to me about buffalo. He planned to be in Rapid City the next week and suggested we have breakfast.

When we hung up, I Googled Joe and learned that he was a very wealthy man. He had invented online stock trading and had just sold his company for an obscene amount of money. Instantly I was intrigued but suspicious. This sounded like another rich but poorly informed guy who was infatuated with the idea of buffalo. I had no idea what his intentions were, so Jill and I were reluctant to go. "I don't like breakfast," Jill said. "But free breakfast in a restaurant is a good idea."

At the time she still had her own restaurant and was running Wild Idea in her spare time. She comes from a family of food freaks and has been a waitress, a dishwasher, a cook, a chef, a hostess, a restaurant manager, and a restaurant owner. She loves everything about food and the food industry, especially restaurants. "It's one of the greatest things about civilization," she says wistfully. She squints her eyes when she thinks about the sheer genius of restaurants. "You just tell them what you want to eat and they bring it to you. They bring you wine. Then take all the dishes away and wash them for you. You can actually participate in genuine conversation."

I think that is what she was expecting when we met Joe Ricketts for breakfast. Though my cynicism was strong, as I thought about the upcoming morning I couldn't help being hopeful. Joe was a businessman who had built an incredibly successful company. In the years to come he would bankroll his son's try for election to the U.S. House of Representatives. He would buy the Chicago Cubs, for crying out loud. He would also invest millions in an effort to prove that President Obama was not a U.S. citizen, but I didn't know that at the time. He was powered by a big, can-do, American-made engine. With his little finger this guy could change my whole world and set the Great Plains back on the road to health and balance.

When we showed up at the local hotel for breakfast, the world-weary cynic in me had been pushed aside. It was the silly, naive, optimist who thrust out his hand and smiled up at Joe. But for the next hour Jill and I only got to talk when we ordered our eggs Benedict. Jill understood the situation right away and asked the waitress if she could keep the menu. She knew that she would need something to read. But over the preceding week, I had brainwashed myself to such an extent that I waited expectantly for my cue to hold forth with my ideas concerning the restoration of free-ranging buffalo and their catalytic value to the health of other iconic Great Plains species. I was ready to talk about the way a huge herd could bolster the spirit of Americans. I wanted to talk about their value as a genuine health food for an ailing nation. I wanted to talk about species diversity, carbon sequestration, and social injustice. But I never got the chance. Instead, I learned that Joe had ordered some of our buffalo meat and thought it was so good that he was planning to start his own buffalo meat company. He was pumping us for information. His scheme was to produce ready-to-eat buffalo TV dinners! "You know, like Swanson's." He already had several high-paid researchers on his staff. He wanted to get a few thousand live buffalo lined up because he figured that Siberia was bound to open up to international investment and hundreds of thousands of acres would soon be available to graze buffalo for a song. Oh, and by the way, would I like to write the biography of his company?

I declined the offer of employment, even though the pay was great and I needed the work. I was so disappointed that after breakfast, Jill had to lead me back to the pickup. She drove and I sat staring at the road that led back to our ranch. When I closed my eyes, all I saw were live, terrified buffalo being loaded into hundreds of ocean-going, steel shipping containers. They were being swung by huge cranes onto decks of ships that were heading back across the Pacific. I wondered what Rocke Afraid of Hawk would make of such a sight.

Halfway home, I asked Jill if Joe Ricketts really was one of our customers. "I recognized the name," she said. "I'll check it out. He probably ordered just to learn what we are up to."

"He didn't learn much," I said. "Tell me that he is not a typical customer. Tell me that our customers get it. Tell me that what we are doing is worth it."

"Most of them get it," she said, "and in the big picture it's worth it."

Though I too was convinced that what we were doing was worthwhile, I was awash with doubt. What was I doing with my life? How did it compare with Joe Ricketts's? He was so sure of what he was doing and I wasn't sure of anything. He seemed happy with computing buffalo into profit. I was the one who lost sleep over the fate of buffalo and their ecosystem.

As we rounded a corner on the road north of Sturgis, Bear Butte was suddenly center stage of our vision. It is a sacred place for the Northern Cheyennes and the Lakotas, and it reminded me of a section in Berry Lopez's great landscape book, *Arctic Dreams*, that describes an Eskimo hunter poised above the breathing hole of a seal that might, or might not, appear that day. My memory of the passage is that the hunter holds a spear aloft for hours, and Lopez implies that the subsistence hunter has never complicated his life beyond the outcome of one measurable event. Sitting in the passenger's seat of the rattling pickup, it dawned on me that for twenty years I had misinterpreted the meaning of Lopez's story. I had always seen the hunter as noble because his life was easy to measure, and that modern man should be less concerned with the complications of his existence. But Joe Ricketts's life was easy to measure too. It was not the simplicity of the action to obtain the coveted object that made for nobility. It was the attitude toward and intended use of the object that was important. It makes all the difference that the hunter intends to feed his family with the seal, and that one seal is enough. What if his intention was to sell the seal? What if he intended to harpoon a thousand seals? What if he intended to sell them? Could that be noble too?

Gervase Hittle came through for us. He agreed to move into a few rooms at the new ranch house and look after things while we organized the final details of the sale and got moved in. We hauled about twenty buffalo down to the Cheyenne River because that was all the buffalo-fenced pasture could hold. Gervase would take care of them while the fencing crew put up the rest of the fence—over twenty miles of it. We planned to build a couple rooms in the barn for Gervase and Erney. Scott had agreed to come up from Florida for a couple months to help with the construction. Unfortunately I had agreed to another semester-long teaching job at Carleton College. It was a tumultuous time and a lot of the work came down on Jill's shoulders. She was the one and only employee of Wild Idea Buffalo Company. My job was to bring in some hard cash, but she had to see to all the details of the move.

Before I left for Minnesota, I wanted to haul as many of our belongings down to the new house as possible. As soon as Scott arrived we started ferrying stuff between the ranches. We would take the first day to load the pickup and trailer with tools, clothes, books, and furniture. We'd drive it down the next day. There were a half-dozen ranch buildings at the Cheyenne River Ranch and we tried to find the right place for everything. We went through the same scenario for four days, and on the trips back and forth I did my best to explain why we were taking such a risk with our lives and livelihood. But I was angry about the timing of things. I resented having to work like that and I felt guilty for having to leave. My explanation to Scott was a kind of justification and, as I talked, I could hear my voice becoming shrill with frustration.

We had almost reached the turnoff for the Broken Heart Ranch and there was still an hour of light. "You want to go over to the Short Horn Saloon for a drink?"

Scott was relieved. "Sure," he said.

The Short Horn was a noncommercial bar set up in a shed in my neighbor's frontyard. It belonged to Sharron and Stan Holsclaw, whose ranch ran along the back of the Broken Heart. They had been our best friends for decades and Jill and I were going to miss them. The area between the house and the Short Horn was filled with ingenious projects in different stages of completion. Most of the projects related to ranching equipment and a lot of them related to horses. Stan was an enrolled member of the Rosebud Sioux Tribe, but he had spent an entire career in the mining industry as a laborer, machine operator, and finally a foreman. He was a machinery savant and an itinerate horse trader with the accompanying character flaws.

I had bought a few horses from him with varying levels of satisfaction, and I was always curious about what he had in his corral. That afternoon, Scott and I parked the pickup beside a hydraulic log splitter that appeared to be in the process of conversion into an industrial-strength trash compactor. We were heading for the house to rouse Stan but first walked over to the corral and peered into the loafing shed. There were five horses inside and the first four came out to greet us. They were Stan's private older horses with good sense. I knew Pepsi and Buck and the pair of Frisian workhorses, though I didn't know their names. Scott and I petted them and rubbed their foreheads while they frisked us, looking for treats. We were about to head for the house when the fifth horse came out of the shed. He was a yearling paint with kind eyes, curious but shy. He stood well beyond arm's reach. There was something about him that attracted me and we stared at each other over the corral rail in mutual appraisal.

I heard Stan chuckle before he spoke. "Finest kind," he said. "He'd go good in your string."

I turned and we smiled at each other. "Yeah," I said, and waved my hand in his face. "I'm still trying to recover from the last time I bought a horse from you."

"I gave you your money back. What more can a guy do?" He moved past me to the corral rail and held his hand out. "This paint, now, he's something special." The horse looked at Stan's hand and took a step back.

"He's never even had a halter on him," I said. I pretended like I didn't care, but there was something about the colt that attracted me. I tried not to let Stan notice.

"Hell," Stan said, "he'll get over that. He's just a baby."

"We came for a drink, not a horse."

Scott had been at the Short Horn before and pushed through the swinging, bat-wing doors like Wild Bill Hickok. Stan is a big man and the Short Horn is a very small bar, maybe ten by twelve feet, but he crawled under the bar that cut that space in half and settled into the bartender's position. We had room for maybe one more drinker on our side of the bar but there were only two stools. Stan just fit between the bar and three rough shelves of odd-ball bottles of liquor that people had given him for Christmas and birthdays—peppermint schnapps, lime flavored vodka, banana cordial, Southern Comfort, and a bottle of whiskey with gold flakes floating around inside. The good stuff was under the bar, and Scott and I knew it.

"I'll have a Crown Royal and water," Scott said.

"No water," Stan said as he reached into the darkness for the Crown.

"Ice?"

"No. No ice either." He poured us each an inch and a half of whiskey in a fairly clean glass. I took a sip and looked at the dirty ceiling and cluttered walls. Old and broken artifacts hung from rusty nails—a single spur with no rowel, a coiled and dried-out bullwhip, a picture of two border collies in the back of pickup, a pheasant's tail feather, a rusty corn knife. It was warm so the potbelly stove was cold. A pane was broken out of the single window. "Damn," I said, "I'm going to miss this place."

"Sure," Stan said. "You guys always drink for nothing."

"What do you mean," Scott said. "We brought you a bottle of booze last time."

"Yeah." Stan pointed to a bottle on the top shelf. "Cream de mint ain't a big seller here." The bottle was covered with dust and the seal was unbroken.

Stan dribbled a little more Crown into our glasses. "Let's talk about that colt. He's the special of the day."

"I bet."

"He's well bred."

I was trying not to be interested but I had to ask. "How's that?"

Stan was standing up with the bottle of Crown still in his hand. "Now that colt there is top-of-the-line breeding. He's out of Montana, by Trailer." Stan chuckled and Scott and I groaned and slid our glasses under the bottle of Crown Royal.

By seven o'clock we were ready to head home. Jill would have dinner ready and I didn't want to miss a minute of our last few evenings together. When we stood up I realized that I had been overserved. We decided to drive through the pastures to our house and that Scott should drive. Sharon waved to us from the porch. "Be careful," she called.

Stan was standing on the porch beside her. He was laughing, "You drive through a fence and you got to fix it." They turned to go inside.

"Yeah, yeah." Scott and I leaned our shoulders against the corral rail and relieved ourselves. The porch light went off and suddenly Stan and Sharron's yard was dark and quiet. The stars popped out at us and I felt an unfamiliar presence standing very close. When my eyes adjusted I saw that it was the painted colt. He stood not three feet away. His two brilliant white spots stood out in the dark like twin ghosts and his gentle eyes were steady into mine. I moved back because I didn't want to frighten him.

In many ways Erney is the opposite of Gervase. He has almost no tenacity but his knowledge is bottomless. While Gervase could pontificate on the metaphoric and stylistic value of every action, Erney cared little about theory. His knowledge is based in practicality, especially about living on the Great Plains. He knows about weather and the germination of plants. He has a sixth sense for what animals need, how they perceive a situation, what we can expect them to do. For these reasons, and the fact that he never wanted to leave the ranch, I depended on him when I had to leave. He was always at the ranch and trustworthy. What he lacked in ambition he made up for in steadiness. His specialty was taking care of falcons. When I was away working, he flew them faithfully; when I was home, he was invaluable help.

When she was small, Jilian loved spending time with Erney, helping him with the falcons and dogs. She would sit for hours and watch him tie flies or sew a scabbard for one of Gervase's knives. She would hand him tools or sort the tiny hackle feathers for him by length and color. She would marvel at how he could tie the hacks onto the smallest hooks and fluff the rabbit fur, deer hair, or wool in such a way that the flies looked real—at least to trout.

Years later, when Jilian was recovering from a relationship with a useless cowboy, she sat bitter and tearful in the passenger seat of my pickup. "I never want to date again," she said. We were driving down a gravel road, and I remember the sound of the little stones on the undercarriage of the truck. "Unless," she said, "I could find someone like Erney."

Erney had only a high school education and had never traveled to foreign lands. Cities made him nervous and driving in cities frightened him. Once I asked if he would be interested in driving to Denver with me. I thought he might like to see the Museum of Natural History. He shook his head. "I didn't lose nothin' in Denver," he said.

Though he had great curiosity it did not extend to travel. Throughout our buildup to moving to the new ranch, Erney never asked to go with us to look the place over. He asked me questions about how the land was situated, what kinds of grasses were prevalent, the number of livestock dams, and the condition of the corrals and the fences. But he did not go down and look for himself. "Guess I'll see it soon enough," he said. "I'll just stay here 'til it's time to go."

Gervase, on the other hand, would go anywhere with me. He loved to travel. He'd never fully recovered from his years as marine. He had been to Europe several times. He traveled to visit old friends and to compete in long-distance shooting contests. He was the long-distance, off-hand silhouette shooting champion in both South Dakota and Nebraska. Unlike Erney or me, he could stay completely detached if he was called upon to handle the rifle when we harvested buffalo in the early days of Wild Idea Buffalo Company. In that respect he was a consummate professional, and during the tumultuous year of the move from one ranch to the other, when I spent five months off at Carleton College, he was the one I turned to. The Sustainable Harvest Alliance mobile harvester was being built and we were still harvesting the buffalo in the field the old way. An excellent and caring marksman was crucial. For that reason I chose Gervase to take over the job.

He took the challenge seriously. The day before every harvest he sighted in two rifles so that he could keep all his shots within a two-inch circle and still be ready if one rifle failed. He worked with the state meat inspectors to devise criteria for humane harvest that far exceeded the minimum requirements of industrial slaughter plants. He encouraged Rocke Afraid of Hawk to "bless" the rifles with sage smoke. He understood the need of the Lakota guys who worked with us to offer tobacco as a thank-you to the buffalo.

On the January morning just before I had to leave for Minnesota, Jill and I watched the harvest from a hundred yards away. "He can do it," I said of Gervase. "You should have enough meat to supply our customers."

"We won't need much."

I barely managed to look at her because of the midwestern guilt that crushed down on me. It was wrong to leave her in the middle of a South Dakota winter with the full responsibility of building our dream. She read my mind and shrugged. "We can do this," she said.

"I know, but there are a lot of balls in the air."

"I've been juggling all my life," Jill said. We smiled at each other.

I wanted to say something that would make the future look clearer. "One of these days . . ." I said.

Jill smiled more broadly when my voice stalled out. "One of these days," she said.

The day before I left for Minnesota, Scott and I made two final trips to the new ranch: one with building materials for the living quarters we planned to build for Erney and Gervase and the other with equipment from our shop—hand-tools, air compressor, welder, drill press, cutting torch, anvil.

For some reason, Scott wanted Jill to come with us on the last trip even though she was bummed out by the fact that I would be leaving in the morning. She was running behind but could see that Scott really wanted her to come. Finally she gave in and we piled into the pickup and started down between the Black Hills and the hogback ridge that tapered out from the northern hills to the prairie that ran clear to the Canadian tundra. Jill was glad that she had decided to come because the sun would soon be setting behind us and those thousand hills, large and small, were beginning to cast shadows that showed the relief of the land. "Beautiful," she said. "And people think it's flat!"

We turned toward the river and the trailer began to bounce hard on the rutted driveway. We drove into the grove of cottonwoods where the springs seep from the hillside and when we turned again, we were right in front of the cavernous machine shop. The sliding doors were open and Gervase was just walking out after a day of building fence. "Damn," he said, "human beings!"

"A little hungry for conversation?" I asked.

"Little bit."

"And a beer?" Scott fished a six-pack from the back of the pickup and held it high.

"I could drink a beer."

"Not until we get all this stuff unloaded," Jill said. "We have to get back at a reasonable hour." She turned to me. "You have to get to that college in a condition to teach kids in thirty-six hours."

Scott backed the stock trailer right into the shop and we started dragging stuff out. We didn't have a plan for how to organize things so we just moved everything to the outside walls. "We'll figure things out as we go" Gervase said.

"And I'll rearrange everything when I get home," I said defensively.

"No doubt."

The trailer was empty and we were nearly finished unloading the pickup when we heard the sound of another truck coming down the driveway. There was still plenty of light but the evening had gone still and we could hear the motor sound for a long time before the pickup appeared. It was Stan and Sharon Holsclaw pulling another stock trailer. I assumed they had come by the Broken Heart and picked up another load. But when the trailer passed me a familiar pair of eyes peered out at me from between the slats. "What the hell?"

Scott was smiling like the pointer that pinned the partridge and Jill was up on the running board. "It's a paint horse."

"It's your wedding present," Scott said.

"We're not married."

"You're getting married, aren't you?"

Jill was coming down off the trailer. "That's what I hear. Not sure when."

Stan was coming from the pickup cab. "I got a delivery. I got a delivery." Now Gervase and I were up on the running board. "Don't stick your hand in there," Stan said. "He's a little green yet."

Sharon was laughing. "It took you three hours to get a halter on him!"

"Hush, hush."

"No sense BS'ing," Sharon said. "Scott already paid you."

"And a helluva deal he got."

Scott was passing beers around. "That was a deal?"

"Clergyman's discount," Stan said. "Where do you want to unload this outfit?"

"Can't we just lead him to the corral?" Gervase asked.

Sharon laughed again. "He might be a little skittish," Stan said. "Better just open the door and stand aside."

Stan backed the trailer halfway into the corral. He chained the corral gate to the side of the trailer and the trailer gate to the corral on the other side. Gervase, though he was a decade older than the oldest of us, crawled through the corral rails like a cat. Scott and I were standing outside the corral and Jill called to us, "This is my *wedding* present?"

Sharon laughed and Stan took control. "Now everybody calm down. He might be a little nervous. Let him out, Gervase."

When the gate swung open the colt came out in one jump. But he didn't run. He just stood there and looked around. Stan seized on this as a sign of intelligence and high potential. "Damned nice horse," he said. "He's going to be a good one." Sharon laughed again. "We let him go too cheap," Stan said. "No kiddin'."

By then it was getting dark but there was still enough light for Jill and I to step into the corral as Stan pulled the trailer out. Gervase closed the gate and left us in the corral with our wedding present. The colt stood under the cottonwoods toward the back of the corral where the dim evening light was defused. His long vertical slashes of brown and white plus black spots made him indistinguishable from the shadows. "He's hard to see," Jill said.

"We should call him Camo," I said.

It was a long semester at Carleton College. I stayed in an apartment supplied by the college and ate at the student union. I taught two classes and did my best to stay engaged. But my heart was on the prairie. There was a time in my life when I had considered pursuing the life of a college professor. Even now whenever I visit a college campus I feel a twinge of regret. I love the slow thoughtful pace, the idea that reading is part of the job, and the notion that almost everyone you meet while crossing campus is willing and able to talk about things that have virtually no practical value. But the honeymoon is short and it doesn't take long before I am feeling bored, trapped by the predictability of the days.

Jill and I managed to get together once during that spring. I had been asked to speak at a tiny nature preserve just east of Minneapolis. Jill flew to Minneapolis to be with me for the weekend. We drove to Afton, Minnesota, to participate in a buffalo release. Afton is on the St. Croix River a half-hour's drive from downtown Saint Paul, and I have to admit, it felt slightly disingenuous to accept a stipend for speaking at a ceremony marking the repatriation of twenty-five yearling buffalo into what amounted to a clearing in the suburbs of the Twin Cities.

I was contacted months before by Steve Hobbes, the executive director of a nature preserve called Belwin, which had recently transformed itself from a private reserve to a nonprofit one. On the telephone Steve spoke earnestly about open spaces and the efforts to restore the tallgrass prairie that had dominated that landscape when Europeans first cast their acquisitive gaze over what they saw as potential farm ground. He was historically and environmentally knowledgeable and obviously dedicated to the cause of Belwin's reclamation, but I had been in the country between the Twin Cities and Wisconsin and I knew what those European farmers had done to it. The truth is, the tallgrass is gone except for a few remnants where plows were prohibited. In place of the switchgrass, big bluestem, and Indian grass are all manner of thorny invasive brush, weedy plants from the steppes of Asia, and cultivated trees. In place of the endless vistas of grass that greeted nineteenth-century immigrants are closed-in overhanging acreages cluttered with homes. It seemed a poor place for buffalo.

When I heard that all of Belwin was only thirteen hundred acres—a fraction of the barely meaningful ranch I was striving to establish in South Dakota—I had my doubts. I almost declined to speak, but Steve seemed a professional conservationist and his dedication came through the phone at me in such a way that I agreed to come. As the date of the buffalo release came closer, I had time to think of what to say to the residents of suburban Saint Paul, likely people who had never enjoyed the feeling that comes with healthy, big landscapes. Where do you begin when you look around and find so little left? Where is the hope? As I taught my classes and waited for Jill to arrive, I tried to think of what to say to those people. I couldn't help but think that the resources and energy to restore what we had ruined might well be a waste. Wouldn't we be better off using all that energy to conserve what, due to serendipity only, we still possess? Where does a nation draw the line? Where do people cut their losses?

Jill and I had our reunion and spent a few days on Carleton's campus. We had a couple of good meals and spent some time with other professors. But Jill was exhausted and she mostly spent time sleeping. I wrestled with what to say when that sorry little herd of buffalo stumbled out of the trailer that was bringing them from somewhere in Wisconsin, where the buffalo habitat was marginal at best.

The Belwin people put us up at the Afton Inn, a quaint and aged gathering spot not too far from the Yacht Club. I was up early, walking the banks of the St. Croix River. To my amazement, I had the river pretty much to myself. My only companions were seagulls and a single old couple fishing a quarter-mile out in the middle of more freshwater than I had seen for years.

While Jill slept, I asked the man who was cleaning the inn to make a pot of coffee, and he asked what I was doing in town. I told him I was there to say a few words when they released the buffalo. He nodded to show me that he knew of Belwin, but he didn't say anything. He stared intently and I felt pressure to explain that I was a writer and that I raised buffalo on a ranch near the Black Hills. He nodded again. "You're going to turn buffalo loose at Belwin?"

"Well, not me. Belwin's board of directors."

His head continued to nod and I knew he was deep in thought. When he spoke, he was brief. "That's about the neatest God-damned thing I've ever heard," he said. "Good for you guys." I couldn't help staring at him as the coffee began to perk.

Jill opted for staying in Afton, so I drove out alone to meet Steve and had to fight a rush of claustrophobia as the alien trees closed in around me. I actually got lost trying to find the site of the buffalo release, and in the process met several of Belwin's employees—an older lady who helped with the educational programs and who called me sweetheart; the maintenance man, who was proud to have built the fence that would surround the buffalo; and a bright young woman who was in charge of the restoration of Belwin's vegetation. They were thrilled to be part of bringing buffalo back to Belwin. I helped load a few tables into a pickup in exchange for a ride to the release site.

The sky was trying to rain but already there was a surprising crowd. I searched for Steve among groups of school kids and interested citizens, and when I found him I was again surprised. He wore a straw cowboy hat and smiled at me through a healthy mustache. He was older than I imagined. We shook hands warmly and I picked up on a twinkle in his eyes that was decidedly conspiratorial and hinted at wisdom known only to guerrilla conservationists. "There's going to be a crowd," he said. "All the TV stations are sending folks." Only then did the potential of an event that I would ordinarily call "token" begin to come clear to me. There was still an hour to go before the buffalo would be released and people were already streaming in from the Twin Cities and the surrounding countryside.

I met the board of directors and the family who, many years before, had started Belwin as a private nature preserve. The matriarch was an elegant older woman who squeezed my hand and thanked me for coming to help. Help with what? I asked myself. But from the flatbed trailer that would serve as a stage for the brief remarks preceding the release, I looked down the county road and realized the answer to my question. This was not so much an effort to reestablish buffalo in a degraded landscape, this was a foot in the door to one of the only forces that could actually help in serious restoration. This was a step in a long-term strategy to educate. I watched the traffic jam moving down the road toward the buffalo release, heard the mothers explaining rudimentary conservation to their children, saw old couples bending stiffly to feel the grass that would sustain the buffalo.

By the time the buffalo arrived, rival groups of children were chanting, "Let them loose! Let them loose! Let them loose!" The television cameras were rolling. Hundreds of people had turned out to see the trailer door open and the buffalo step out onto Belwin's prairie, and I was scrambling to mentally rewrite my prepared comments.

I may be a conservationist snob but I can count, and I can add. There were more people standing around that tiny buffalo paddock waiting to see the gang of twenty-five than would probably ever see the hundreds of buffalo I planned for our new ranch. The economic and philanthropic power that spread out from the stage was immense. In a land that is often written off for conservation potential, here was real strength. Judging by the numbers that had sacrificed their Saturday morning, I had miscalculated the importance of the event. But there was no time to rethink, only time to react to what I felt. I stepped to the microphone and began my remarks. "You are standing on sacred ground," I said. "It is about to become more sacred."

Six

BY THE MIDDLE OF APRIL I WAS ENGULFED IN A HIGHER education malaise. Spring was burgeoning, but in a Minnesota way. The birds were returning, to be sure, but in Minnesota you have to stand still or creep slowly around a tree trunk to see them. The geese are of the golf course variety. They exude none of the mystery of the long-distance flyers that are heralded by faint honking and appear over the grasslands a mile high and five miles out. There are no diurnal owls to speak of. Things are always moist. The greening of grass is a certainty. No magic there.

The trip to Belwin lingered in my mind. I continued to think about the tallgrass prairie that once had stretched along the eastern flank of the Great Plains from far southern Canada to parts of eastern Texas. Scholars divide the Great Plains into three parts. Ostensibly, the differentiation is by vegetation: tallgrass, mixed grass, and shortgrass. Vegetation type and fertility in the form of increased organic matter are determined mostly by rainfall, with the height of the grass diminishing as the rainfall tapers off—from over thirty inches of moisture in the eastern tallgrass to around ten inches in the shortgrass along the Rockies. The lines between the grass types are not hard and fast, and elevation and proximity to water courses play a part. But the bulk of the Great Plains, where buffalo are most at home and where the Cheyenne River Ranch is located, is mixed grass. In many places the suite of species that historically made up the mixed grass prairie, though stressed, is still intact. The tallgrass, of course, is nearly gone.

Buffalo probably did not spend much time in the tallgrass. The big herds likely moved from the west to Missouri, Iowa, and Minnesota after sections of the fuel-rich tallgrass had burned with summer thunderstorms. They would have loved the new, fast-growing grass shoots. There were some visitations of fair-sized herds after the homesteaders began to fill those regions, but sighting a buffalo was something special. In fact, prairie species began diminishing as soon as Europeans began violently changing the ecosystem in the early 1800s. Because of the ample rainfall and the deep topsoil, built from eons of decayed tallgrass, European agrarian lust for that land was understandable. What is less understandable is the contemporary American nostalgia for tallgrass prairie that no living person remembers.

In the historic tallgrass landscape there are scores of postage-stamp-sized restoration projects that can never right the wrongs of the past. Those museum-scale preserves can only serve as perpetual reminders of the already past wrongs. Without a paradigm shift they will function only to salve the consciences of the beneficiaries of the great tallgrass exploitation. Carleton College has such a reminder that is called, ironically, Cowling Arboretum. It was established in the1920s by college president Donald Cowling and Professor Harvey Stork as an educational open area adjacent to the college. It is a tremendous asset to the college and has grown to an 880-acre laboratory for the enjoyment and study of what was once the northeastern edge of the tallgrass region of the Great Plains.

What is most striking to me is that the perception of its value seems to have shifted in the ninety years since the "Arb's" inception. The genesis seems to have been rooted in the same nineteenth-century landscape philosophies that led to a cascade of ecological catastrophes. By its name we know that the arboretum's founders held trees in high regard. There is a hint of European landscape control and "improvement" in the early plantings which can still be discerned from the seeming chaos of Mother Nature clawing her way back to dominance. Somewhere in the Arb's history, restoration ecologists embedded in Carleton College's faculty were able to wrestle control away from the nature controllers; now the educational thrust is focused on 150 acres of tallgrass prairie fighting to reestablish itself. It is a ferocious battle that may not be winnable.

In the last century the perennial grasses were expatriated by an onslaught of mechanical and chemical farming. Naturally occurring fires were outlawed, so even in the field corners where the tractors could not reach, the more fire-vulnerable invasive annuals were given the advantage. Weeds of all sorts leaped to fill the niche left vacant by the indigenous tallgrasses and, with little competition, they were no doubt well established by the time the Carleton administration realized that the Arb would never be a Parisian garden. That realization may be the most important lesson that the Cowling Arboretum will ever teach.

As my semester at Carleton wound down, I found myself taking my classes out to wander the Arb. We helped other classes perform miniature controlled burns of the invading vegetation. We watched crews chopping tenacious and vicious buckthorn trees that were never a part of healthy tallgrass prairies. We searched for seedling bluestem and were thrilled to see a single meadowlark. My message to my students was that restoration of an ecosystem was often much more work and cost many times more than was supposedly gained by the destruction of the ecosystem. I told them that the next ecosystem in line for destruction was the mixed-grass prairie where I lived. I told them that I was ready to head back to South Dakota, that I missed Jill, and that I missed the coming of spring in the land of endless sky.

I had been calling Jill three times a week, so I knew that almost everything had been moved to the Cheyenne River and that the buffalo fence was nearly complete. She said that things were a mess. Jilian was planning to move temporarily into what would be my office, if they were able to find enough room for her bed among the jumbled books. Scott and Gervase were pretty much camping out, but they were getting ready to start remodeling the cattle shed into a place where Erney and Gervase could live. Guilt over my comfortable digs and soft teaching life twisted inside of me. It drove me out of Minnesota as fast as possible and I had my grades ready to turn in twenty minutes after holding my last class. I was on Interstate 35 heading south by ten in the morning, with nine hours of driving ahead of me.

The route took me near the border with Iowa, a state where almost nothing but people, feed grains, and hogs survive. I thought about a similar semester I had spent at a college in the tiny town of Grinnell, Iowa. I recalled a tiny graveyard with ancient tombstones bent at odd angles by the heave of frost and the pounding of eternal winds. During that entire semester I had wanted to visit the graveyard because I'd been told that it was one of the very few places left where the old tallgrass prairie can still be seen. I was interested in the grasses that I might find there but what I really wanted to find was the drab, once-common prairie butterfly called the Dakota skipper.

I never made it to that cemetery but if I had, there was little chance that I would have actually found a Dakota skipper. Of the millions that once fluttered from one prairie flower to the next over a vast 200,000-square-mile range, only a few remain. The reasons for this great decline are fairly clear: an estimated 99.9 percent of the Dakota skipper's habitat has been destroyed and the remaining .1 percent is under siege. The semester I spent at Grinnell came long after the great plow-up of the twentieth century but occurred right in the middle of the new plow-up driven by the ethanol scam. For many years I have visited the cemetery in my mind and, as I walk from tombstone to tombstone, huge John Deere tractors nibble at the field edges as they try to find a few more acres to plant their corn.

The only reason there is any native grass in the cemetery is out of respect for the human dead who lie beneath the undisturbed sod. A few road ditches and railroad right-of-ways still exist where the grasses have found sanctuary—out of respect for government entities and large corporations.

The winter I visited Grinnell College as a temporary instructor I felt right at home in the little prairie town, complete with four bars, the locally owned bank, and the town square. The winter weather and the monochromatic pallor of the countryside kept me focused on the college community. I ventured into that countryside only once, and when I did, I got the feeling of walking across the deck of an ocean-going ship that had somehow come loose from its moorings. In winter the town of Grinnell is surrounded by deep-tilled black soil, highlighted only by the miniature snowdrifts behind each dirt clod. It is a world that has indeed been turned upside down. What was for hundreds of thousands of years a thriving forest of tallgrass has, relatively recently, had its roots turned skyward and the leaves plowed under for mulch to feed corn and soybeans. Winter was not a good time to go in search of grasses or butterflies, and it was all too odd for me anyway. After that first and only trip into the Iowa countryside, I kept to the town—the classrooms, the library, one of the four bars—and myself.

During that Iowa winter is when I first learned of the Dakota skipper. They rarely travel more than a mile from where they are born, they are known for their elusiveness, they are likely important pollinators of particular prairie plants, and they are mostly dependent on the tallgrass prairies that are nearly gone. In fact, the Dakota skipper is a candidate for endangered species status. I found a photograph of one and stared hard at it in the dim Iowa winter light coming through a library window. It is a simple brown butterfly that would pass for a moth, with streaks of rust on the wings and lighter-colored antennae. The Dakota skipper is no bald eagle, it is not a massive polar bear, and it is not a peregrine falcon stooping at two hundred miles per hour. It is no unicorn. Its plainness startled me and I knew immediately that its humbleness would doom it to extinction. No matter what the value of this little butterfly, no one was going to piece together enough remnant tallgrass prairies or restore enough cornfields to build bridges for Dakota skippers to search out mates and perpetuate the species. The Dakota skipper's is a cautionary tale. If the Dakota skipper of the tallgrass can disappear, how are the burrowing owls and long-billed curlews of my ranch safe?

The thought of that cemetery and the imaginary last Dakota skipper haunted me for a long time after that winter in Grinnell. I lived with an image of that little lovesick butterfly, shy and evasive, genetically unprepared to cross the miles of barren cornfields to find a mate. I dreamt of the tallgrasses against my thighs and saw the names chiseled on the tombstones. I would wake from my bed and stand with my hands on the windowsill, staring at the four o'clock sky, thinking of all that had been lost.

I longed to wander among that tiny cemetery's tombstones thrusting up through the remnant native grasses, and search the stems of the Indian grass, the dropseed, the compassplant, the blazing star, cornflowers, asters, and goldenrod. I wanted to ask the sunflowers, the June grass, and bluestem if they had seen a skipper. Did one pass this way? Was it desperate? Was it weak with the drive to survive?

Finally, the challenges of establishing the Cheyenne River Ranch crowded out my early morning vigils for the Dakota skipper. The nightmares stopped and I was fine, at least until I got a call from my good friend Mike Forsberg. I knew he had been out photographing in the tallgrass. He was after photographs of endangered and threatened species: searching for western prairie fringed orchids in Minnesota, then back along the Missouri River to get some shots of hatching least terns and piping plovers. As naturalists go, Mike is one of the most positive and hopeful I know. Over the years he has been a welcome counterbalance to my cynicism, but when I heard his hello, I knew that something had changed. It sounded like he was nearly in tears.

He had been staked out for several nights beside a few western fringed orchids in hopes of catching them in the process of being pollinated. This particular threatened orchid was only pollinated at night, and Mike had been sleeping in a road ditch, waiting for the night-flying insects that might be attracted. He was dirty and tired by the time he got his picture, but he had had a meeting that same day with tern and plover biologists on the Missouri River. By noon he was wading on the fragile sandbars that the birds need to breed. The Missouri could be viewed as the boundary between the tallgrass and the mixed-grass prairies, but the Missouri is barely a river anymore. It has been dammed and channelized for irrigation, flood control, and barge traffic. With most of the sandbars having been destroyed, the federal government has been compelled to build a few artificial ones to keep the terns and plovers viable.

Mike had planned his visit carefully so that he could get pictures of the tiny birds hatching and running, flightless, along the sands. The pictures were to be happy, celebratory shots, but it didn't turn out that way. What he found was that the Corps of Engineers had, that very morning, released a huge quantity of water from the upstream dam to raise the water high enough to accommodate a single barge on its way downstream with a load of turkey feed for a farm in Tennessee. The scene was desperate: frenzied biologists doing their best to save day-old chicks from the rising water. "Almost all of them drowned," Mike said. His familiar buoyancy was gone. He had retreated to his vehicle to make some sense of what he had seen when he got the call saying that a maintenance crew had just come down the road he had camped on the previous few nights. "They mowed the road ditch," he said. "The orchids are gone."

The line went silent on both ends. Gone, I thought.

After that the Dakota skipper dream returned and, during my remaining time at Carleton, I was repeatedly awakened by the gentle patter of butterfly wings against the window screen. Each morning of that long semester I went to the window, but there was nothing to see. When I returned to bed the sound would come again. It gave me no peace. I believe it was the last Dakota skipper—seeking refuge.

I turned onto Interstate 90 and drove west as if the ghost of the last Dakota skipper was chasing after me. I did not slow down until the farmland of the eastern part of South Dakota began to break and pitch on its way to the Missouri River and the grasslands beyond. I sped up as I crossed the bridge and held my breath as if it might collapse under me.

I stopped at Al's Oasis, a famous tourist trap right on the river. I longed for a buffalo burger, and even though Al's buffalo meat was the low-quality feedlot variety, it was better than anything I had found in the tallgrass. I filled the pickup with gasoline first, then went in and ordered a buffalo burger and salad. While they were overcooking the buffalo I called Jill. I planned to begin the conversation about how much I missed her and grass-fed buffalo meat, but the instant she answered I knew that more immediate problems had burst into our lives.

"Where have you been?"

"Driving."

"Erney had a stroke."

"Oh, shit. Dead?"

"No, we found him out on the shop floor about noon. He was at the Sturgis hospital in a half-hour but they took him right on down to Rapid City Regional."

"How is he?"

"They won't let anyone in to see him. The doctor says it's critical. I was there all day. Just came home to take care of Jilian and I'm going back."

"I'm three and a half hours out. I'll meet you there."

When I got to the hospital I found Jill in the critical care waiting room. She was hanging tough, but she looked worried. "They won't let me in to see him because I'm not related, but I was with him in the ambulance. His eyes were open but he just stared. I don't think he knows where he is."

"Did he try to talk?"

"No."

"Did he recognize you?"

"No."

She gave me a hug and we sat down. There was nothing to do but wait, but we didn't have to wait for long. A harried but kind intensive care nurse came to tell us that a neurologist was with Erney. When Jill asked if there was any change, the nurse shook her head. "He's not responding," she said. She smiled and went back into Erney's room.

When the doctor came out, he too looked harried. "How is he doing?" I asked. The doctor didn't answer but he offered his hand. I shook it and told him my name.

"Mr. O'Brien," he said, as if he had been wondering when I was going to show up. "You are Mr. Hersman's . . ."

"Best friend," Jill said, as she squeezed my arm.

"And this is my wife," I said with a solemn face. "We are all he has. Could we see him, now?"

The doctor pulled his wire-rimmed glasses from his face, closed his eyes, and pressed them with both hands. It was nearly nine o'clock at night and he looked like he'd put in a long day. "Sure," he said. "But briefly, and understand that he's in critical condition."

"Is he going to make it?"

The doctor took his time responding. He took a deep breath and replaced his glasses. "We don't know," he said. "But it would be good for you to see him now." He stepped aside and let us precede him into the intensive care room.

The room looked just like I had imagined intensive care rooms to look. There was a single light shining yellowish beams down on Erney, the corners were shadowy. and every space contained machines with blinking LED lights. There were monitor cords, like spaghetti, across Erney's chest, which disappeared under his flimsy white robe. Bottles of saline and other liquids hung from stainless steel hooks and terminated in needles that were taped to the back of his hands. They looked so small against his meaty hands, and the missing right thumb drew my attention, though I had seen it a million times before.

The sunburned, weather-beaten color of his skin was gone. He was white with a greenish hew. His lips were parted and a thread of spittle seeped toward his neck. The big nose and unkempt whiskers no longer seemed to match, and his blue eyes were wide open but without a hint of surprise. I could see his chest moving up and down, slow and shallow. It was all horrible, but his eyes were the worst. He didn't blink and seemed to be staring beyond the ceiling. When I put my hands on the gurney and moved above him to see his eyes better, I could have sworn there was a glimmer of recognition.

I looked hard into his eyes and felt Jill watching me. I was ready to admit that I had been mistaken about the glimmer of recognition until I felt something moving near my hand that rested on the edge of the bed. Jill and I looked down at the same time and saw Erney's big, thumb-less hand reach out to grasp mine as tight as it could. He made a sound that could have been, "Dan'l."

Except for that, Erney showed no sign of recovery. For two days there was no real change, which the doctor said was not a good sign. Several falconer friends from years before came to join the vigil, and we all took turns sitting at his bedside. When I finally made it to the new ranch I was again struck by how dry the land looked. The specter of drought added to the paralysis of fatigue and worry. I was daunted by the amount of work that was ahead of us. Many jobs had been started but only a few were finished. Jilian had moved into what I had hoped would become my office, and she was working at a golf course for the summer, driving the forty miles back and forth to Rapid City. Jill was struggling with getting the house in living order, returning calls for Wild Idea Buffalo Company and making the ninety-minute commute to our rented shipping headquarters. Gervase and Scott were plugging away at the new living quarters but, with Erney in such bad shape, it looked like there would be no need for two apartments. He never got to see the Cheyenne River Ranch.

I was depressed. Though there were many jobs that needed to be done, from moving the last of the buffalo to driving a semi-tractor to Bellingham, Washington, to pick up the newly finished Sustainable Harvest trailer, all I wanted to do was spend time in the corral with Camo. When I wasn't at the hospital I was plying Camo with treats, leading him around the corral, holding the saddle pad and halter to his nose to sniff, picking up his feet one at a time.

Erney did not improve, and one night, when I was at his bedside with Gervase and an old friend, Dave Graham, the doctor broached the question of a living will. "Does anyone have his power of attorney for healthcare decisions?" the doctor asked.

I shook my head. Erney and I had talked about it over the years and we both agreed that living on life support was not something we wanted to do. We knew that we both needed living wills, and he had even told me that he would want me to have the power to "pull the plug." But we never found time to actually write something down. "No," I told the doctor, "he doesn't have anything like that."

Dave, a retired veterinary pathologist, is a big man with a full beard. When he stepped between the doctor and me, he commanded everyone's attention. "I'll bet he's got a living will," he said to the doctor. Then he turned to me and looked me straight in the eyes. "I'll bet you just haven't looked hard enough for it." It seemed like an odd thing for Dave to say because he hadn't spent much time around either Erney or me for years. "No," I said, "he was never organized enough to get something like that done."

Dave stayed between me and the doc. "No," he said. "I think he's got one. You need to look a little harder in his cabin." He was acting strangely and he even poked a finger in my direction. I looked at him and then I looked at Gervase, who was nodding his head.

"That cabin's a mess," Gervase said. "I'll bet it's in there somewhere." He was ogling me and nodding his head and I still didn't catch on. "He probably filed it with his important papers."

Erney did not have any important papers. He had never even paid income taxes. I started to ask Gervase if he was crazy. Then it dawned on me what these good friends of Erney were trying to do, and I froze. The doctor was looking at me and I knew I would stutter if I didn't pause and take a deep breath before I continued. "Oh yeah," I said. "He probably put that in his filing cabinet." I could feel my palms sweating, but Dave and Gervase were nodding and smiling. "I'll bet Gervase is right. In with his important papers." I tried to think of what important papers Erney would have. "Maybe with his ah . . . falconry license." I looked at the doctor, and even he was nodding.

"That's good," the doctor said. "I certainly hope you find it. Any idea who the executor might be?"

"Ah . . ." I looked from Dave's face to Gervase's. They were nodding, urging me on. "I think I remember him asking me," I said. "Yeah. Me. I think it's me."

"Well, I hope so," the doctor said. "There might be some very serious decisions to be made."

That night, Dave, Gervase, and I composed a brief document and scribbled Erney's name to the bottom. It was the most illegal thing I had ever done, and I wasn't able to sleep after doing it.

We had found a buyer for the Broken Heart Ranch, and the thirty years I had spent there were already receding into my past. I should have been focused on the future, but with Erney lying in a hospital bed, barely conscious, and a hundred loose ends and unexpected complications to greet me every morning, my spirits could not rise to the task.

Jill's nephew Terrance had moved in to help on the fencing crew, and Gervase and Scott were framing out the new living quarters. Terrance is a big, tough, enrolled tribal member. He and the fencing crew worked hard. There was no rain to delay the honest, measurable work, and they ended each day with a wonderful sense of accomplishment that I envied. Normally I would have been either helping them or Gervase and Scott, but the best I could do was to visit the projects every day or so and offer a listless comment or two. Even my time with Camo was complicated by the fact that he was corralled with my old horse, Blacky.

Blacky was thirty years old and was the first horse I had had at the Broken Heart Ranch. I broke both his mother and father, and I had broken and trained Blacky from when he was a day old. By the time Camo came to us, Blacky was long retired. He was old and thin, and when I saw those two horses standing in the corral, I couldn't help thinking of all the years gone by. Erney had been there when I first rode Blacky. He had held the halter as I prepared to climb aboard for the first time. "Crank 'er down tight, Dan'l," he said.

I rode him for twenty years, and when I moved onto younger, stronger horses, Jill began to ride old Blacky. She loved that horse and he taught her everything she knew about horses. Seeing the old sway-back with the cloudy eyes standing in the corral next to the tricolor colt with bright, curious eyes filled me with such confused emotions that some days all I could do was stand between them with a hand on both of their necks.

Some mornings the fencing crew was long gone and sawing sounds were already coming from the barn by the time I stepped outside. Jilian was already mowing grass at the golf course and Jill was on her way to Wild Idea's new shared office in Spearfish, South Dakota. People left me alone. Every day I moved from the house to the water tank, which is plumbed into a perpetual spring at the near end of the corral, mentally measuring the stream of water and noting that it was slacking. I had been through droughts before and knew what they could do to poorly capitalized ranching operations. When the horses saw me standing there by the water tank, Blacky would come to me straight away, but Camo would stand perfectly still behind the barn where the ground was a lattice work of cottonwood shadows. It was not rare to see just the kind eyes looking out of the landscape mosaic before I could sort out the horse. Sometimes he would trot out of the backdrop and kick the air as if he knew he had fooled me.

Before Scott and I left for Washington in the semi, there was some good news from Erney. He was still immobile but his eyes had begun to track and he could struggle with a few simple words. It looked like I would not have to use my fraudulent power of attorney. But the news was only marginally good, and we still worried, so I added the possible eternal care of Erney to my list of self-pitying stresses.

It is over twelve hundred and fifty miles from the Cheyenne River Ranch to Bellingham, Washington. Using part of Jim Borglum's donation to Sustainable Harvest Alliance we purchased an over-the-road semi tractor and, since I was the only one with a CDL, I had to be the lone driver to Bellingham to pick up the harvest trailer. Over the two years that we had been working on getting the mobile harvester, I had been looking forward to the day that we could actually head out, over the Rocky Mountains, to pick it up. But with all that was happening, my enthusiasm had begun to flag. It would be a five-day trip and even though Scott planned to go with me, I would have to do all the driving. The thought of it exhausted me further.

The semi was a fairly new Sterling, made by Ford for hauling heavy trailers across country. Of course, we would be driving to the coast with no trailer behind. Truckers call that bobtailing, and to the uninitiated it might sound like that would make things easier. But it doesn't. Semis are made to pull loads, and without a trailer behind, the powerful drive wheels tend to spin and are notoriously dangerous on slippery roads. The plains were bone-dry but the forecast was for snow on the mountain passes around Missoula, Montana.

We had a sleeper behind the seats with a decent double bed and we intended to stop every five or six hours for a nap. But we were barely out of the Black Hills when my eyelids began to get heavy. We stopped in the dusty town of Broadus, Montana, to fill our coffee mugs and then pushed on to the gas station just across the road from the Custer Battlefield. I had only been driving four hours, but I told Scott that I couldn't keep awake. "Let's just take an hour," I said. "I'll be good in an hour."

We crawled into the sleeper, pulled the curtains, and turned the stereo system down low. It was dark and the bed was comfortable enough. I fell instantly into a dreamy asleep. I could feel Scott beside me and heard the sounds of Van Morrison quiet in the background. "Drop it straight into the deep blue sea."

When I awoke we were moving. I sat up on the bed and pulled the curtains back. It was dark, we were on an Interstate highway, and big wet snowflakes were hitting the window. Scott, even without the proper license, was driving. "Where are we?"

"Just past Butte."

"I've been asleep for five hours?"

"Six," Scott said. He couldn't take his eyes off the slippery road but he nodded. "Figured you needed the rest."

The new mobile harvester was beautiful. It was thirty-six feet long, weighed sixteen thousand pounds, and was antiseptically white—inside and out. The builders spent most of day with us to be sure that Scott and I understood how all the systems worked. The harvester was divided into three sections: the mechanical room, at the front of the trailer and accessed through a side door, held the generator, water supply, and cooling units; the skinning floor opened from the rear and a heavy aluminum ramp connected the floor to the ground to make an incline plane for winching the dead buffalo up and onto the skinning cradle; the cooler, beyond the skinning room, was large enough to hang and cool up to forty buffalo halves. The harvester was built to be pulled into pastures and be completely self-sufficient. Though there were a couple similar rigs in use around the country, this was the first designed specifically for harvesting buffalo and capable of handling cold weather.

When I first talked to Shane Brown about being a skinner for Sustainable Harvest Alliance, he looked at the pictures of the trailer while it was still under construction and took a moment to respond. He was from the Cheyenne River Reservation and had worked with buffalo most of his life. "Pull it right out in the fields, hey?" I nodded and he looked back at the photograph and began to nod, too. "What'cha callin' it?"

"The trailer?"

"Yeah. We need to call her 'The Buffalo Girl.'"

I didn't give it much thought until we were standing in the builder's parking lot and looking up at the trailer's huge white side. The builder was standing between Scott and me. "She's a sweetheart," he said.

I had to agree. "She is indeed. The Buffalo Girl," I said.

Scott backed the tractor under the Buffalo Girl and I latched the hitch down tight. The night before, we had gotten a decent night's sleep and intended to make the twenty-four-hour run back to South Dakota nonstop. I had long since ceased to worry about Scott driving without a CDL. There was something about the sleeper and the rumble of the three hundred horse power Caterpillar engine that put me out like a light. Scott had done most of the driving on the way over and I was hoping he would do most of the driving back. We had worked a way for him to wake me at the first sign of a weigh station and I could slide into the driver's seat behind him without even stopping the truck.

There was snow in the mountains just east of Seattle but the truck pulled better with the trailer behind. I called Jill from a truck stop in Wallace, Idaho, and she told me that they planned to move Erney out of the hospital and into an assisted care facility. He had no additional insurance so Jill found a facility that would take Medicare patients. "Sturgis Long-Term Care," she said. "It's depressing. There are people in wheelchairs lining the halls. Half of them are gorked out. A lot of them just stare into thin air."

"How's Erney?"

"Three days ago I would have said that he'd fit right in, but he's starting to talk a little. He's hard to understand and can't remember words or walk. No control on his right side."

"Jesus."

"No kidding."

The Rockies were covered with snow but we made good time. I slept most of the way and Scott lasted until the Black Hills appeared as a dark line just below the rising sun. I took the Buffalo Girl down out of the Northern Cheyenne Reservation and across the dry prairie flats to the South Dakota line. At about noon we stopped in Belle Fourche for fuel. The next town was Sturgis, and I called the long-term care facility to see if Erney had been checked in.

The nurse said that he was there but she thought he was having trouble adjusting. She suggested that this might not be a good time to visit, but I told her that I was coming through town and planned to stop. "Well, you might as well join the parade," the nurse said. "A man and a woman just left. They didn't get much out of Mr. Hersman. They brought him a gift and he paid no attention."

Sturgis Long-term Care is attached to the small Sturgis hospital. It is not one of those fancy assisted living facilities. The halls are narrow and drab, the windows are small, and the yellow walls could use some paint. Just as Jill had told me, the halls were lined with wheelchair-bound seniors in varying stages of decline. Many looked up at me as I made my way toward the single nurses' station. I could see where years of wheelchairs had rubbed against it. An old woman in a wheelchair smiled at me and tried to speak, but nothing intelligible came out. I smiled at her then turned to the nurse in charge. "I'd like to see Erney Hersman," I said.

She was a grandmotherly type and as she adjusted her bifocals and ran her finger down the columns on a clipboard, I could see that she was over worked. "Oh yes, Mr. Hersman. Room 234." She stood up and called to a young woman who was talking to an old man leaning against his walker. The man had the bearing of a rancher. His clothes were neat and his thin hair was combed back over his ears. When the young woman excused herself, he nodded and smiled politely.

"Miss Fleming will take you down there," the head nurse said.

Miss Fleming's nametag read "Tina, Volunteer," and she seemed pleased to be helping me find Erney's room. "Mr. Hersman came in yesterday," she said. "Things are still unfamiliar to him." She was maybe twenty years old and overweight. She smiled steadily as if there was nothing on Earth she would rather be doing. When I passed the old rancher he nodded seriously to me.

Tina and I walked side by side and I tried to get her to venture an opinion about Erney's prognosis. "It's so hard to tell with these darn strokes," she said. "He's gotten out a few words and that's a good sign." When I didn't answer, she tried again to raise my spirits. "Now, as soon as you leave, I'm going to try to get Mr. Hersman out of bed and into a chair."

"He can sit in a chair?"

"Well, he hasn't yet." We were at Erney's door and she stopped to let me go in first. "But I bet he recognizes you."

Erney lay on his back and stared at the ceiling, but when I said hello his head moved slowly in my direction. His color was still greenish and his eyes were wild and suspicious. When he saw me the eyes softened slightly, though it was clear that he was confused. "Here's a friend to see you," Tina said. The eyes rolled and locked on Tina. "Now you remember me. I'm Tina." She went to his bed and fussed with his blanket and Erney lay still, as if he was frightened.

"Scott and I are on our way back from Washington with that mobile harvest trailer." His eyes came back to me and I thought he understood. "He's asleep in the truck."

Tina moved to the door. "Now don't stay too long, Mr. O'Brien." She beamed and looked to Erney. "I'll be back in a few minutes and we'll try your chair." She nodded to the battered leather chair that stood near the window.

After Tina left I sat on the arm of the chair and tried to tell Erney about our trip over the mountains. His eyes were on me, and at first I thought he was listening to the story. But after a minute he began to move his lips and I could see that he was searching for a word. "Ho . . . ho . . ." I moved closer, as if the word might come out too soft to hear. But when it came it was distorted, angry, and loud. "Ho . . . ho . . . home!"

I thought for a moment before I responded. Erney and I had always been honest with each other, and it didn't seem like a good time to start lying. I paced the length of his bed, looked out his dirty window and then down at an open cardboard box at the foot of his bed. Inside the box was a bag of wild bird food and a small bird feeder. I pulled the feeder from the box and held it up. When I looked at Erney his face was contorting again and I knew he was looking for another word. "Jerry," he said.

I nodded. "Jerry and Margret brought this to you?"

There was another long wait. "Y . . . y . . . yes," he finally said.

I sat on the edge of the bed and examined the feeder. But I was still wondering how to answer his question. I knew what I had to say, but when I saw his defiant eyes I almost chickened out.

"Ho . . . home! I wa . . . want to ga ga. Go home."

Both of our eyes filled with tears and I leaned close. "Erney. You can't come home. We don't know how to take care of you."

"I wa . . . want to . . . go home," he said again.

"You have to get better," I said.

He shook his head.

"Yes," I said. "You have to make yourself better."

"No." The resentment in his eyes was fierce.

"Yes," I said. I leaned even closer and my voice came out like a growl. "I'm not wiping your ass for the rest of your life."

I pulled away and his head rolled back to look at the ceiling. He was embarrassed and angry. I paced to the window with the bird feeder still in my hand. The only thing outside was a utility dock and a neglected patch of lawn. But a scraggly elm tree grew four feet on the other side of the glass. I was pretty sure that Erney was done talking. "I'm going to go hang your feeder in that tree."

Having something to do made me feel better. I borrowed a piece of twine from the head nurse and stepped outside. The old rancher with the walker was outside sitting on a bench, not too far from a half-dozen people in wheelchairs. He nodded to me as I moved around in search of the loading dock and the elm tree.

I tied the bird feeder to the highest branch I could reach and poured most of the bag of birdseed into the plastic reservoir. When I passed the old rancher again he was standing up, looking at the sky. "Don't look much like rain," he said to me.

I stopped with my hand on the door handle and took a moment to look at the sky with him. "No," I said. "Don't look much like rain."

I intended to say something more to Erney, but when I got to his room, Tina was with him. She had lowered him into the chair and stood with her hand on his shoulder. Erney's head lolled against the headrest and his eyes wandered. I watched from the doorway until I could catch Tina's attention. Then I held up what was left of the birdseed so she would see me set the bag just inside the door. She understood and smiled. Before I left, I looked once more at Erney. His head still rested, slightly akimbo, against the back of the chair, but his eyes were fixed out the window. When I looked, I saw that a group of white-crowed sparrows had already found the feeder. They jockeyed fiercely for position and swirled around the feeder like a tornado of life.

Part Three

Seven

THE LAST OF THE BUFFALO WERE MOVED DOWN TO THE Cheyenne River Ranch in late May. Our plan was to graze them for the summer on the part of the ranch that we owned then move them to the National Grasslands—government permitted land—in the fall. We had two grazing permits—Indian Creek and Big Corral—and when we bought the ranch the permits were set up with the Forest Service to allow 273 mother beef cows and their calves to summer-graze at a fraction of the cost of a lease on privately owned land. The area was large enough to handle about 500 cow/calf pairs and the neighbors had permits for the remaining 250 pairs. Because the other permit owners were nervous, albeit needlessly, about letting their cattle reside in the same pasture as our buffalo, I had asked for the Cheyenne River permits to be changed from allowing summer cattle to allowing winter buffalo.

Some of the neighbors were not friendly and I suppose I understand why. Even though Jill and I had lived in the general area for our entire adult lives, we were new to the Cheyenne River drainage. Almost all the people within thirty miles had known each other since they were children. They had gone to school together, worked together, their kids played sports together, and they were all in the cattle business. To cattlemen, buffalo meant change and nobody likes the unknown.

A neighbor at the Broken Heart Ranch who eventually became a good friend came over one morning in the mid-1980s, after I had been on the ranch for five years. He was a good Catholic man and he wanted to get something off his chest. "I wasn't too sure about you," he admitted. "I mean, you used those chicken hawks to hunt with and you were always messing with books. I figured it was some sort of a front. You know, witness protection program, maybe some sort of Russian spy keeping an eye on the missile silos around here." Had I been able to speak just one sentence in Russian, that would have been the perfect time to try it out.

He said he was sorry that he hadn't been friendly to me from the start. He knew it was wrong and he had talked to his priest about it. "Father told me it was fear," he said. "I'm done being scared."

"Of me?"

"I guess I was," he said. "But no more." He put his prejudice against me behind him. He began to wave when we passed on the gravel roads. He asked questions that he had wondered about for years. And he changed the minds of others. I was hoping to find someone like that around the Cheyenne River Ranch, which was why Gervase and I jumped at the chance to go to the first branding we were invited to.

There were lots of mounted cowboys and cowgirls, and there were plenty of old-timers like Gervase and me leaning on the corral rails as the cattle herd was gathered from the pasture. The important jobs of vaccinating, castrating, and branding were assigned to more familiar old guys, and by nine o'clock calves were being roped and drug in a steady stream toward the branding fires. Gervase and I did what we could to help, but these people were professionals. The job could have been accomplished with half the help, and it occurred to me that this branding event was as much a social occasion as it was a big job that needed communal help to accomplish.

A group of serious cowboys were doing most of the work. From a short laconic man I learned that these neighbors had been moving from place to place, branding each other's calves, for the past six weeks. It was easy to see that they were used to working together. Three riders rotated slowly into the pen of several hundred calves. In turn, the ropes would circle a cowboy hat a couple times and then snake out to catch a calf's hind hocks. The other end of the rope would be dallied around the saddle horn as the horse slowly turned with a nearly unperceivable touch of a leg and rein. Two "wrestlers" stepped out as the calf was dragged past the branding stoves. With little effort, one of the men would secure the front of the calf and the other the rear. In unison they flipped the rope, and the calf was on its side with a cowboy at each end. The rope would already be loose and being recoiled as the horse moved steadily back into the sea of calves.

"Complete with the Budweiser," I said, and nodded toward where the second-tier cowboys were reaching into the beer coolers.

Gervase followed my nod and smiled. "Look there," he said.

When I looked a tall, scruffy cowboy was pulling out three cans of Bud. His hat was greasy where he'd been pulling it on and off for years. While he needed a shave, it was clear that he didn't need another beer. He was young and his smile was not without charm, despite the Copenhagen stained teeth. He turned and handed one of the beers to Sarah Rausch, the daughter of the family that owned the cattle. He handed the other beer to Jilian. "What the hell?" I said.

Gervase shrugged. "Jilian and Sarah are friends."

"Who's the guy?"

"Beats me."

We wandered over to where Sarah and Jilian were leaning up against a pickup truck. Jilly didn't hide the beer, but she didn't drink any while I was standing there. She introduced me to Sarah and to Cody Crawford, who offered Gervase and me a beer. It looked pretty good but I refused. "No thanks, I think they are about ready to have lunch."

"Well, heck, beer goes good with lunch, too." Cody grinned and bobbed his head.

There was an awkward silence until Sarah spoke up. "I better go in and help Mom get the food out to the shop. You want to come, Jilian?"

"Sure." She left her beer on the tailgate of the pickup and followed Sarah toward the house, leaving Gervase and me with Cody and the awkward silence. We were relieved when Sue Rausch called out that there was soapy water in the pans by the shop for washing up. Lunch was on the way. Cody took two more beers from the cooler and we followed him toward where everyone was gathering.

The neighborhood ladies had pulled out all the stops: big foil pans of roast beef, chicken, scalloped potatoes, bean casseroles, Jello salad with carrots on top, chocolate cake, fig bars, and oatmeal cookies. It was real plains cooking, fuel for the embattled horse culture that the whole world loves. These were coveted recipes that were not often shared. There were rumors that some of the very best neighborhood recipes had gone to the grave with Grandmother so- and-so. "Guess it's sort of a way to be remembered," one of the ladies said.

There were half a dozen long banquet tables set up in the machine shop. The drill press, air compressor, welder, cutting torch, and hand tools had been pushed into a corner to create room. Children played on the floor and cowboys filled their plates to overflowing. The ranch owners sat around one of the tables with their cowboy hats pushed back. They were older men and, though we weren't invited, it seemed natural for Gervase and me to join that group.

Gervase had met a few of the ranchers at the volunteer fire department meetings and they nodded to him. I got a nod and smile only from Richard Rausch, who was just getting up to check that everything was ready for the afternoon branding. He held out his hand. "Glad you could make it," he said.

I juggled my plate and coffee to the table and took his hand. "Thanks for asking." Then he was gone and I sat down with Gervase to a table that had gone oddly silent. The kids went on chasing each other around the tables and the middle generation joked as they shoveled in food. At our table you could hear people chewing.

It didn't surprise me that the ranchers were introverts. "Western hospitality" is certainly different from "Southern hospitality." But I couldn't stand the silence and tried the old standby conversation starter. "Sure is dry," I said. "When does it start raining around here?"

There were a couple of snorts to communicate that I was right about it being dry, but silly to even wonder when it would start raining. There was the sound of more chewing and a couple men stood up and collected their empty plates. One announced that he was going for coffee. "Anybody want a cup?" Two hands went up, but no one spoke until one of the ranchers that I barely knew turned to me and asked how I liked working for the UN.

I knew that he was one of the men who shared the National Grassland pastures with us. He had his black hat pushed back and stared at me as if he wanted an answer, but I didn't understand the question. "United Nations?" I wasn't sure I had heard him right.

"Yeah," he said. "They control the Forest Service. They own the National Grasslands."

I was trying to follow him. The National Grasslands are part of the U.S. Forest Service all right. And the Forest Service is part of the U.S. Department of Agriculture. I wanted to respond, but wasn't sure what to say. Then it dawned on me that this must be a joke. The entire table was silent, and I looked for hidden smirks or rolling eyes. But no one gave any sign that the United Nations owning the public grasslands of the United States was nonsense. Finally I said the only thing that came to mind: "How did the United Nations get ahold of our National Grasslands?"

The rancher shook his head like that was the dumbest question he had ever heard. "Well, hell," he said. "They bought 'em from Castro."

I caught my breath and again looked around the table. Surely someone was about to crack up. But no, the only strange look I got was the one of incongruity on Gervase's face. I couldn't help thinking that now would be a great time to say something in Spanish. But I was too dumbfounded to even try.

We all moved into the Cheyenne River Ranch, except for Erney, who was still locked in the Long-Term Care Unit. He still had never gotten a chance to see the place, but every time I went to town for supplies I stopped in to let him know what the new ranch was like. He would usually ask how things were going and I would say, "Good. Dry, but good."

"Dry," he would say. It took him a moment to remember how to say the next words. "Dry-is-never-good."

"No," I said. "I was looking forward to seeing what kinds of grasses are out there." He was in his chair by the window and I was sitting on his bed. Tina had been getting him dressed every morning and he watched the birds at the feeder most of the day. "It's hard to tell one grass from the next when it doesn't rain."

"It-will-rain." His head lolled back from the window and his eyes searched for mine. When they latched on, he looked like he might have forgotten what he wanted to say. But it just took time. "It—always—does."

I had to smile. "Well," I said, "it always has."

His lips couldn't smile, but I could tell that he wanted to. "Yes," he said. And something in the way his eyes lingered on mine made me know what else he was thinking.

"You want to go down and take a look at this desert that we bought?"

"Yes."

That day I had been sent to town for material that Gervase, Terrance, and Scott needed. The pickup was about half full and I had a dozen more things on my to-do list, but none of them seemed important. "When do you want to go?" The eyes just stared so I pushed right ahead. "What are you doing right now?"

I didn't think he would be able to respond, but he did. "Nothing."

The head nurse was not supportive. "Oh no. He's not ready to leave."

"We'll be gone for four hours."

"No. No, the doctor would have to okay something like this." She was scrambling on her computer. Working to pull up Erney's charts. I let her run down the screen. "No," she said, it doesn't say anything about him going for rides."

"Does it say he can't go?"

"Not in so many words."

"Then, what the heck?"

"But you don't know what he needs."

I let her think about that before I said, "Yes, I do."

We were eyeball to eyeball when Tina stepped up to the podium.

Her demeanor was tentative but her voice was strong. "I think it would be good for him."

"So do I," I said. "Might be just the thing."

The nurse tried to remain steadfast but we could see that she was weakening. In five minutes we were moving Erney from his chair by the window to a wheelchair. It was a warm day but Tina wrapped a blanket around Erney's shoulders and put a few things into a paper bag—medicine, a bottle of water, and an energy bar. Erney was looking at me like a baby being wrapped in a snow suit. "Jesus," I said, "we're not climbing Mount Everest." That was the first time I'd seen Erney smile for months.

We made our escape out the back door to avoid the nurse's station. Tina came as far as the pickup and helped me load Erney. She was gentle and fussed with his blanket, adjusting his useless arm in his lap. She put a pillow behind his head. "Don't spoil him," I said. "I'm just going to unload him like a sack of feed." Tina clicked her tongue and shushed me.

We were standing between Erney's open door and the wheelchair. "Why don't we throw that wheelchair in the back," I said. "I'll need it down at the ranch."

"That's the facility's property, I don't know if I could . . ."

"Just tell them that I stole it."

"Oh, I couldn't . . ."

"Tina, don't make me move him around in a wheelbarrow."

That made Tina giggle and when I glanced around, I saw that Erney had been paying attention and that tiny smile was again at the corner of his mouth.

We didn't even try to talk on the hour and half trip down to the ranch. His head was turned away from me and laid back against the pillow. He watched the pine trees as we came down from the Hills and onto the prairie. I had my first cell phone by then and I tried to call Jill—but we were already out of tower range. I wanted to point things out to Erney but I wasn't sure if he was asleep. He would have known what he was seeing. Even though he might not have been in that exact place before, he knew even the tiny draws eventually wound their way to the Cheyenne River, that the ridges between the draws would be dry and rocky, that the clouds gathering over the Hills might well turn into violent thunderstorms and, even with the violence, the storm would be welcome.

When we came to the deserted village of Folsom, I broke my silence. "That's Spring Creek." I pointed straight south toward a line of trees and Erney struggled to straighten his head. "We go east here for a few miles." We made the gradual turn and when Erney finally got facing straight ahead I told him that the table land in the distance was our National Grasslands grazing permit and beyond that was Badlands National Park. We continued east and mourning doves began to explode from the edge of the gravel road. A hundred. Two hundred. Probably more. Both of us knew that they had arrived only weeks before and that somewhere in a low tree or on the ground they already had laid two tiny, perfect white eggs per pair. They fluttered up in profusion in front of the pickup. The Northern Plains invigorates mourning doves and the prairie was having the same effect on Erney. He held his head upright for the last two miles of our driveway. When we broke over the bluffs above the river he raised his good hand to the dashboard and leaned forward to the point where I thought he might topple into the windshield.

Below us, and a half mile off, was the thread of cottonwoods that marked the course of the Cheyenne River. Erney's head bobbed as he tried to hold it steady enough to study the scale of the landscape. We made the gentle turn at the foot of the driveway and moved into the shade of the giant cottonwoods growing on both sides of the cedar-sided house nestled halfway down the bluff. We pulled up between the house and the machine shop and Erney looked slowly from one building to the next. He took in the water tank through which one of the springs flowed. A colorful bunting perched on the edge of the tank and I saw that he was trying to form its name.

"Lazuli," I said. "Lazuli bunting." It was a bird that we did not see at the Broken Heart Ranch.

Erney nodded and the bunting flitted away in a rush of blue and buff. He reached across his chest and fumbled at the door handle. "Hold on, Big Fella. Let me help you out of here."

He continued to fumble as I moved around the front of the pickup but there was no chance that he could escape without me opening the door for him. I could hear the tractor running at the steel barn. Terrance, Gervase, and Scott were leveling the ground where we had set drain tile before pouring the cement slab that would become the base of the dog kennel and the living quarters. I unloaded the wheelchair before I popped the door and took hold of his legs. My plan was to get his legs pointed the right direction and ease him down, then around into the chair. I had no experience with this sort of thing and had no idea if I could push the wheelchair in the loose gravel of the driveway. "Now we got to work together here, Ern."

I gripped his legs and moved him until he was sitting sidesaddle in the pickup seat. "Now, easy." He pushed himself off into my arms and landed with knees bent. I started to swivel him into the chair, but he held firm, then rose onto his own two feet.

He put his good hand on my shoulder and spoke loud and clear. "Let's—see—what—Ger . . . is doing." We left the wheelchair forlorn in the driveway between the house and the machine shop and moved, very slowly, along the corral panels and past the ancient horse barn toward the modern steel barn and the sound of construction.

Terrance, Gervase, and Scott were stripped down to their t-shirts and sweating in the midday sun. Heat was pounding off the steel building, and it struck me for the hundredth time that the building was a waste. It was a hundred feet long and sixty feet wide and had been considered an expensive asset when we bought the place. It was pretty new, intended for use as shelter for cattle when they were having their calves in early spring. Killing March and April storms are common on the northern Great Plains and the cattle market is configured so that the earlier the ranchers arrange for their calves to be born, the more money they will get for them in the fall. The timing of breeding is pushed back so that calves come right at the most dangerous time. A good, solid, steel barn is a way for ranchers to thumb their noses at nature. But buffalo are not domestic; their breeding is not controlled by the rancher but rather by photoperiod—the length of daylight. They have evolved to have their calves when the weather is most conducive to survival. I have never heard of a buffalo calf being killed by a spring blizzard. Even if they have access to a big steel barn like the one that came with our ranch, they never go inside. They calve as they have calved for tens of thousands of years: out on the prairie where everything is clean and healthy. We had to think hard to find a use for the steel barn.

The work crew was building concrete forms in the open, shed portion of the barn. They were hard at it and didn't notice us inching in their direction. All work stopped when Gervase looked up and said, "Well, I'll be go to hell."

Scott squinted into the sun. "Is that Erney or is it Lazarus?"

Erney looked up from where he was carefully watching each of his tortured steps. He smiled. He hung on tight and we crept into the shade of the barn. Terrance produced a five-gallon pail for Erney to sit on. We stood around him and chattered out our happiness to see him. But it became obvious that he could not carry on any kind of conversation, and things got awkward. He moved his hand in a way that let us know that he wanted us to keep working so we tried to carry on as if everything was normal.

I glanced up at Erney as I drove wooden stakes into the ground and pulled a level line between them. He watched what we were doing and let his eyes wander to the rafters in the barn. Cliff swallows zipped in and out. A pair of crows cawed in the distance. It was only a few minutes until we saw that he was going pale and his eyelids were sagging. Scott poked me. "You better go get the truck."

Erney slept all the way back to the extended care facility. I was worried that we had overtaxed his strength, but Tina reassured me that it was not unusual for stroke patients to need great amounts of sleep. "He's all right," she told me. She patted my arm as if I was the patient.

The drought had become too serious to ignore. The Cheyenne River bottom southeast of Rapid City is only seventy miles from the old

Broken Heart Ranch but it is in the rain shadow of the Black Hills, so the ecosystem has adjusted. Most of the grasses, birds, and animals are the same as those further north, but the spectrum of species has shifted toward the dryer extreme. On the new ranch we found more sage and very few marsh grasses. There were more prairie dogs, burrowing owls, and rattlesnakes. Only in the springy hillside, where the house is located, did we find orioles and goldfinches.

Even in the early spring the stockponds were withering; only a muddy ring circled the shrunken water where cattails and canary grasses should have been. The chorus of frogs I had heard before we bought the place had gone silent. Russian thistle and kochia weed appeared in the old farmground as soon as the grasses had hunkered down for the hot summer. The wild sunflowers came on strong but stunted, and the hillsides turned yellow early with their blossoms. The skies were powder blue all day long. A hundred degrees was common and the wind was relentless.

Only occasionally did thunderheads rise up over the Black Hills. The most they yielded was a quarter of an inch, which usually evaporated within an hour of falling. When I complained to Shane about the drought he shrugged and said, "I should do a rain dance." At this point I should have sensed that a Lakota joke was coming, but I was hungry for rain and wanted to believe. "Do rain dances work?"

"Oh yeah," Shane said. Then he shrugged. "Eventually."

He reached out and slugged my arm and I groaned.

"'Specially if I wear my walleye skin loincloth!"

Among the invasive grass species that plague the Great Plains, two are particularly good at exploiting drought: downy brome grass and Chinese brome grass. Both are Asian annuals that probably stowed away in wheat seed imported in the late nineteenth and early twentieth centuries. Collectively they are called "cheat grass" but they are really two different species. Downy brome and Chinese brome both green up early and rob the native grasses of early spring moisture. They also seed out early, producing billions of seeds that are ready to sprout whenever they get a shot of moisture. Like almost everything out here, they are opportunistic: when conditions are right they spring from the earth to hog the moisture and sunshine, then they die and leave the pastures brown with their noxious seed heads, unfit for other grasses to grow. That first summer almost the entire ranch was covered with cheat grass. The buffalo waded through it looking for native perennials but they ate the cheat grass and they survived. In fact, as we moved through a blistering August and September, the buffalo looked much better than the grass on the ranch. An old friend and buffalo guru came out to look and confirmed my observation. "They do all right even on cheat grass," he said. "It doesn't do much for cattle or for peoples' spirits, but buffalo do all right."

The heat waves rose from the brown hillsides beginning in midmorning. The whole world quavered as the heat bounced off the land. The river ran low and a cloud of dust followed the buffalo as they moved around in search of anything green. The bulls fought, as they have always done. They battled for the attention of the females and stood beside them as they came into heat, trying their best to stay between them and the main herd, fending off would-be suitors. The drive to pass their genes on to the next generation was so strong that the best bulls seldom ate. They stood, single-minded and vigilant in the choking heat. At night, when the temperature nosed briefly downward, I could hear them roar. The breeding season moved forward as if the drought was inconsequential. To the new mortgage holders of the land, however, the lack of water was consequential indeed. The hay crop we had been counting on did not materialize. We knew that if we could make it to November there would be plenty of grass for the buffalo on the Grasslands permit, but I began to have my doubts that we would make it to winter.

The looming catastrophe seemed only another part of the loss of Erney as a confidant. I missed having him to talk to, but when I called Tina to check on him, I was heartened to hear that he was doing better. "He's not as grumpy as he was at first. He wanted a walker."

"A walker? He can't walk."

"Not very fast. It takes him a half hour to get to the nurse's station and back. That exhausts him and he sleeps the rest of the day."

"Is he watching television?"

"Some, but when he's awake he fiddles with a pencil and the legal pad we gave him."

"He can't write. His right hand is useless."

"He tries to use his left. But no, he can't write. He scribbles."

Like a child, I thought. "Mere oblivion, sans teeth, sans eyes, sans taste, sans everything." It was a struggle to find the bright side during those first months.

Early that summer, Jill nailed down Wild Idea Buffalo Company's first commercial customer, a restaurant in Chicago that had caught wind of us and wanted to serve healthy meat raised responsibly. Jill talked to the managing owner of the restaurant, Heartland Cafe, and got the impression that it was not run in a traditional way. We found out later that the Heartland is a full city block in Rodgers Park. The next year when we visited Michael James, one of the owners, and his wife, Paige, we learned that the Heartland was a left-wing hangout, complete with a bookstore, bar, theater, publishing house, and a darn good restaurant. Michael was the driving force behind the complex. He was an old Chicago organizer who was doing his best to put a friendly, socially conscious face on his businesses.

A month after the Heartland became our customer, Michael called me. "I want to come out and see the buffalo," he said. It caught me a little off-guard because we had not yet realized that Wild Idea customers would be interested in visiting the ranch. "I got a passion for buffalo," he said. "I got a passion for lots of things. I write, organize a sports program for Mexican kids. Politics. I do a little acting."

"Acting?"

"Small parts in movies."

"And you want to come out here to see buffalo?"

"Yeah. Came through the Black Hills and the Badlands when I was young, and never forgot it. There is a huge 1920s photograph of the Badlands hanging in our kitchen." He seemed like an interesting guy.

"I don't see why not."

Michael flew in from Chicago. He was a big guy with thinning light-brown hair who started talking as soon as he saw me. "It's really good to meet you—good to be here—haven't been here since I came through after college, in '67—helluva trip—Black Hills—killer, man." All the time his eyes were fixed on me and he smiled a slow, pleasant smile that didn't match the language. I would find out later that Michael is a very articulate and intelligent man, but when he gets excited, which happens a lot, all his thoughts come out at once.

When we got into the pickup, heading for the ranch, the monologue continued. "Yeah, I was traveling with some good old friends—right on through here—Mount Rushmore, Pine Ridge, Badlands, Crazy Horse—man." He was digging in one of his white socks that emerged from his worn tennis shoes and I thought he was scratching his ankle. "Not a bad connection—Chicago, Minneapolis, Rapid—but, man. You want a smoke?" He pulled a small plastic bag of pot out of his sock and was rolling a joint.

"You carried that on the airplane?"

"Oh yeah, I figured, what the hell—they're not looking for weed—where we headed?—Cheyenne River this way?—Boy, been a long time."

By the time we got to the ranch we were both much calmer and the conversation had settled into a more normal tempo. I was looking forward to the dinner that Jill had planned to entertain our one and only commercial customer: greens from the garden, buffalo chuck roast, mashed potatoes, and pinot noir. However, when we pulled into the ranch, Gervase was waiting for us. "The buffalo are out," he said.

"Where?"

"Heading west."

We were instinctually moving toward where the ATVs were kept. "How did they get out?"

"A gate got left open. Probably rock hunters." We were all calm but in motion and, as we walked, I introduced Gervase and Michael.

Buffalo are not difficult to herd back to where they came from if you work at it slowly, but they can move a long way in a short time so it can be difficult to find them. We needed to hurry but we needed to be careful, and I was worried about Michael. Though he seemed a capable guy, he was a city boy. His tendency toward excitability made me think he might get cranked up. But the pressure of the situation seemed to calm him and he walked with us to the shop to get the ATVs. He pulled a small tape recorder from his pocket. "Rock hunters?" he asked, then raised the recorder to get our response.

"Little semi-precious rock called a Fairburn agate," Gervase said. "People go nuts for them."

Michael nodded as the engines were starting up. "Pretty nuts," he said to himself, "to let a bunch of buffalo out for a rock."

Nearly two hundred head of buffalo had wandered through an open gate onto a portion of the Buffalo Gap National Grassland, where they were not supposed to be. A couple friends, Sam Hurst and Duane Lammers, had already been contacted and were on their way to help. Sam Hurst was in his truck and Duane and his light airplane would be in the air in a few minutes.

We picked up the missing buffalos' tracks at the open gate and followed them up onto the public land to the west of our deeded land. Michael and I rode in the pickup; Gervase and Sam went on ahead on ATVs to try to locate the buffalo. The buffalo could have easily been ten miles away and take several hours, or even all day, to get them back. But there was little chance they would disappear completely so, just as in dealing with all animals, there was no sense getting excited. Michael had a cell phone and called Duane as soon as we saw his airplane above us. I marveled at the way Michael took charge of the communications. He later told me that it was just like acting. "Just like playing a part in a movie called something like 'The Great Buffalo Escape.'"

Duane spotted the herd about the time Sam appeared on a hilltop and waved us in his direction. "Rodger that," Michael said into the cell phone. He turned to me. "The air corps and the ATV recon confirm sighting." He smiled and clapped his hands together with joy. "Over that hill," he said.

His excitement tickled me. "Rodger that," I said. We turned onto a two-track road and I stepped on the gas.

When we got to the top of the hill, a dark smear of buffalo grazed in the distant grassy depression below us. The ATVs were making their way to the other side of the herd and Duane was tipping his wings to indicate that he was heading back to the airport. Michael and I picked our way down the incline and joined the ATVs in a line on the other side of the buffalo. By then I was sure we would have no trouble herding them back into the right pasture, and once they began to drift in the right direction I turned my attention to Michael.

The tape recorder had been on the dashboard for an hour and now he picked it up, checked it, popped it open, and flipped the tape over. He sat back and looked thoughtfully out the windshield at the herd of buffalo moving slowly ahead of us and then at the rolling brown hills that stretched to a vanishing point in every direction. A slight smile twitched at the corners of his mouth. I could have sworn that the light-colored eyelashes blinked back tears.

That night Michael helped Jill in her kitchen. In addition to Gervase, Jilian, and myself, Jill had Wild Idea Buffalo Company's first commercial customer in her house for dinner and she intended to show him the versatility of the meat. Michael's head chef at the Heartland Cafe came from Mexico, so there was a south-of the-boarder flare to some of Jill's offerings. Beside the buffalo roulade—a butterflied roast stuffed with spinach, sliced into little pinwheels—there was a hybrid Mexican-Thai buffalo salad with Asian fish sauce, jalapeños, sweet garlic, salt, and peppers. We also enjoyed a buffalo New York steak on skewers with more peanut sauce; buffalo enchiladas; a green chili stew with buffalo and pheasant; and hot and spicy buffalo wings. Jill smiled. "They are smaller than you might think."

"Don't tell me," Michael said. "They taste like chicken, right?"

There was also a sampler of Jill's "Buffalo Blues"—new red potatoes stuffed with seasoned ground buffalo, blue cheese, and a little salsa.

Michael took it all in and talked about his restaurant staff, all of whom came from the same little town in Mexico. He had first come across them when he was setting up an international basketball camp with a friend who played in the NBA. His views on immigration and the power of business for social justice fascinated us all.

The food continued to come while the hilltops across the Cheyenne River changed with the light to the shade of dusk in a Russell Chatham painting. We sampled little buffalo sliders, and Jill and Michael talked about searing roasts, breaking them down, shredding them for fajitas and barbecued sandwiches. There was much talk of food costs and changing last night's entree into today's soup special.

Jilian was quiet. I don't think she knew what to make of this Michael James. It was nice to have her around to meet our "exotic" new friend; the school year had just begun and she was already spending a lot of time away from home. Jill and I worried about what she was up to. Though we were proud that she had already applied for admission to the University of Hawaii at Hilo for the coming fall, we worried that her worldview might be narrowing. No men like Michael lived in our new community, so I pressed Michael to keep talking because I wanted her to hear and understand how big and varied the world really is.

Knowing Jilian would be interested, I asked Michael the question that I thought might be on her mind: "Do you have any acting jobs lined up?"

"Not really," he said. "My agent is working on a little part, but who knows."

"What's the part?"

"Just a bit part. Kevin Costner is doing a film about a coast guard rescue outfit."

"And you are auditioning?"

"Probably won't be any auditions. Just an agent deal."

"So it's just like an extra?"

"No, no. There's some action—you know."

We were all outside enjoying the cool evening on the deck. Michael was smoking and Jilian was slightly shocked. "So, is it a speaking part?" she asked.

"Yeah, the script has some words, but probably mostly ad-lib stuff."

"Like what?" Jilian asked.

Michael looked at her and smiled. "Well, right now the script just says something like, 'Help. Help.'" The smile had grown even larger.

"If I get the part, I'll play a guy who's drowning." He shrugged his shoulders. "I'll probably put in some poignant arm gestures."

Jilian shook her head. "You're going to flop around in the water and wave your arms?"

He shrugged again. "I was made for the part. I've been flopping around waving my arms for years."

Before we turned in for the night, Jill, Michael, and I sat at the kitchen table and talked about food, business, and Wild Idea. "Hard to do good things and be a businessperson," Michael said.

He was an old warrior for justice and the years showed in his face. "If you're just making things that people don't need, it's easy to be successful."

"Isn't that what the system does best?"

"Yeah. It gets harder if you consider people's lives. The health of the planet, food. The stuff that's harder to measure."

"You're a revolutionary," I joked.

"You bet," he said, without smiling. "Have been my whole life. All you can do is keep pounding away at it." Now he smiled broadly, raised his arms over his head, and waved them wildly. "Help! Help!" he said.

The traditional name for the place where falcons are kept is a mews; it is nice to have the kennels close by so that the birds and the dogs get used to each other. We had a mature, white gyrfalcon named Oscar who was a joy to hunt with, but with Erney gone and way too much to do at Wild Idea, everyone knew that Oscar would not get flown that fall. There would be no time for the bird or the dogs, so the mews and kennels would just be places to house them until times got less crazy.

Nevertheless, we wanted to build a good mews and good kennels. Gervase and I agreed about what the dogs and the falcons needed, but there was some difference of opinion about how the human living quarters should go together. We delayed the living quarters decision and turned our attention to finishing the mews and kennels following the design of what we'd had at the Broken Heart. In midsummer Scott and Terrance went back to their own jobs, and Gervase and I plodded on.

Creating an apartment for Erney had silently disappeared from our mental blueprint, and the project had morphed into a single set of living rooms for Gervase. We knew he needed an apartment with running water, a kitchen, and a place to sleep. We knew it would be adjacent to the mews and kennels, but beyond that there was little agreement. To avoid confronting the details of our disagreement, we concentrated on the basics of running water and electric lines to the existing barn. The sizzling heat persisted, so we rose for work early: 6:30, 6:00, 5:30, 5:00, 4:30 a.m. The temperature stayed in the upper nineties. No rain came. The nightmare of withering pastures haunted us. We became grumpy and we argued about the details as the heat of every day built to the one-hundred-degree mark.

When I called Tina to check on Erney, she told me that he was still walking, slowly and with assistance, in the air-conditioned hallways. He couldn't really handle the telephone, but he had let her know that he wanted to talk to me. "You should come up," Tina said. "He's trying hard, but he's not very happy. He's gotten kind of nasty toward the other patients again."

I was not surprised that Erney wasn't being nice to the other patients. What did surprise me was that he was exercising. I had never known Erney to commit any physical act that wasn't absolutely required. It would have made more sense to me to hear that he was starting to loll around the waiting room with the other wheelchair-bound inmates. Deprived of all the things that gave him joy, I figured he might give up.

When I arrived at the facility, Erney was in his chair, looking out his window and holding a legal pad in his lap. His eyes panned the room to find the source of my voice.

When he found me there was an odd contortion of his face that I took to be an attempt at a smile. "How's it going?" I asked.

Erney shook his head to let me know that it was a dumb question. "Crum-bee," he said.

"Yea, crumby with me too."

"No rain?" he asked.

"No. No rain."

He stared up at me and his mouth worked as though he was trying that old bar trick of tying a cherry stem into a knot with his tongue. His eyes filled with frustration and I knew he was trying to find a word. Finally he looked down to the legal pad lying in his lap and slowly he grasped it with his left hand and pushed it toward me. "Here," he said.

I took the pad from him and looked down at the jagged sketch. I could only imagine the effort it had taken Erney to produce the drawing. The lines moved along for an inch or two, and then shot off wildly at oblique angles. The pressure of the pencil against the paper was not constant and some lines were so faint that they were hard to see. Others were thick and dark where his renegade muscles had pushed down too hard. I wanted to understand the drawing for Erney's sake. I looked at it as if it was a Rorschach ink blot, but I saw nothing.

"No bathroom," he said.

It seemed like a non sequitur but I nodded and smiled as if I understood his meaning. "Good." I tore the page off the pad and nodded my head as if I saw what Erney was trying to depict.

He nodded back at me. "See what," he swallowed before he finished the sentence, "you think."

"Yeah, Jill will want to see this." I folded the paper and put it in my shirt pocket.

Erney seemed satisfied and struggled in his chair. "Have a look," he said as he reached out and slowly dragged the walker toward him.

"Whoa, whoa." I said. "We'd better get Tina."

"Don't need–Tina."

I took his arm and helped him rise to his feet. His arm, which had always been heavy and as solid as a horse's shoulder, now felt boney and weak. When he was standing I looked him straight in the eyes. "Don't be showing off here."

"Stand back," he said.

I took a baby step backward and stood poised to leap forward in case he started to tip over. But he didn't tip over. He set his jaw and somehow stood solid as he pushed the walker forward. He shifted his weight and shuffled his feet forward one at a time very slowly. He allowed himself one small triumphal glance at me before he refocused on the walker and slid it forward as carefully as an eye surgeon.

I backed out of Erney's room as he moved toward the corridor. Halfway to the nurse's station it was obvious that he was not going to fall. I moved to the side and let him come up to stand abreast of me. We moved passed the nurse's station and I nodded to Tina, who stood smiling as if Erney was her child. We walked down the hall, turned, and walked back to Erney's room. We walked very slowly but we walked together.

"What is it?" Jill asked after I unfolded the yellow legal sheet and laid it on our kitchen table.

"I have no idea," I said.

She stared at it and rotated it ninety degrees to the left. "It's a diagram," she said. Then she rotated it ninety degrees in the other direction.

"Of what?"

She turned it a hundred and eighty degrees and twisted her head from side to side. "I don't know," she said.

We agreed that it bore a likeness to the crayon drawings that hung in our bathroom. Jill had framed them years before, when Lucas and Jilian were in grade school. I had always found the drawings charming, but I needed to have Jill interpret them for me the first time I saw them. When I looked at Lucas's giant stick horse, the free-floating cowboy hat, and the sunflowers twice the size of the house I could not understand what I was looking at. "Sometimes," Jill told me, "appreciation requires a unique perspective."

When we looked at Erney's scribbles she said, "We need an interpreter with a different point of view."

"Or from a different planet," I said. And then we looked at each other because we were both having the same thought.

Gervase took one look at Erney's drawing and said, "It's a plan for our living space." He looked a little closer. "He wants me to live above him. Looks like he's figuring on sharing the downstairs with the dogs." He pointed to some squiggly lines that formed a rough box. "Falcons here. Looks like storage behind this door."

Jill and I looked at each other. "He can't live with the dogs," Jill said.

"There's a separation here." Gervase pointed to a crooked line. "It's like an attached kennel. Oscar goes over here." He leaned closer. "But I don't see a bathroom. He's got a bathroom for me, but none for him."

"He's got to have a bathroom," Jill said.

"Is he coming back here to live?" Gervase was smiling but clearly doubtful.

I was staring at the drawing and beginning to see what Erney had put down on the paper. Jill was shaking her head. "They'd never let him out," she said.

"He's like a ward of the state," Gervase said.

"There's probably a way," I said. "Could we take care of him?

Jill was still shaking her head. "He can't live with dogs and no bathroom. The social services people will come."

"We could widen the doors for a wheelchair and add a john." I pointed to the drawing as if I understood it.

"We're going to spring Erney?" Gervase asked.

I really hadn't considered doing so before that moment, but we needed Erney. "He'd spring us," I said.

There was a pause as we thought about what we were saying. Then Jill shrugged. "I'm in," she said. "As long as he has his own bathroom."

In the end there was compromise. Erney was talked into a bathroom, Gervase got the entire upper level, and the dogs and falcons were separated into adjoining rooms. Erney continued to exercise in the hallways of the Long-Term Care Unit until the rooms were finished. We simply showed up one day and brought him home. We told only Tina what we were doing, and she was thrilled. "It's the right thing for him," she said. "I won't testify against you."

That afternoon I called his doctor and the social services people to inform them that Erney was again living with us. They were upset and threatened to call the police. We settled on visits from a social worker, who came out in few days to check on the "facility." Jill had the new place as clean as a Hyatt Regency and we must have passed muster because all they did was assign a rehabilitation nurse to come out once a week. But she only made a few trips out to the ranch because Erney took charge of his own therapy and was as uncooperative as a scalded badger.

A couple weeks later the doctor called to chastise us one more time. He said we weren't trained and we'd get tired of caring for Erney. It was a long, one-sided conversation and, though he finally admitted that Erney was doing well, he told us his improvement would plateau and he would never fully recover. The doc was right, but by the time the blistering summer was over and the buffalo were ready to cross the Cheyenne River and go onto the National Grasslands, Erney was able to shuffle around the ranch headquarters well enough to feed the dogs and keep an eye on Oscar. He was there in the passenger seat of a pickup when we rode out on horseback and moved the buffalo into the corner of the sad summer pasture. Rocke Afraid of Hawk was there to drum and sing as the buffalo passed through the gate and onto the east side of the river for the first time in a 150 years.

Once the gate was opened, the buffalo wasted no time leaving our pasture and lining out toward the river. Since they were not familiar with the ins and outs of crossing rivers, I thought they would hesitate. But their genetic memories kicked in and one old cow waded right into the water—with her calf at her side. She did not stop to drink, and neither did any of the others. They plowed across the Cheyenne and up the bluff on the other side. They did not run, but they moved steadily to the top of the high ground on the government side while the eerie Lakota music filled the immense void. Erney sat in the pickup truck and nodded his approval. "Quite a sight," I said.

He nodded. "Finer than frog hair," he said.

Eight

THE DROUGHT WAS BROKEN BY AN EARLY WINTER STORM, followed by months of continual snow and wind. Jilian drove back and forth to school and played basketball for the New Underwood Tigers. She was accepted at the University of Hawaii. What had been a year of constant worry about the ill effects of too little rain morphed into dealing with the stress of traveling on treacherous winter roads. For weeks at a time the buffalo were out of our sight, and Jilian was nearly the same.

She took to her new set of friends without reservation, and they took to her. She had been drifting toward the kids who, in my day, would have been called the wild ones. The new community that we found ourselves in was full of such kids. College was not necessarily one of their goals. Alcohol use was common and, for a community that professed strong support for law and order, underage drinking laws were taken lightly. Like the supposed abhorrence of farm subsidies, government laws and regulations were respected mostly when it was convenient.

Jill and I were no exception. We accepted the inexpensive grazing rates on the grassland and we said almost nothing when Jilian and her friends threw late-night beer parties on the Cheyenne River. We told ourselves that at least we knew where she was. Not until the fuel started disappearing from the storage tanks near our workshop did we put a limit on who was driving in and out of our yard. From our bedroom window we could see their campfires on the snowy riverbank and often wondered what we should do. At least we could see their fires, and the river was rendered safe due to the fact that every stretch that was deep enough to be dangerous was frozen solid.

Thankfully, the basketball season started before winter got too bad. The coach announced that the girls were in training so no alcohol or late nights would be tolerated. Jill and I slept a little better, though we were not foolish enough to believe that the danger had passed. We made it to almost every game despite the difficulty of navigating the mile and a half of drifted driveway before we got to the county-maintained road.

Part of the ranching philosophy that Jill and I developed over the years was to own and operate as few fuel-guzzling machines as possible. Implement dealers and banks are happy to lend money to ranchers who pay their bills and the income tax structure is designed to encourage borrowing money to pay for farm implements, tractors, and pickup trucks. The temptation to buy such wonderful machines is great, but many farmers and ranchers end up in a trade-in game of making ever-higher payments on more and more expensive equipment. It was something that I had always avoided and perhaps one of the ways that I survived the boom-and-bust cycles of agriculture. In my entire life I had owned only one new pickup truck and I had borrowed no money to buy it.

It is an old-fashioned way to live and it was sometimes difficult to watch what looked like the entire world racing up and down roads in constantly renewed and shiny equipment. It is particularly difficult to ask a neighbor to clear the snow from your driveway because your piece of junk, forty-year-old tractor can't put a dent in the drifts. My miserly attitude was born in the agricultural credit crash of the 1980s that ruined many ranches and almost ruined me as well. I learned to never borrow money if you aren't willing to find a second job to pay it back. Our first full winter on the Cheyenne River Ranch reminded me of the winter of 1981 just before that crash.

At the time, I was in my early thirties and got caught on a ranch on the North Dakota–South Dakota boarder. I had been hunting grouse with a falcon and had been too engrossed in what I was doing to notice the wall of black clouds that had suddenly filled the western sky. I started down the twenty miles of gravel toward the asphalt road that connected to a small town, but I didn't make it. It was rolling country that blended into the Grand River breaks and I was lucky to make it back to a line-shack near the southern boundary of the ranch that I had been hunting on. I spent the next three nights on the couch of the creaking building where the hired man was stationed for the winter. It was his winter job to watch over several hundred cows. He had to see that the cattle's water was thawed every day and make sure they got enough hay to keep them alive. It was December and, with three months to go, the winter had already been tough. "We winter rough," the hired man said. He was talking about both the cows and himself.

The shack was about as remote as a person could get in the Lower Forty-Eight. Just a board-and-batten rectangle of wood surrounded by a broken-down wire corral and a couple hundred tons of loose-stacked hay. There was no insulation in the walls or roof, and the wood-burning stove was brought to a roar whenever we were inside. But, as soon as the blizzard winds stopped blowing, we were outside trying to get the cattle fed in several feet of snow that the wind had piled into every draw and depression. The hired man was older than I but still young. His face and name are lost to me now, but I can remember that he had a late 1940s Dodge Power Wagon. It was one of the first four-wheel drive vehicles made available to civilians—the huge cousin of the World War II Willies Jeep. It was a full ton truck with chains on all of the four knobby tires, which came up to my waist. "She's got a little age on her," the hired man said as he slapped the Power Wagon's dented front fender. "But runs like a Swiss watch."

We were both bundled up inside the cab, wearing all the clothes we had: stocking caps, hooded parkas, wool gloves covered with leather, felt-packed boots. The outside temperature was far below zero, but the air was still and the sun was coming up clear and bright over an endless white landscape. The undulations of the land were only revealed by the gradated shadows cast by the rising sun. The stillness that came in the wake of the storm was insulted first by the bellowing of cattle standing at a wire gate a half-mile away and then by the labored chug of the Power Wagon's flathead in-line six cylinder engine.

"It started," I said with surprise.

The hired man smiled and unplugged the heater that was screwed into the engine block. "With a little help from the Grand River Electric Co-op," he said.

The plan was to get the Power Wagon through the snowdrifts to the huge stacks of loose hay, pile the flatbed of the truck full of hay with pitchforks, drive the hay out to the cattle, and pitch the hay off. We needed to repeat that procedure until the cattle quit bawling. While the engine was warming up we locked the front hubs into the four-wheel drive position, tossed a couple pitchforks onto the flatbed, and lashed them down beside a heavy scoop shovel. The hired man wedged a pint bottle of Black Velvet between the windshield and the dashboard, reloaded Copenhagen into his lower lip, and eased the Power Wagon into the lowest gear he could find. "We'll start out in 'grammaw'," he said. "We won't bash nothing unless we have to."

It turned out that we had to bash some drifts. We could move right along where the snow had fallen straight down, but where the wind had piled and packed it, we had to gather some steam. We moved out to the stacks of hay that had been cut the summer before. The hay had been piled twelve feet high with a front-end loader that swept it up from the ground and deposited it, one bunch at a time, until the stacks held ten or twelve tons. The summer days when it was stacked were likely deadly hot; now, on an arctic day, it had to be spread back out onto the ground.

The largest drifts between the buildings and the hay corrals were only three feet deep and no longer than the length of the truck. At a speed of fifteen miles per hour, the Power Wagon made it through with only the very softest top layer rolling up and onto the hood. But, even then, I could feel the tires spin and grip, spin and grip. "We're spinning," I said, with a note of warning.

"Yeah, once we get a load on she'll settle down and pull like a Clydesdale."

Working in extreme cold is a special kind of desperation. At first the cold air stings your face like wind-driven sleet. Once you begin to exert yourself you believe that the air might be frosting your lungs and you slow down. Soon you get used to the surging blood and begin to move like a metronome. Finally you start to heat up, and the layers of winter clothing begin to peel away for fear that you will sweat your clothes wet and not be able to stop working for fear of freezing to death.

We were down to our flannel shirts and no gloves by the time the hay was loaded six feet over the flatbed. We must have looked like a huge arctic tortoise as we lumbered away from the hay corrals and through the virgin snow toward where a herd of noisy black cattle continued to gather. It turned out to be true that a load of a few tons of hay enhanced the traction of the tires and we moved easily over the flat ground and only lugged down slightly when we hit drifts and the snow puffed onto the windshield. The windshield wipers were run by a vacuum system off the engine and they sped up as the engine accelerated. There were times we could not see well and times that we should have stopped until the wipers caught up. But we needed to keep our speed up, so we plunged ahead whether we could see or not.

I was beginning to think that we might make it, until the wipers surged and revealed that there was a deep draw ahead of us. It was clear that the draw was fifty yards wide. The drift in the bottom might be as high as a man's head. "We're going to get this thing stuck," I said as we started down.

"Hang on," the hired man said. He romped on the accelerator and the Power Wagon roared. Snow exploded all around us and we bucked and surged like a space capsule during reentry. The sun was blocked out by flying snow, but we continued to move until the trajectory of the hood began to point upward. At that point we were slowing fast and I held my breath, hoping that if the windshield wipers caught up we would see the opposite lip of the draw. The nose continued to point up and the Power Wagon fought like the old war horse that it was. I could feel the tires spinning and catching as she chugged in seizures. I rocked in my seat as though the shifting of 160 pounds might make the difference. We lurched in descending surges until the engine finally died.

The roaring of the engine had masked the silence that enveloped us. The entire cab was covered with snow. It was dark and, with no movement or sunlight, the truck cab went still, padded, and suddenly tomblike. I was in a panic but knew the doors would be useless, so I fumbled at the window crank. "That side don't work," the hired man said from the darkness. He had cranked his side window down and some of the snow that had been banked against it fell away so that clear bright sunshine came mercifully into the cab.

I shimmied out after him and sank beside him into the drift that was higher than the hood. We had plowed another foot onto the windshield and even the heavily loaded bed was only inches above the snow line. "Damned near made it," he said.

We were still fifteen feet from the top of the draw where the land leveled out. Behind us was a hundred feet of churned and battered snow with a four-foot-high wake thrown up on both sides. It took a moment for me to calm my panic, but when I did, all I could do was stand up in snow as high as my waist and shake my head. "Jesus," I said. "We're really stuck."

The hired man snorted as he waded to the bed of the truck and dug in the snow just in front of the mountain of hay. "We're not stuck."

"Yea," I said. "We're stuck."

"We ain't stuck." He raised the scoop shovel into the air and shook it defiantly. "We ain't stuck 'til this son of a bitch breaks." He waded to the front of the truck and started digging at a drive wheel.

Here's the lesson I learned in the winter of 1981: you aren't really stuck until the shovel breaks. It took hours for the two of us to move enough snow to rock the Power Wagon a few inches. In another hour we were again bashing toward the top of the draw. By early afternoon we were again in shirt sleeves, pitching off that first load of hay to the still-bawling cows. Each of the next three trips through the draw got easier. We ran the last load out during the twilight on a road that we had practically built by hand.

Our first winter on the Cheyenne River ranch was a lot like that winter of 1981. The snow started in October and the driveway blew in for the first time on Halloween night. Storm warnings had been reported all day, but Jill, Jilian, and I changed the bulb in the porch light and had a big bowl of candy ready just in case some of the neighbors brought their children by. If our new neighbors took their kids out that night, they didn't bring them to our house. The wind started moving before it was even dark. By morning the three of us had eaten half the bowl of candy and the yard light glowed yellow against a foot of puffy snow, drifted onto the porch.

The trees around our house slows the northwesterly wind, and snow empties out of the blizzard and makes the yard look more like New England than the Great Plains. Gervase came trudging through the snow early that day. I saw him coming with Hank, Tootsie, Al, and Trixy frolicking around him. The scene could have been from a Currier and Ives lithograph. When I stepped outside to meet him I could hear the wind still whistling in the tops of the cottonwoods and I knew that the scene likely was very different at the top of the driveway, where there was nothing to slow the blizzard for miles.

"Happy Halloween,"

"Trick or treat?"

"Trick."

"The trick is going to be getting out of here," I said.

"You think the tractor will start?"

"Probably not." I knew that Gervase, at seventy-two years old, had met a woman who lived in the Hills. He was anxious to get access to the county road. So I bugged him. "Maybe we should coffee up and think this over."

"Let's just get at it," he said. When I looked at him, he got nervous. "I mean, what if Erney has another stroke or something?"

I looked up into the treetops, where the limbs were whipping slower against the bright blue sky. "If you get out of here and get to chasing that woman, you're more likely to have a stroke than he is."

Gervase puffed up a little and laughed. "You might be right. Blizzards invigorate Old Ern. He's bundled up, trying to shovel out the dog kennel."

"He can't be doing that." I had given Erney charge of the dogs, in addition to Oscar, because I thought he needed a chore to keep him sane. But no one expected him to shovel snow.

"Can't stop him," Gervase said. "He's moving real slow—about a quarter-scoop of snow every five minutes. But you can't stop him."

"You go shovel his snow. Make him think that he's doing it. I'll go fight the tractor."

Our tractor was always a piece of junk. It was a Rhino, an underpowered and underengineered little tractor made in the late 1970s in the Shanghai Tractor works in Shanghai, China. It did not have a cab, so there was no heat or air conditioning. Things slipped out of adjustment easily and repairs were common. The technology was about the same as U.S. tractors made in the 1940s and 1950s: less than fifty horsepower, weak hydraulics, oil leaks from every gasket. The loader was terribly weak and the hydraulic hoses squirted fluid whenever the bucket was under a load. That winter, starting with the Halloween blizzard, the loader was often under a load of heavy snow, and every time I used it I swore and beat the wrenches I was using to fix it against the cheaply made crankcase, u-joints, and transmission. Jill told me to quit bellyaching and go buy a new tractor.

"Go get one of those Bobcat loaders you're always talking about." She knew that I loved Bobcat loaders—small, four-wheel-drive, skid steer jobs—that would be perfect for our ranch. Though she knew that we couldn't afford one, she thought we should find a way.

"Right. And pay for it with my good looks?"

"They have banks. Banks lend people money so they don't drive their families crazy."

That morning, when I plugged in the Rhino's block heater, I promised myself that I wouldn't lose my temper or let the piece of inanimate junk push me into a funk. We left it plugged in for ninety minutes before we even tried to start it. That gave Gervase and me a chance to shovel the deck and help Erney finish cleaning out the dog kennels. It was a Sunday, so Jilian didn't have school and Jill, who had moved Wild Idea's office into a closet in our bedroom, was unhappy to find that the newly installed Internet connection was not working, so they both came out to help. By the time we got the tractor running and we were ready to tackle the five-foot drifts in the driveway, they had let the dogs loose again and were playing in the polar landscape just below the lip of the bluff, with an old inner tube for a sled. The wind died down, the sun came through bright, and the snow shimmered like a Canadian lake.

Gervase and I pounded away at the drifts and the old Rhino puffed and belched black smoke. By noon it had warmed up, and as I stood beside the idling tractor, pulling off my insulated coveralls, I realized that—not withstanding the hours of work ahead of us—it was a beautiful, early winter day. A trio of sharp-tailed grouse cut across the blue sky and landed in the cottonwoods high above me. Their usual food source had been covered with snow, and I watched as they pecked at cottonwood buds in the tall branches.

The Rhino only broke down once that day—a blown hydraulic hose for which we happened to have a spare. We were running again in forty-five minutes and made it out to the main gravel road by two o'clock in the afternoon. When I came into a late lunch, I was able to announce that Jilian would be able to make it in to school the next morning. She grumbled a little, but a week later a strong northwest wind pushed all the snow back into the driveway and she got some time off. The next full-blown blizzard hit us on the day before Christmas.

It was difficult not to worry about the buffalo. They were, after all, the mainstay of our income, and, because they were in an eight-mile square pasture with no access road, we had no way to check on them. Weeks passed without catching even a glimpse of them. Every time I drove into the ranch, just before I dropped down off the bluff and through the cut where the snow drifted deep with every hard blow, I stopped the pickup and scanned the distant hills with binoculars. Across the Cheyenne River all that could be seen were endless stretches of glistening white snow. It was part of our experiment. If large-landscape, free-ranging buffalo couldn't thrive on the winter prairies without the heavy cost of constant care that domestic grazers demand, then our gamble was surely doomed. In my heart I had no doubt that they were all right. Their kind had survived much more severe winters than our first winter on the Cheyenne River. But every time my binoculars found an unusual black line at the top of a far-distant wind-blown butte, I held my breath as I twisted the focus knob. If a grazing herd of buffalo emerged from the blurry black line, I shouted like a high school cheerleader.

Tom Fredrick and his son, Wayne, were managing a herd of three hundred buffalo for Sinte Gleska College on the Rosebud Reservation. Sinte Gleska means Spotted Tail in the Lakota language. I had always liked the name because it reminded me of the plumage of an immature prairie falcon and because I held Chief Spotted Tail in high regard. Chief Spotted Tail, the uncle of Crazy Horse, was chief of the Brule Band of the Lakota people during the latter half of the nineteenth century. His negotiating skills were probably responsible for the reversal of a plan to ship the Lakotas off to the Indian Territory in Oklahoma. The tribal college was named for him. In photographs Spotted Tail comes off as strongly elegant with an intimidating bearing.

Tom and Wayne have a similar bearing, and when they came to ask me if Sustainable Harvest Alliance could visit the Rosebud to harvest about a hundred buffalo for them, I paid close attention. It was our first foray into harvesting other people's buffalo and, although those animals would become food for the reservation, it dawned on me that it might be possible to someday buy a few of their best ones for Wild Idea. I agreed to give it a try.

To that point we were harvesting only about two days a month. The crew varied because the job was part-time. Shane Brown and Cliff Allen arranged their schedules so that they could get off work on most harvest days to come for the hard job of skinning a half-dozen buffalo. I filled in where needed, though my main job was to drive the semi. If I had any strength as a buffalo harvester it was that I could do all the jobs—even if I couldn't do any one of them well. Just like driving the semi, keeping a knife sharp enough to skin a buffalo baffled me and I simply do not like shooting buffalo. But I am able do those jobs in a pinch.

Shane and Cliff were good skinners. They believed in what we were doing, and they made sacrifices to work for us. They had both worked in the meatpacking industry most of their lives and they knew that Sustainable Harvest and Wild Idea had a better way. But they needed more work than a day or two a month and hoped that the job would someday become full-time.

In many ways my "day jobs" were not flexible. The curse of a free-lance writer is that you cannot afford to say no to any possible work because there is no telling when the phone might ring again. I could not make ends meet by driving a semi or shooting and skinning a dozen buffalo a month. When I was summoned to a university I had to go, and if there were buffalo to be harvested I needed to figure out how to get that done in my absence. I knew several months ahead that the timing of the harvest of Sinte Gleska's buffalo was going to overlap with my planned time at Carleton College. I also knew that interest in our meat was increasing and that Jill was adding customers, slowly but steadily. The SHA truck could not shut down just because I was not there.

I placed an advertisement in the help-wanted section of the local news paper and I was as honest and specific as I dared to be: "Part-time worker needed. Must be handy around dangerous machinery and animals. Must possess a Commercial Driver's License, and be a good rifle shot."

Everyone who answered the ad was taken seriously. On the strength of their hunting prowess they all claimed to be great rifle shots, but SHA shooting was not hunting and the job had nothing exciting or romantic about it. It was a technical job that required patience and serious training. I asked all the applicants if they had been trained in the military but no one had, and though a few had driven semis, none had the license to make it legal.

A couple people didn't bother to call back after our first phone conversation. One guy showed up drunk. The winter continued to dump snow on us. I was pushing snow from the driveway about once a week and my Carleton job was approaching fast. Even if we found someone decent to fill in for me, it would take a few harvests to train them. I was nearly in a panic when I found a message on my cell phone from a guy named Jerry Blanks. When I called him back, a woman answered and, after I explained who I was, she called Jerry without holding her hand over the mouth piece. "It's him!" she yelled.

Then her hand must have found the receiver because there was hollow silence until Jerry Blanks came on. "Hello?"

"Hello."

"Is this the guy that's looking for a truck driver who can shoot?"

"Yes. We need someone with a commercial driver's license and some marksmanship training."

"I've been driving a semi over the road and I was trained in the Marine Corps."

"We're looking for a jack-of-all-trades."

"That's what I am."

"Why'd you quit driving over the road?"

"I got tired of it."

"What are you doing now?"

"Looking for the perfect job."

"This would be just a part-time job. We'd be out harvesting buffalo a couple days a month. There is a lot of cleanup involved"

"Buffalo, huh. I like buffalo. That would be even better. Could I sort of do cleanup at odd hours?"

"What do you mean by odd hours?"

"I like to work late at night."

I was intrigued, and it just so happened that we were going to the Rosebud Reservation for a harvest that week. "Why don't you come along with us to Rosebud? Just to see what you think."

"Okay."

"I can't pay you."

"Okay."

In those days we kept the SHA semi and trailer at my nephew Terrance's barn because it was too big to get down our hill, especially with all the snow. When Gervase and I left our house it was still dark.

We drove his pickup because he liked to shoot from the driver's seat, where he was completely comfortable. It was nineteen degrees and the snow snaked across the seven miles of gravel road to Terrance's. I was pretty sure that the driveway would be blown in again by the time we got home that night, but the weather on Rosebud was supposed to be okay.

Shane and Cliff pulled in at five o'clock, just as we were pulling the SHA truck out of the barn. We let the truck idle as they tossed their gear into the sleeper then we stood around in the cold darkness. I was disgusted that Jerry Blanks was late, but I wasn't surprised. He would have had to leave his home at four o'clock a.m.

Cliff jumped into Gervase's pickup and they were pulling out to lead the way to Rosebud just as Jerry pulled into the headlights of the semi. I stopped the truck and the air breaks hissed as Jerry came running to the passenger door carrying a pair of insulated coveralls. It wasn't a good start between us, but he popped into the cab with a smile on his face as Shane moved to the bunk behind the seats. After we shook hands, Jerry pumped his fist at the air. "Let's rock," he said.

He was a stout guy with a day's growth of beard, a butch haircut, and a grin that showed a misshaped tooth. He was bubbling with excitement but trying to keep a lid on things. He explained that he thought I had meant that he should leave Rapid City at five o'clock. He honestly figured that he was fifteen minutes early. "I've been up all night," he said, "waiting." We were rolling by then, and from the height of the tractor cab the fingerdrifts across the road seemed distant and inconsequential.

It takes about three hours to drive to Mission, South Dakota, the main town on the Rosebud Reservation, and Jerry and I talked the whole way. I found out that the woman who had answered the telephone was his wife and that she was a librarian at the Rapid City Public Library. "I'm not much when it comes to books," he said, "but she is."

"What did she think when you left at four o'clock in the morning?"

"Oh, I wasn't at home," he said.

"Where were you?"

"At my girlfriend's house." He smiled and shrugged his shoulders in the blue lights of the dashboard.

When we got to Mission, Cliff and Gervase were waiting for us at the Antelope Motel cafe. There was enough time to grab some bacon and eggs before Tom Fredrick and the state meat inspector showed up. The sun was just peeking red over the snowscape when we pulled into the buffalo pasture.

The buffalo are killed out on the prairie, where they are comfortable, but the skinning and eviscerating takes place inside the Buffalo Girl. Once the rear door is shut the trailer resembles the kill floor in a very small meat-processing plant. The difference is that the live buffalo never see the white walls and the stainless steel equipment. They never hear the grinding of machinery or smell the blood and disinfectant. Like all kill floors, a lot of very hot water is used, so the trailer has to be set up so that everything drains properly. The idea is that the nutrition-rich water is returned to the soil, but there is a trick to getting the slope just right. Jerry understood exactly what was needed without any explanation. He also knew that the driver can not see everything around a big truck, so he was out of the truck and guiding me backward as soon as we had slowed enough for him to jump free.

When I set the air breaks he was on the running board just outside my window. "With this snow, we're going to need the tire chains to pull out of here. Might as well put them on now while the engine is running and before we get more snow."

"Those chains are a pain in the butt to put on." I said. "Why don't we wait until we need them?"

He shrugged. "They're no big deal," he said.

By the time everyone was out of the truck, Jerry had the chains laid out behind the drive wheels. "Just back her up a couple feet," he said.

I did as I was told. By the time Cliff and Shane had the generator running and the hot water flowing to the trailer, Jerry was finished with the chains and standing at my elbow. Gervase was busy getting the outside of the trailer set up and shipshape. I pointed to the mechanical room in the front of the trailer. The inspector was leaning over the improvised desk, going over the paperwork in a thick three-ring binder, checking to see that all was in order. "He checks everything in that book," I said.

"HACCP?" Jerry asked.

I was surprised. "Yeah," I said, "Hazard Analysis and . . ."

"Critical Control Points," Jerry said.

I was even more surprised, and looked sideways at him. He shrugged. "I worked in a commercial kitchen" he said.

"You've worked in a lot of places. Why'd you quit?"

Another shrug. "Boring. I like not knowing what is going to happen."

I almost said that he had come to the right place, but instead I went on with my explanation. "When the guys complete their pre-operation cleanup, the inspector will check it out and then we can get going." We walked to the aluminum ramp that Gervase had just attached to the wide back door of the trailer. "We slide them up here with those winches." I pointed to the twin three-thousand-pound winches attached near the ceiling, positioned at the same level as the meat rail where the carcasses would hang. We stepped into the trailer.

"Stand back," Shane said. "Hot water, hot water."

We just ducked the 180 degree spray of water. The air was filled with steam and we skirted around Cliff, a giant of a man who had boxed briefly as pro heavyweight. He was in his late fifties and was as kind as he was big. He grinned down at us as he sterilized knives and we moved back to where the overhead rails disappeared into the eight-by-twelve-foot cooler where the rails split into four separate rails. "Here's where we cool and store the split carcasses."

Jerry looked up at the system of rails and switches. "At the end of the day, this place must look like a scene from that Rocky movie."

"That's the idea. But no punching allowed." I looked up and found Cliff watching me. He smiled and his eyes narrowed to slits. When I checked the cooler temperature I found it plenty cool.

We met the inspector as we stepped into the snowy pasture. He stepped through the boil of steamy air and closed the door behind him before he began his final inspection. He emerged again in a couple minutes. "Good to go," he said.

Tom, Wayne, and Gervase had been sitting in Gervase's truck keeping warm, but when they saw us gathering, they stepped out and came to the rear of the Buffalo Girl. We all stood by the ramp where the first buffalo would soon be laying, and Shane took the floor. "Okay," he said. "We need to be safe today. We got winches and sharp knives and that floor is going to be a little slick until things warm up." He turned to Gervase. "Nothing but good clean shots. Nobody get in a hurry. Safety first. Respect the buffalo." He nodded to Tom, "You want to say a prayer?"

Tom stepped forward and took a cigarette from his shirt pocket. He broke off the filter, twisted the tobacco out into his hand, and stood for a few seconds with his eyes closed. Then he turned to where the herd of buffalo was standing a quarter-mile away. He sang to them in Lakota and sprinkled the tobacco in the four directions. He turned in a complete circle and then raised a pinch of tobacco up to Father Sky and one down to Mother Earth. I glanced over to Jerry. Though all of this was new to him, he stood as solemn as any of us. It was the last time that day that I saw him without a smile on his face.

We harvested seven buffalo that day. Jerry rode with Gervase and, after the shot, helped chain the animals to the tractor loader. He helped winch them into the trailer, watched the skinners take the heads and hocks off before they each skinned one side and winched the carcass up to be eviscerated, split, and washed. Halfway through the day the generator stopped working, and together Jerry and I took off the fuel filter and cleaned it out by blowing through it backward. He stood under the ladder and handed pieces of wire up so I could wire the perfect carcasses to the rail for transport. On the way home I asked him to drive and he took the wheel with glee. When we arrived back at Terrance's barn, I asked him if he thought he could work into helping Gervase with the shooting.

"You bet," he said with a giddy smile. "I'd have to learn how to move around the herd, but I catch on fast."

"You seem to like what you saw today."

"It's just what I'm looking for," he said.

"You'd be wearing a lot of hats. Lot of stuff to go wrong."

"I just love a challenge." He giggled like a ten-year-old.

"You like this kind of work?"

"Oh yeah," he said. "When it comes to this kind of stuff, I'm enthusiastic." Then he shrugged. "But I'm lazy."

"You're lazy?"

"Oh yeah. But that's a good thing."

"How is lazy good?"

"That's how people figure out the easiest way to do something. Lazy is the mother of efficiency."

I stared at him until I was convinced that he believed what he had just said. Then I offered him the job.

Jill was taking orders for Wild Idea Buffalo Company from the ranch house. With the help of friends who knew many times more than Jill and I about such things, we built a basic website. Jill embraced the web and its associated technologies much more readily than I did. I could barely type a manuscript on a computer and the first website I ever visited was our own.

She had her computer and a telephone set up in a closet behind the bi-fold doors in our bedroom. When she got home from the restaurant at night or early in the morning, she would push the doors aside and roll an office chair up for an hour of contacting people who had questions or had ordered buffalo meat. We had an answering machine for the new 800 number, but when she was not around I would occasionally answer a call. I was clumsy compared to Jill but our policy was to talk to everyone who ordered, introducing ourselves and explaining what we were trying to do. We learned there were three kinds of people who ordered our meat: foodies in search of a unique culinary experience; conservationists concerned with biodiversity on the Great Plains; and people who loved red meat but chose not to eat anything from a feedlot. Of the last group there were two categories: those whose doctors had told them to cut out grain-finished meat (grass-fed buffalo was okay) and moral vegetarians.

I always got the sense that the moral vegetarians did not want to divulge their names for fear that I knew one of their friends and might reveal that they had called us. One young woman from the East Coast told me that after fifteen years of standing firm against industrial red meat, she still woke up in the middle of the night dreaming of rib eye steaks. An older vegetarian told me that he felt creepy and dishonest ordering meat and wanted me to talk him through it.

I told Jill that psychotherapy was above my pay grade and referred those cases to her. My responsibilities were mostly limited to taking care of the live buffalo and bringing in some cash by working away from the ranch. Jill gave up her restaurant but she did her share of catering for special parties while she worked to expand Wild Idea's business. The Sustainable Harvest truck produced enough grass-fed buffalo to meet the orders that came in by phone and increasingly via the Internet. A local processing plant was accepting the carcasses from the SHA truck and by late that winter there was too much traffic for us to do the shipping from the commercial cold storage plant where we kept our inventory. We made a deal with another company that shipped frozen food to help with fulfillment. Jill began making the ninety-mile trip to Spearfish, South Dakota, every Monday and Tuesday morning and spent those days making sure that every package was right before Fed Ex picked it up. On Mondays and Tuesdays she wasn't home until after nine o'clock p.m.

It was the end of Jilian's last basketball season. We were on the icy roads a couple nights a week, cheering for the New Underwood Tigers and supporting Jilian, who was playing well. There was some talk about her playing basketball as a freshman at the university. The night of her last game she played particularly well. Her coach approached us and asked if we would be interested in sending Jilian to Australia with a group of other girl basketball players. It was sort of an all-star summer program for graduated seniors to play in a large tournament in Sydney. The coach hadn't said anything to Jilian, but we knew that she would be thrilled. She was chomping at the bit to get out into the big world and we wanted her to have the chance. But the trip wasn't cheap and we were already wondering how we were going to pay for her first year of college. On the way home that night, Jill and I talked it over.

The road ditches were iridescent white with snow and the sky was black as a falcon's eye. Pure white jackrabbits as big as medium-sized dogs appeared on the black highway and ran crazily in the headlights. "Wild as March hares," I said.

"Must be mating season," Jill said.

"Right around the corner," I said. We glanced at each other in the blue dashboard lights. "You're thinking about Jilian aren't you?"

"Yep."

"Australia?"

"Partly."

"I've never been to Australia," I said.

"I've never been to Hawaii." We laughed because we both knew that we would find a way to send her to both places.

"It's the right thing," Jill said. "Big world."

"And she's ready."

"I'm not so sure." I saw her shoulder shrug at the edge of my vision as another crazy rabbit shot across the road.

"What do you mean?" I asked. "She's the most adventurous kid I know."

"She's got a boyfriend."

"She's always had a boyfriend," I said. "Who is it now?"

"Cody Crawford."

"Oh, for God's sake. How do you know that?"

"I just know. He stays clear of you."

"That's probably best."

"Yeah," Jill said. "He's an idiot."

"Is he even working?"

"He's a welder."

"Another reason to send her to Australia."

Jill nodded. "I hope she knows that I'm going to visit her in Hawaii."

I kept my eyes on the road because of the jackrabbits. But without looking at her I knew that Jill was thinking about all she had missed by never going to college. "You've earned a little Hawaii time," I said.

There was a silence and on a roadside snowdrift two rabbits leaped three feet straight into air. "I might move into the dorm with her," Jill said.

"Have you talked to her about that?"

Jill laughed out loud. "No," she said. "Not yet."

The buffalo were supposed to come off the National Grassland at the end of March and I was due at my teaching job in Minnesota on the first of April. I was worried about bringing the buffalo back over the river because we had never done it before and I wasn't sure if we would even be able to find them. The foul weather had eased, but snow still covered everything except the miniature cedar trees along the ridgelines. The plan was to wait until the herd came down to the river to drink, then lure the buffalo over the river and through the gate into the proper pasture using bales of good hay as the enticement. Day after day I parked my pickup high up on the bluff above our house and scanned the east side of the river with binoculars. Some days I saw a few buffalo standing out stark on a wide, windswept plateau several miles away. Most days I saw nothing.

As the date approached, Gervase and I spent more time watching. Worrying about not being able to get the buffalo back to our side of the river kept me up at night. If we couldn't get them back on time I would have to cancel my yearly teaching gig and we were counting on that extra cash. In the last week of the month Gervase and I saw a few scattered buffalo grazing high above the river on the rolling highlands called Zebell Table, but we never saw them come down to the river. "They must be eating snow for their water," Gervase said.

I agreed. "Unless some are coming down to the river at night."

The last week of March we were getting desperate and so, on a warm day, we drove an ATV down to the river to look for tracks. We found none on the west side but there was a disturbance in the mud on the other side. I drove the ATV as close to the water as I dared but still couldn't tell if the tracks on the other side of the river were from buffalo or not. I stopped with the front wheels touching the huge chunks of ice that had been pushed up onto the bank. I goosed the engine and we popped up onto a ten-foot-square slab of ice.

"You're not going to try to cross it, are you?" Gervase was looking at me and had one foot out of the ATV.

I didn't bother to answer him and we idled to the edge of the water and looked at the water rushing past. We had crossed there many times during the summer drought and knew that the best place was where the water ran fastest. The movement of the water washed the mud and sand from the rocks and left the bottom solid. But now that some of the snow was beginning to melt and the ice jams were pushing the channel around, everything looked different. It was hard to tell how deep it was but it looked like there might be a narrow shallow place just in front of the ATV. I leaned over the steering wheel and looked at the river. "Don't do it," Gervase said. He jumped out and stood on the ice with one hand on the roll bar of the ATV. "You'll go down like an engine block."

"I'm not going to just drive into the river."

We both watched the rushing water for a full minute. "What do you think we should do?" Gervase asked.

"We should check the depth of the water."

"How are we going to do that?"

"Well," I said, "one of us should wade out there a-ways."

He looked at me through the ATV roll bar. "Which one of us?"

"Well, you're already standing there."

"No, no."

But I knew how to get to Gervase. "Come on. We have to check out those tracks and you were the marine."

He straightened up bit taller and I knew I had him. "That was fifty years ago," he said.

"Yeah, but you never forgot all that survival training. Besides, this is sort of an amphibious operation." I thought that might get him to smile, but when I looked, his jaw was set. He stood with his hands on his hips.

I eased out the other side of the ATV and picked up a lariat that was coiled in the bed. "I'll stand right here and, if you start to go downstream, I'll throw you this rope."

His hands were still on his hips and he was shifting his weight from one foot to the other. He slid out of his heavy jacket and tossed it into the back of the ATV. He took a couple steps forward and pointed to a pile of rocks beside the water. "Stand up there," he said. "Get ready to throw that damned rope."

He stepped off the ice and onto the gravel beneath three inches of water. He took another step and the foot went in over the boot top.

"Cold?"

"Colder than hell," he said.

By the time he got to midstream the water was up to his knees and I was afraid it would sweep his legs out from under him. He stood with his feet wide apart and his arms out like a tightrope walker. He teetered and took another step. It came up to his crotch. "This isn't working," he called out.

I started to swing the lariat around my head. "Hell," I said, "you're halfway there. No sense coming back."

He rocked again and staggered two steps forward. The water was a little shallower and he took an instant to turn and grin at me. He slogged three more steps and stood dripping with just his feet submerged. "No sweat," he yelled. "Got to be the shallowest place on the river." He took two more steps and looked down at the tracks in the muddy river bank. "Looks like one came down here to drink."

"We have to follow that track," I said. "You think I can make it?"

"I don't know, but I don't feel like walking back across."

I tossed the lariat into the ATV bed and slid into the seat. I backed up a few feet and revved the engine. The last thing I saw before the wall of water sprayed over me was a soggy Gervase hustling to get out of my way.

Within ten minutes we were 150 feet above the river and bumping onto the shoulder of Zebell Table. From the west side of the river Zebell looks nearly flat but it is actually a thousand acres of undulating grasslands and draws. There is a big prairie dog town up there and the table is cut by several deep draws wide enough to hide small forests of cedar trees and a thousand head of buffalo with ease.

What snow had not blown off in the March winds was melting fast where the exposed dirt of the prairie dog mounds soaked up the sun's radiant heat. We were both wet, but the air was still, so we idled along beside the fresh buffalo tracks. "What are we going to do if we find him?" Gervase asked.

"I don't know," I said.

We moved slowly over the soft snow and prairie dog mud for half a mile, then down a long flat to the rim of one of the deep draws that transect the table. A small herd of antelope raised their heads to look at us, then ran a quarter mile arc around us and stopped to have another look. There was still a lot of last year's grass sticking up through the snow and the warm sunshine was releasing more. In places it stood thick and a foot high. It made the buffalo track hard to follow, and we occasionally lost it completely. When we did, we circled very slowly back to where we had lost it. Gervase hung out one side of the ATV and I hung out the other. Our faces were barely three feet off the ground and we were lost in concentration.

On we went and the track joined several more. We dipped down into a bowl and found where a lot of buffalo had spent considerable time, but those tracks were old. A pair of crows, no doubt early prospectors for a prime nesting site, scolded us from the top of a cedar tree. Neither of us knew exactly where we were but we knew we could always go to a high place and locate the river. We scanned the rim of the bowl in front of us then slowly turned to look behind.

Silhouetted on the horizon in the direction from where we had descended were the heads of a half-dozen curious buffalo. They were adult females that had known Gervase and me since they were calves. They were friendly, and because they had never been hassled, were comfortable around ATVs. As soon as they figured out what we were, they began moving slowly toward us. Their horns stood out against a clear blue sky and their bodies rose up as if they were coming out of the earth. Their expressions were calm and their heads swung back and forth with the rhythm of their gait. More buffalo were following behind them, and by the time the first few cows were fifty yards from the ATV, a hundred more had come over the rim and were ambling our way.

"We found the buffalo," Gervase said.

"Kind of looks like they've been waiting for us." Dozens more were coming over the hill, most of which were youngsters. They butted each other playfully and a few ran great arcs to join the leaders of the herd, who were now standing twenty feet away, looking at us with deep dark eyes. I had never seen spring buffalo in better shape. Their manes were long and shaggy and the coats covering their backs and sides were as thick and uniform as sheared chocolate-colored mink.

"So what do we do now?" Gervase asked.

"Maybe they'll follow us."

"We don't have any hay."

"Maybe they'll trust us."

I put the ATV into low gear and turned it for home. I didn't dare look back, but Gervase sat sideways in his seat. "They're coming," he said.

I held my breath for most of the time that it took us to travel the mile to where we had to begin our descent into the river bottom. We had led buffalo many times but seldom this far and almost never without tidbitting them as we went. We knew that sometimes they balked at walking down a hill. So this time I took one hopeful look over my shoulder before we started down. There were buffalo strung out behind us for a half-mile. I turned back to the task of negotiating the descent and didn't breathe until we were nearly at the bottom. Gervase supplied a running commentary: "They're coming. Damn. They're really coming. Step on it. Goddamn, they're *really* coming."

We were just getting to level ground when I looked back to see the hillside alive with running buffalo. They chased each other, twisting and turning, swarming like insects in the huge landscape under an infinite sky. Gervase was slapping my shoulder. "Don't say whoa at horse race! Move it."

It was all we could do to stay ahead of the herd. A few youngsters even beat us to the river. It crossed my mind that they were thirsty but none put their heads down to drink. They lined up at the water's edge downstream from where we had crossed. In front of them the water raged fifty yards across and who knew how deep. "They'll never cross," I said, as we pulled up in the tracks we had made on our way over.

"How about us? Are we going to cross?"

"We're going across where we know it's shallowest," I said. "Maybe we can get to the house and back with something to coax them across." I was suddenly obsessed, worried this might be our best or only chance to get the herd into our pasture. The gate that we needed to put them through was only a couple hundred yards away on the other side of the river. We had left it open and I could see it beckoning to us.

I stomped on the accelerator and a wall of water again blocked out the sun. I was hoping we'd be able to make it back to the tractor and bring out a bale of hay. But somewhere in the middle of the river the ATV bogged down. It jumped on the rocky river bottom and water surged through the floorboards. I pumped the gas but the engine was failing. Gervase and I were soaked with ice-cold water. The ATV bucked but it was no use. The engine gave out with a glug and we were still thirty feet from the west bank.

We sat on the ATV seat with water coursing over the floorboards up to our thighs. We'd be coming back from the house with the tractor alright. But only after a long cold walk and only to pull the ATV out of the river. By then the buffalo would have scattered back into the hills. "Shit," I said, and punched the steering wheel with my palms. I lowered my head, closed my eyes, and listened to the water rushing through the ATV.

Gervase tapped my shoulder again. "Have a look," he said.

When I glanced up, buffalo were pouring into the river. An old cow was just sinking into a swimming position with everything but her head below the water. She moved more like a muskrat than a buffalo and dozens of buffalo were right behind her. We watched in silence as hundreds of buffalo slipped into the icy water and moved across as if they had been swimming frigid rivers every day of their lives.

By the time the last buffalo made the plunge, the first ones were on the opposite bank and the lead animals had nearly reached the gate.

I was free to leave for my job. But a day after the buffalo came home the wind came up in the afternoon and the temperature again slipped below freezing. By eleven o'clock that night the stars were invisible and the sharp wind blended with a wet, heavy snow.

Jill found me staring out the patio door, watching the big flakes streaking through the deck light's beam. She touched my shoulder. "You all right?"

"Sure."

"You worried about the buffalo?"

I shook my head. "No. This won't bother the buffalo. Just wondering if the driveway is going to blow in again. Worried about getting to Minnesota on time."

"Wish you didn't have to go."

I put my arm around her. "Me too. But it's a job."

"I'm going to miss you."

"I'm going to miss you, too."

The flakes were getting larger and Jill shook her head. "Where was all this moisture last summer when we needed it?"

In the morning eighteen inches of heavy, wet snow sat on the level and three feet had packed into the driveway. I had a day to get it cleared out.

Gervase and Erney were, of course, already up by the time I waded out to their living quarters. It was a replay of the previous three times that the driveway had been snowed shut—Hank, Tootsie, Al, and Trixy were running around like puppies and Erney was inside one of the dog runs fighting with a scoop shovel. Gervase was trying to help him clear the snow from the concrete floor. With grumpy, halting words Erney was telling Gervase that he didn't need any damned help and Gervase was standing back, bundled up in coveralls and a wool stocking cap, saying things like, "Go ahead, then, have another stroke!"

As soon as Gervase saw me he dismissed Erney with a wave and came my way. We watched for a moment and saw that Erney was using the shovel, not only to move tiny portions of snow but also to keep his balance. "He won't listen," Gervase said.

"Never has," I said. "We'll be around the yard for awhile. Let's just let him go."

"We don't have any choice, unless we want to beat him up."

"We don't have time. We have to move some snow. I have to get out of here tomorrow, first thing."

We were already walking toward the accursed Rhino. "Wouldn't hurt to roll out a bail of hay for the buffalo," Gervase said.

I agreed. "But we have to get through that driveway first."

We plugged in the Rhino's block heater and, while we were waiting, checked on Erney. He had scraped away a foot-wide strip a quarter of the length of one of the runs. It was heavy, dangerous snow and I didn't bother to debate with him. I slogged to the machine shop and grabbed shovels for Gervase and me. We each took one of the runs and were finished with ours by the time Erney had move another two feet. He was leaning against the chain link of his run and looked up at us with a wild, sweaty face. While Gervase finished the shoveling I helped Erney walk inside and sat him down in front of the television. "Hell," he said, "I'd-a got it before it melted."

We should have known that something major was going to go wrong when the Rhino started on the first try. It coughed and blew blue-black smoke from its stack. The diesel fumes drove us to the upwind side and we stood back, amazed that it continued to run. I felt a grave sense of urgency. I hadn't even packed for my two months away from the ranch and now I had a full day of work ahead of me. I stepped on the clutch to put the Rhino into gear and found no resistance. The clutch went straight to the floorboard and stayed there. My heart went with it.

The clutch had been grinding for years and I knew instantly that it had finally given out, but I tried to pop the transmission into first gear anyway. It made a horrible grinding sound but I tried again. I stomped on the clutch pedal a couple more times and tried to put it into gear once more. When it was clear that the clutch was completely shot, I calmly turned the key and shut off the engine. I slid out of the seat and stepped down off the tractor. I forced a smile as I walked past Gervase. All I said when I passed Jill in the house was, "The shovel broke." She had no idea what I was talking about but knew it was best not to ask. I was courteous when I called Rick Messer, the vice president of our bank. It made complete sense to him that he should lend us the money to purchase a brand new Bobcat loader.

Nine

WHEN YOU HAVE TO BUY A PIECE OF MACHINERY OR YOU want to send your little girl on her first international trip or away to college, it is wonderful to have a good-paying job. Though I didn't want to leave home, I considered myself lucky as I streaked eastward through the upper reaches of the Pine Ridge Reservation, where the rate of unemployment hovers chronically at 80 percent.

The snow petered out just as I crossed the White River and turned north to where I picked up Interstate 90, which took me four hundred miles east. The scattered ranches turned slowly to farms and the farms grew thicker until I got to Sioux Falls, the largest city in South Dakota. From there on the agriculture turned from a lifestyle to an industry; three hours later I was within the influence of the *real* city of Minneapolis, where the very idea of buffalo that thrived on nothing but grass, water, and distance had become so implausible that I was already homesick.

I missed the last months of Jilian's senior year of high school, but I returned with enough cash to pay for her trip to Australia. We took her to the airport in Rapid City, where she joined the rest of her basketball team. A prettier, greener group of eighteen-year-old girls never gathered at a United Airlines ticket counter. A few boyfriends had gotten off work to send the girls off and Cody Crawford was among them.

I managed to be civil to Cody, but Jill could barely look at him. He had come in his welder's clothes, was sporting a couple of days' beard growth, and didn't bother to wipe the tobacco juice away from his lips when he kissed Jilian good-bye. Jill's fingernails dug into my arm, and the barely audible noise she made reminded me of a cornered bull snake.

It was a long ride home from the airport. I tried to tell Jill that this was a day we should celebrate. Jilian was off into the big, crazy world. She would be in Los Angeles in a few hours, then heading for Hawaii and finally an entirely new continent. "Her horizons are about to explode," I said. "She'll be off to college in the fall and then Katie-bar-the-door." But Jill only stared straight ahead.

"Come on. This is a time to be proud. Our little girl graduated with honors, she's a hard worker, and she's venturing off on her own."

"I hate that Cody Crawford."

"Oh, come on. You're being an overly protective mom. Don't you remember your first attraction to a guy like Cody?"

I was driving but glanced over at Jill just as she turned to look at me. Her chin quivered. "Yeah," she said. "I remember it perfectly."

Gervase, Jerry, Cliff, and Shane had been working in the Buffalo Girl, mostly on the reservation. They waited until I returned home to harvest buffalo from the Cheyenne River Ranch. While I was gone they had harvested only a handful of days. I had no idea how I was going to be able to keep our crew together with so little work to keep them busy. I figured that Gervase would stick with us for awhile no matter what, but for Jerry and Shane to come out to work for only a day or two a month, they had to take a day off their regular jobs, which I knew their employers were not happy about. Shane and Jerry each had a young family to provide for—in fact, they both had a couple of families to provide for—and I worried about the fallout from home in addition to what might happen at their jobs. Cliff was an old warhorse who was partially retired, but he worked with us because it gave him something worthwhile to do. "I've slaughtered enough animals in my life that I don't need to slaughter any more," Cliff told me. Then he winked. "But this is a little different. I'm going to stick around and see what happens here."

While I was gone, the number of orders for our meat had increased.

There was enough volume that Jill was thinking about hanging out a shingle in Rapid City. She joked that it was time that Wild Idea came out of our closet, but she had doubts that there were enough buffalo raised strictly on grass to fill the orders. "Christmas is coming," she said.

"Christmas? It's still June."

She handed me a profit and loss statement. "What's this thing?" I asked.

She grimaced as if she was afraid I would be mad. "I bought QuickBooks software," she said. "I entered everything I could find from the last few years. Look at November and December sales."

I ran my finger down the column she had indicated as if I knew exactly what I was looking for. She ended up guiding my hand to a tally page. "November and December are 40 percent of our business. If we keep trending this way, we are going to need 7,600 pounds of saleable meat in storage this fall."

"7,600 pounds?"

"That's figuring super quality grass-fed animals." She was reading from a yellow legal pad. "Thousand pounds on the hoof. Figured conservatively at 50 percent of live weight to carcass weight. Gives us a 500-pound carcass hanging in the SHA truck. By the time the processing plant gets them cut and wrapped, I guessed each carcass at about 380 pounds of saleable meat. That's 7,600 pounds of meat ready to sell over the holidays." She looked at me and smiled.

"How many live buffalo?" I said.

She glanced back at her notes and ran her finger up a column. "Mmm, better figure twenty-four in addition to the fifty that we'll be harvesting off our own ranch."

"Twenty-four additional buffalo? Where do we get twenty-four more buffalo?"

She dug through a pile of papers on the kitchen counter and came up with a list of four buffalo producers whose animals we had harvested in the past. "You should contact these guys first," she said. She turned the paper over and showed me a second list. "Here are the guys that called while you were gone."

I squinted at her as I took the paper from her hand. There were eight buffalo producers on the list of people who had called, but five had been crossed off. Behind the crossed-off names were notes like "Feeds corn," "Hormones," and "This guy is a jerk." Of the three producers who passed muster, two were Lakotas: Black Feather and Iron Cloud. The third was the guy who had bought the Broken Heart Ranch. He still owned buffalo and let me hunt for grouse on his land with my falcon. These were good leads. I looked back to Jill, who was shaking a finger at me. "Now the catch is that we only want buffalo that meet our criteria. You are going to have to go out and look at every one of them."

"And talk these guys into selling them for SHA to come harvest."

"Right," she said. "For around a thousand dollars a piece."

I laughed. "And if I should happen to find twenty-four perfect buffalo and convince their owners to sell them for a thousand dollars a piece, where will we get the twenty-four thousand dollars to buy them?"

"We have to go see Rick Messer at the bank."

"And beg for twenty-four thousand dollars."

Jill was sitting down at the kitchen counter, shuffling papers. "Ah," she grimaced, "more like thirty-two thousand."

I moved around the counter and when I locked eyes with her, she shrugged. "We need a bigger computer and there are some other bills."

"We haven't even made the first payment on the Bobcat."

Jill smiled. "Well, that's why we need to go in person." She raised a handful of papers and shook them. "And I'll bring my brand new QuickBooks profit and loss statements."

The next morning I was leaning against the pickup waiting for her to get ready before we went to see Rick when Camo came out of the shadows behind the barn and nickered to me from the corral fence. His head, shoulders, and rump had muscled-up and he was nearly grown. I met him at the fence and reached to touch the dark chestnut jaw muscles that tapered to his valet muzzle. He nosed my hands, probing for a treat. I felt sad and ashamed that I had not spent more time with him. "You're not a baby anymore. Two years old." I rubbed his hard head between his bottomless eyes. "About old enough to ride." I heard Jill come from the door behind me and move toward the pickup, but I laid my forehead against Camo's. "It's a promise, buddy."

It took almost an hour to get to the Pioneer Bank and Trust building on the other side of Rapid City. Our land mortgage was held by a big international agricultural lender, but our checking accounts and the Bobcat loan were with Pioneer. The bank was started by a ranching family in northwestern South Dakota whom Jill and I knew. As a young man working for South Dakota Game, Fish, and Parks, I had surveyed their family ranch for nesting birds of prey. Jill knew the boys that had grown up to guide the family business into the modern banking age. Now they were respected and stately men who had passed the reins, and our accounts, on to an able staff of young bankers. Our accounts had been with them for many years but we were insignificant customers, distinguished only by the fact that what little money we had borrowed over the years had been paid back on time.

Rick was a vice president with his office in the branch where we banked. When he spied us from his glass cubicle he came to meet us with a genuine smile that you don't see at national chain banks. "How are the buffalo?" he asked as we shook hands.

"Well," I said, "they need a little cash."

Rick continued to smile but squinted one eye. "Is this about that Bobcat loader we bought?"

Jill and I shook our heads in unison. "No," I said, "it's running fine."

"This is about a business loan," Jill said.

"You want a production loan for the ranch?"

I shook my head. "No. This is not really so much about ranching."

"A business loan," Jill said. "Like I had when I had my restaurants."

"Ah ha," he said. "Business loan. We do business loans." He waved us ahead of him and toward his cubicle.

Jill laid it all out on Rick's desk. She had a small brochure that, along with the website, constituted Wild Idea Buffalo Company's complete advertising campaign to date. She had a few numbers written down on a yellow pad which showed that we hoped to increase our buffalo meat sales by 20 percent over the next few years. She had a list of our assets: an old computer, a website, and five thousand dollars worth of frozen meat. She had her newly minted financials from the previous eighteen months. Rick looked everything over.

"You want to buy more buffalo because you have more demand than you can meet from your own ranch."

"Carcasses, really."

"You want to buy dead buffalo?"

"Yeah," Jill said. "The really good ones. Grass-fed, free range. Happy buffalo."

"You want to buy happy, dead buffalo."

We nodded and he looked back down at Jill's paperwork. He shifted things around the desk a little but I could tell that he wasn't really reading things. "How much you going to need?" he asked without looking up.

"Thirty-five thousand," Jill said with false bravado. I noticed that she had bumped her request by three thousand and I knew why. We had the nonrefundable down payment on Jilian's first semester of college to meet.

"Thirty-five thousand dollars worth of happy, dead buffalo?"

"And a computer." Jill pointed to the asset sheet. "Our computer is really old. And, ah, we have a little bill with our good friends who did the brochure and the website for us."

"What would you say for the computer and the outstanding bills?"

"Probably about four or five thousand dollars?"

Rick was doing some figuring on a piece of paper. "How many buffalo?"

"Twenty-four," I said.

"A little over twelve hundred a piece?"

I couldn't believe he figured that so fast. "We were hoping to get them a little cheaper than that." I mumbled my words because I was afraid that Rick had already found the extra three thousand Jill had thrown in for a life cushion.

He looked up at me then looked at Jill. "Is that enough?"

We nodded and he nodded back. He looked back at the figures he had written down. "We took part of your buffalo herd for collateral on the Bobcat." He shifted his eyes to the note we had signed for the Bobcat, studied it for awhile, and looked up again. "I'm talking the live ones, now." He glanced over at our financial statement. "But you have enough left for this."

"So you'll give us the money?" I was amazed.

"No," he said. "We don't give money away here. You'll have to pay it back, with interest, over three years."

I had to smile. "Oh," I said. "I knew there was a catch."

We harvested buffalo at the Cheyenne River Ranch at the beginning of July. Because the days were long and the afternoons temps had been pushing up over ninety degrees, the crew showed up at the truck, parked behind the newly rented Wild Idea office in Rapid City, at five o'clock in the morning. By six o'clock the big white Buffalo Girl pulled into the pasture at the north end of the ranch.

I drove the Bobcat up from the ranch house to move the dead buffalo from the field to the Buffalo Girl. Jerry and I had welded log-chain hooks to the corners of the loader bucket so that a short chain choker could be wrapped around a buffalo's hind hocks and the other end could be easily attached to a hook on the bucket then raised eight feet into the air. It worked like a charm, except that moving the Bobcat very far was quite bone jarring. I was glad to turn the job over to Jerry. He was thirty-eight years old but when he got the chance to drive the Bobcat, he grinned like a third-grader on a new bike.

Gervase and the inspector were already out in Gervase's pickup doing the ante mortem inspection of the herd. I had heard him checking the zero on his rifle before five that morning. When I had stepped out of the house that morning he was just climbing into his pickup. He held up a small piece of cardboard with a two-inch circle penned in the center. Three perfect bullets holes touched each other in the circle's center. Cliff and Shane had come out of the sparkling bleached trailer and reported to me on the safety meeting they had had before I arrived. "We are 100 percent shipshape, Boss," Shane said.

Cliff towered behind us. His strong hands drew the blade of his skinning knife carefully over a sharpening steel. He looked intently through tiny, John Lennon–style glasses. "Going to be hot one," he said.

Jerry was in the Bobcat and already two hundred yards into the pasture, bouncing toward where the pickup was stopped in the midst of the buffalo herd, when I heard the shot. I looked out to see all the buffalo standing stoically around the pickup as Gervase and the inspector got out and approached a prone buffalo not fifty feet away. They would have collected the required blood samples by the time Jerry reached them.

"Well," Cliff said, "looks like we got our first customer."

Shane was looking out to where the buffalo was being hoisted skyward. Shane's Lakota face was catching the morning sun and he elevated is chin in a way that made it seem that the coming day would be a good one. The Bobcat turned in place and we could hear the RPMs increase. A large flock of buffalo birds arched over the men, the machine, and the buffalo. A breeze rattled in the grass and Gervase and the inspector were on their way back; the three of us continued to stand quietly at the back of the Buffalo Girl. Shane was fiddling with something in his hand as he stared at the distant Black Hills. When I looked I saw the cigarette. The filter had already been broken off and he was stripping the tobacco into his left hand.

The next fall we got a call from Vin, a Wild Idea customer who lived in Boston. He seemed keenly interested in what we were doing. It was not entirely unusual for a customer to let us know that they supported our efforts, but this call was different. The voice was friendly but deep, slow, and authoritative. "My wife, Carla, and I eat your meat," Vin said. "We like it. Recommend it to our friends." This was a good way to begin a conversation, and I thanked him.

"We were wondering if we could stop by your ranch and meet you this fall." This, too, was good. Jill and I welcomed customers to take a look at the ranch and see exactly where their meat was coming from. We had been putting people up for a night or two and feeding them, but if they were interesting we always got into the wine and had too much fun. It was breaking us and having strangers in our home was becoming disruptive. We wanted to switch policies to an eco-tourist model, charging for overnight stays and for white tablecloth meals of buffalo. We were in the process of fixing up an old house at the other end of the ranch. We thought customers could stay there, and this guy and his wife might be a good test run. "We could probably arrange something." I said. "When were you planning to be out this way?"

"Carla and I are going to be in Denver on . . ." He paused to check his calendar. "Probably be out there on about the twenty-eighth of August."

The date rang a bell with me but I was pretty sure that we had nothing planned. I pretended to check our calendar. "Well . . . yeah, that would probably work. Give me your email and we'll get back to you."

"Great," he said.

Who knew where this might lead. It could be that this couple simply liked our meat, that they were retired science teachers or social workers. But, on that first Internet search, I found out that these folks were investors and their range of investment was wide and varied. They were involved in big and small projects and seemed to have a knack for making money. Maybe they were investors in earthmoving equipment like the kind Cody was fixing for the oil fields in Wyoming. The date of their visit turned out to be the date of the Democratic National Convention. It seemed incongruous that Boston financiers would be in Denver that day.

For days I had flashbacks to our breakfast with Joe Ricketts, who was spending millions building a buffalo meat business that sold highly processed frozen dinners of buffalo meat from buffalo that had stood in feedlots for the last months of their lives. I had second thoughts about offering to host Carla and Vin.

Erney was always ready to listen to me, and I spent an hour or so every day sitting on a broken chair commiserating with him. "Just relax," he said. "Wealthy guys run everything. Just the way it is." The television was blasting a commercial at high volume.

"Turn that down," I shouted.

He looked at me through his rheumy stroked-out eyes, and said, "What?"

"Turn it down." I pointed to the TV and turned my thumb downward. He fumbled with the remote. "But they do a lot of damage," I said.

"Commercials?"

"No, rich people. Industrialists. Venture capitalists."

"Poor people do a lot of damage too."

"You're poor," I said. "You don't do any damage."

"I don't do anything."

I shook my head and watched the silent television. Andy Griffith was explaining something to Don Knox. "Well," I grumbled, "a lot of wealthy people don't do anything that's good."

"They do some good things," Erney said. Now we were both watching the muted television.

"Like what?"

We watched in silence, and finally I looked over at him. He pretended not to notice that I was watching him. I could see that the old wheels in his head were turning as they always had, but since the stroke it was as if a layer of thin, opaque plastic engulfed him. He blinked his eyes and turned to face me. "Give me a little time, Dan'l. I'll think of something."

Jill was worried about Jilian's impending return from Australia. "I've got this sick feeling in my gut," she kept saying.

"What? How much trouble could she get into in Australia?"

"She could get into a lot of trouble in Australia. In fact, I hope she has. I'm more afraid of her coming home."

"Cody Crawford."

"I can't reach her on her cell phone."

"Maybe she's busy calling Hawaii, ordering her school books."

"No, she's texting that tobacco-chewing cowboy."

"No. Why would she waste serious time with him?"

Jill looked at me and her eyes welled up with tears. "Because she didn't get the kind of love a kid needs when she was young."

"Oh, come on."

But it was no use. For the three days before Jilian's return, Jill did not sleep. "A mother knows," she said.

For the first time in our lives we were early to meet an airplane. Jill was a wreck. She could not stand still in the waiting area. She had brought the season's last gumbo lily: a tiny, white, exquisite native flower she had picked that morning from our pasture. She brought it as a welcome-home present and she shifted it from hand to hand. She paced like a trapped leopard and would not listen to my whispers of reason.

I thought that Jill was being irrational until I saw a small middle-aged man with long sideburns watching her. He was with a woman who I figured was his wife, and a hefty teenaged girl who must have been their daughter. The man watched Jill and spoke to his wife, who looked our way and smiled. Finally the man crossed the waiting room floor and approached us. "You must be Jill," he said with an obsequious smile.

Jill froze in place. "Yes," she said.

"Well, hell, I told Ma over there," he nodded to his wife. "I told her that a good-looking thing like you just had to be Jilian's mom. Hell, you're just a dead ringer. Let me go get Ma and Trinity."

He sprinted across the room and I turned to Jill. "Who the hell is that?"

"Cody's father."

"How do you know?"

"I just know."

Two minutes later Cody came strutting down the corridor with a dozen red roses in his hand. He wore a colorful cowboy shirt with pearl snaps, tight, straight-legged jeans, fancy cowboy boots, and a black cowboy hat. Mr. and Mrs. Crawford were standing behind us. "Here he comes, Ma. Don't he look proud?"

Jill felt behind her for a chair and sat down as Mr. Crawford turned to me. "Cody's got him that job welding over there in the oil fields in Wyoming. Fixing that big-rig stuff. Damned good money, too."

Passengers were coming off the airplane and I watched Jill's eyes. "I just don't know who missed who the most," Mr. Crawford said. "Did little Jilian miss Cody more or did Cody miss Jilian more?"

The mother weighed in. "That's sure the question, ain't it."

Cody was now standing beside me. His father elbowed him. "You didn't forget the most important thing did you?"

"Shit no, Dad." He smiled and pulled the ring box out of his pocket just as Jilian came through the door.

I looked to Jill and her face had gone white. Her shoulders slumped and her hands dangled beside her chair. She let the gumbo lily slip to the floor and reached out to take my hand.

Part Four

Ten

JILL AND I WERE AT LOOSE ENDS BECAUSE CODY HAD rented a house in the energy boomtown of Gillette, Wyoming—150 miles away. He was putting in long, lucrative hours welding the broken parts of huge earthmoving machines that tore coal, oil, and gas out of the earth. Jilian would join him very soon. The fact that she was being spirited away from us had made me skeptical of the world and of people with the power to do us harm.

Before Jilian announced that she was leaving, we had agreed to take on a young French woman as an unpaid intern at Wild Idea. She was the daughter of a Parisian acquaintance and, with Jilian lost to us, Maeve became a sort of surrogate daughter. She was confident and wise beyond her years. Wise enough to know that there was a hole in our hearts and convinced that Cody was just a phase for Jilian.

Phase or not, Jill and I knew that Jilian was in dangerous territory. She had backed out of going to college and there was a nauseating tension when we were alone with her. Maeve and Jilian became friends before she moved to Gillette, and Jill and I clung to the dream that Jilian would be inspired by Maeve's spirit of independent adventure then change her mind about Cody and head for Hawaii. On one of the last weekends that she was home, she and Maeve went to one of the lakes high up in the Black Hills with a group of Jilian's friends. When they came home they showed us pictures of their outing on Jilian's cell phone. I watched as pictures of the two happy, carefree young women came up on Jilian's phone. It was easy to see that Jilian was no longer the chubby, grinning little girl that had awakened the parent in me. But even though the two girl's smiles would have looked identical to most observers, they were not the same for me because I felt I could see their futures.

Maeve and Jilian were laughing at their images while I sat on the stool in our kitchen and watched the pictures blink past. Jilian must have detected the melancholy on my face because after she had left for Gillette, I found that she had somehow transferred one of those pictures to the background of my cell phone. Two years later I lost that phone in a buffalo pasture but I can still see that picture. The two young women smiling in midair with arms and legs akimbo. They had evidently jumped from one of the cliffs that overhang the lake. They were falling toward dark water, but you'd never know it by the joy on their faces.

Maeve stepped into Jilian's place as though they were sisters. She attached herself to Jill, to Wild Idea, to the ranch, to the buffalo, and particularly to Hank. By then he was a big, beautiful, mature black-and-white English setter that seemed to know what everyone was saying and thinking. Jilian was sick to leave him. When she left, Hank, too, showed signs of depression. Eventually he glommed onto Maeve and accepted her presence in Jilian's old bedroom. He had, of course, come from France, and, as though he remembered his early puppyhood, took commands in either language.

It was a sad day when Maeve went back to France. She had buffered the pain of our loss of Jilian and the house went suddenly lifeless without her. No more cell phone ringtones during dinner. No more help preparing meals or cleaning up. Hank wandered through the house looking for a lively girl to pet him. The evening laughter was dialed back to nearly nothing, and Jill and I found ourselves gloomy and irritable almost every night.

Even Gervase seemed to desert us. The old goat had gone head-over-heels for the woman in Hill City. Her house was ninety minutes from the ranch and about half of the route was on a gravel road. Gervase was wearing the tires off his pickup and I marveled at his stamina. He was always an early riser and would often be up doing something in the shop by five-thirty in the morning. The difference was that, since he had met this woman, he was no longer going to bed early. Now he would jump in the pickup about five o'clock in the afternoon and not be back until dawn.

Love is an incalculable source of renewable energy but, finally, even Gervase began to weaken. It started with a note on my desk saying that he might not make it back from Hill City until noon the next day. A month later it was rare to see him two days in a row. I wasn't concerned. In fact, I encouraged him. There was barely enough work to do around the ranch to keep us both busy. Even though we could have had some jobs done in half the time, I was able to handle them alone.

Of course there was also the safety factor. At my age it was a good policy to have someone around to call for a Medivac extraction. That policy goes double when it comes to breaking young horses. For a week I'd been saddling Camo every day or two as he stood tied to the corral rail. He had bucked when I first tightened the girth, but he was only startled—just a few leaps at the end of the lead rope. From then on, whenever I saddled him he just turned his head and looked at me as if to ask what I was doing. There was no trouble getting my left foot up and into the left stirrup, and he didn't mind my weight hanging on the side of the saddle. But I had not gotten up the nerve to swing my right leg over. I needed someone to hold his bridle and distract him while I crept into the saddle. Gervase would have been the perfect guy because he was fearless and fancied himself a horseman. But he was otherwise occupied.

Standing there alone in that dusty corral, a sensation of mortality wafted over me. I was over sixty years old and ever since a saddle girth had snapped on me two years before, I was more timid. Before that accident I had never thought much about the possibility of getting injured. But more than a few ribs broke inside of me when I came off that running horse. For two days in a row I stood beside Camo, easing my weight up to lay across the saddle. Jill was not good in that sort of situation. Jilian and Gervase were AWOL. My only option was Erney.

I found him sitting in his Easy Boy recliner, watching *The Golden Girls*. He had grown his beard back and thrown a buffalo hide over the chair. Except for the television, he looked like a nineteenth-century beaver trapper. "Hiya, Dan'l."

"What are you doing?"

"Nothin.'"

"You want to give me a hand?"

"Sure." He began to struggle to get out of the chair.

"Don't you want to know what I need?"

"Nope." He thrashed around until his good hand got ahold of his cane.

"Hang on. Let me help you."

"I got it. I got it." He came to his feet and stood there puffing.

When he caught his breath, he raised a finger to my face. "I been thinkin'," he said.

"What about?" I was guiding him toward the door.

"That wealthy guy that's coming out. Is he a man of discriminating taste?"

"I don't know."

"Well, that's the way Teton Park got goin'. 'Course, it's mountains, but Old J. D. Rockefeller Jr. went out there and got interested. Hadn't been for him, all that country south of Yellowstone would be mobile home parks and tourist traps. Now, that's something good that a wealthy guy did."

"Boy, you have been thinking." I said. "How do you know all that?"

We were outside now and moving at the pace of growing slime mold. "It was on TV. But here's the thing: any guy can appreciate a bunch of snow-capped mountains. That's easy. This buffalo stuff takes a little more sophistication. But the right guy could do for this prairie country what Rockefeller did for the mountains."

"Yep," I said. "This place just needs a little appreciation."

"It would take a special person," he said. "But it's possible."

"He might be xenophobic for all I know. Probably freak out when he crosses the Missouri River."

"No," Erney said. "Those guys are tough as nails."

It was painful to watch him moving toward the corral but he wouldn't take my hand. Camo raised his head, but when he saw it was just us, he let it sink again toward the dust of the corral. "I just want you to stand in front of him and talk while I climb on," I said.

We had finally made it to the corral and Erney smiled. "Little rodeo, huh?"

"I hope not. He'll probably just stand there. What I want you to do is operate this. I pulled my cell phone from my pocket. "Can you work one of these things?"

He tilted his head back and looked at the phone through his bifocals. "Never have," he said. "But I've seen 'em do it on TV. Who do you want me to call, the undertaker?"

"Let's start with 911."

Erney hung his cane on a corral rail, slipped the cell phone into the breast pocket of his one-piece jumpsuit, and leaned against a post. Camo was half asleep. His eyes were partly closed and his tail swished mechanically in the August sun. "He doesn't look too savage," Erney said.

"He's not. But he's young."

"And we're old," he laughed. "You want me in there with him?"

"No way."

"Good. He could knock me over with a fart."

"I just want you to rub his head from this side of the fence. Just talk to him while I ease on."

"You don't want to leave him tied to the rail, do ya?" I had Camo bridled with the reins looped over the saddle horn, but I also had a halter and lead rope tied to the corral rail. "If he gets to fightin' that rope, might pull him down with you on top."

Erney was right. It would be best if he took the lead rope. If Camo pulled back, the rope would have some give and the horse wouldn't get frightened. I'd have the reins in my hands, so I could pull his head up and make him stop bucking if it came to that. "We could untie it, but you've got to stay on that side of the fence," I said.

"No worry," Erney said. "I'm not comin' in there."

"Okay." I untied the lead rope and Erney took ahold of it with his good hand. Camo was still dozing and I felt a little silly for going through all of this. "Just keep talking to him," I said as I stepped into the stirrup.

"He's not gonna do nothin'," Erney said. "He's about as active as I am."

I swung my leg over and settled into the saddle. Camo didn't move. He chewed on the bit and stretched his nose out for Erney to scratch. "Tame as chicken," Erney said.

I sat quietly. He was so used to me hanging on the side of the saddle that he hadn't noticed that I was aboard. Erney looked up at me and wiggled his shaggy eyebrows. I smiled back, then reached down and patted Camo's neck. That's when he looked back and realized that there was something on his back. For the first time since I'd owned him, I saw the white ring around his eye. Then he ducked his head and started to buck.

When a horse bucks, you have to pull their head up hard. They can't really buck when their head is up, so I pulled on the reins. But Erney had ahold of the lead rope and wouldn't let his head come up. He wasn't going to let Camo take off bucking across the corral if he could help it. With one hand he held on like a barnacle. I couldn't pull Camo's head up so he continued to buck—but he had nowhere to go. I held the reins high to try to get his head up while Erney held onto the rope which kept his head down. I was going up and down like a jack-in-the-box with every powerful lunge, and Erney was going back to the end of the rope then hard up against the corral rails. By the time Camo wound down, I was hanging off the side of the saddle and Erney was halfway strained through the fence.

It's best not to get right off a horse after he's bucked—it gives them the idea that they won and that it might work again. So I straightened up and sat there while Erney got his legs under him. "You all right? I panted.

"Was that eight seconds?"

"Maybe three," I said.

He tied the lead rope to the rail and looked up at me. His thin hair was disheveled; beads of sweat stood out on this forehead, and his eyes were not focused. He leaned against the corral post and labored to catch his breath. "Three seconds? I thought time was supposed to fly when you're having fun."

From that day forward I rode Camo three or four times a week. At first it was just a few turns around the corral and eventually outside the gate and across the buffalo pastures. He learned to move away from the pressure of my legs and the feeling of the reins against his neck. He'd turn when I used the leg and the rein on the same side. It wasn't long before he'd sidestep a little if I touched him on one side with my leg and the other side with the rein. I enjoyed those days because it got me outside and gave me time to think. By the end of August I had had many hours to consider what Erney had said about Rockefeller and the Teton Mountains. I knew the story because I'd worked there in the seventies and eighties and had haunted the museums and Park Service interruptive center.

J. D. Junior saw those mountains for the first time in 1924. He was awestruck by the natural beauty but also stunned by the budding commercialism that was already compromising the scenic resource. His response was to form a land company to buy up all the budding tourist traps that were gathering at the foot of the mountains, all with the idea that the land would be donated to the federal government. The anti-government crowd did everything they could to retain their "right" to profit from despoiling the Tetons. They held Rockefeller and government planners off for twenty-five years. But eventually the piece of land between Yellowstone National Park and Jackson Hole, Wyoming, was protected from unrestrained capitalism. Now tourists, environmentalists, and outdoor enthusiasts the world over agree that what Rockefeller did was a good thing indeed.

Could something like that happen on the Great Plains? Erney was right that it would take a person, or a group of people, with a special vision. They'd have to be folks of means and I figured that people like that were more likely to be impressed with blue ribbon fly fishing than biodiversity on a prairie dog town.

In an email, Carla and Vin suggested that they stay in Rapid City. I answered by commenting that, although we appreciated the consideration, it was a long and winding gravel road between the nearest motel and the Cheyenne River Ranch. I insisted that they stay with us and made it sound like I was simply being hospitable. But, in fact, we were nearly finished upgrading the second house and wanted to try it out on some guests. The timing was perfect.

We had put a lot of work into knocking down and burying several unredeemable outbuildings, hauling many tons of trash and junk to the dump, installing some rough landscaping in the building area, and completely changing the floor plan and exterior of the little house. In the summer, just before Carla and Vin came to visit, Jill had redone the interior of the house in a decorating style she called "Homestead."

We had bought the place from Bill O'Neill when is brother, Jim, died. Their homesteading parents and grandparents were long gone and Bill had moved away many years before in search of greener pastures. He ended up running a sawmill in Montana and didn't come home often.

Jim lived alone and worked at a gravel pit ten miles down the road. The house and grounds were a world-class mess—something you might see on a reality show about hoarding. There were lots of cats, Louis L'Amour books, and cowboy boots. There was a heavy wood-burning stove in the tiny kitchen and a huge coal oil stove with no thermostat in the living room that was either on or off. The outbuildings were like a time warp to pre–World War II: chicken feeders and waterers, kerosene heaters, and countless farm implement parts and pieces from the early days of horsepower to the 1960s. Some of the machine parts and some of the clothes in the house were brand new and still in their packages.

The heart attack came on a cold winter's night while Jim was working out on the treadmill that his brother had given him. He apparently just keeled over and flopped onto the floor, dead. But the oil stove was turned way up. After a couple days, one of Jim's coworkers from the gravel pit found him. The smell hit him when he got out of his pickup. He said that the stove had run out of fuel but the house was still too hot to enter. Apparently old Jim had exploded. Some of the walls were sticky.

Jill worked on the largest dark stain on the living room floor for a week before she rented a sander. The coal oil stove was one of the first appliances to get hauled to the dump. When the place was completely cleared out, Terrance and another neighbor came in to tear out walls and add a porch. Jill took everything that she considered worth saving down to our shop and mounted a cleaning campaign that lasted for most of a month. Under the clutter we found a metal sink-cabinet with an immense drain board, a round oak table with lion's feet, and chairs that almost matched. We found Depression Glass and china from Jim's mother or grandmother. There were kerosene lamps and framed pictures of cowboys on bucking horses.

The tasks that fell to me had to do with plumbing and animal control. Because no one wanted to get into the walls and because we figured this would be strictly a summer place, I re-plumbed the bathroom and the kitchen by running pipes along the baseboards, with petcocks for fall drainage. The toilet stool must have been one of the very first ones mass produced. It was short and the flushing mechanism was like nothing I had ever seen. I considered replacing it, but the fitting coming out of the floor did not match anything at Lowe's or Hardware Hank's. Besides, no one—not even Gervase—had the nerve to venture into the crawl space.

In addition to the full complement of feral cats that had to be dispersed, skunks lived under the house and rattlesnakes had taken over the foundations of most of the outbuildings. All the cats that were not dangerously wild were scattered to ranches in need of mousers, but the skunks had to be trapped at the back of the house where they had gotten under the floorboards. We tried to seal the holes with rocks and dirt, but the skunks dug them out, sometimes within hours. Jim must have operated under some sort of truce with the skunks or he simply didn't mind the smell. The rattlesnakes seemed beyond the tolerance of even St. Francis—and Jim O'Neill was no St. Francis.

We must have disturbed the snake dens as we demolished the outbuildings. For awhile they seemed to be everywhere: basking in the sun on the south side of building remnants, slowly crossing the driveway on their way to who knows where, coiled on the warm concrete of the new porch. I don't like killing snakes, or skunks, for that matter, and as long as the O'Neill place was not being used, we left the fauna alone. But when we made the decision to start using it for summer guests, our attitude had to change. While Jill rearranged walls, cleaned, painted, and purchased thrift store furniture, I trapped, shot, transported, and smoked out as many varmints as I could. My job was much less pleasant than Jill's but just as essential for building a safe and comfortable place for humans to live.

In some ways it was a snapshot of the ancient relationship between expanding humanity and the natural world. Of course, in this case the concentration of troublesome species was created by the human structures that had sprung up on the O'Neill homestead. The small predators that had since made their homes there were rarely found on that acre of prairie before the O'Neills showed up because such a patch of native grasses could only support a small population of the rodents that the gathering varmints fed upon. Our ranch policy was to live and let live outside the confines of the building area and to make sure that the human habitats were poor habitats for things like skunks and snakes.

Of course some skunks and snakes continued to stop in at the O'Neill place on their natural rounds, and Jill and I worried that a Wild Idea customer, intent on an authentic ranch visit, might come face to face with a little too much authenticity. On the day that the Ryans were scheduled to arrive, we took Hank up to the house. Jill went through the house making last-minute tweaks to the decorating while Hank and I checked the grounds for intruders. Hank took his ranchland security job very seriously and seemed to know that, now that the O'Neill place was cleaned up and ready for guests, his responsibilities had expanded. He walked ahead of me with his head and tail high and occasionally stopped to peer in all directions, like a canine Peter Sellers. When we went back to the house he laid down on the porch, extraordinarily alert, while I went in to help Jill.

After she finished putting the prairie sage in a vase we stood back and looked at her creation. Nothing about the house was extravagant. There was economy in every feature, from the low ceilings to the miniature toilet. She had somehow brought the prairie light inside and, though it was still basically the same house that Jim O'Neill had inhabited, it sparkled like never before.

It turned out that Carla and Vin's first visit landed on the day Barack Obama was scheduled to give his nomination acceptance speech at the Democratic Convention and Jill and I wanted to watch it on television. To avoid embarrassment, we hoped to have our guests in and out of our house before Obama accepted the nomination. We planned to have them up at the O'Neill place not long after dark so that we could settle down on the downstairs couch all by ourselves.

We emailed our standard driving directions from the airport to the ranch. The directions had been used by lots of folks. They were perfect—down to the quarter mile—but still, not everyone made the trip without mishap. Following those directions was a sort of character test that several other guests had failed miserably. It's actually quite easy to get from the airport to the ranch, but you have to believe that the given directions are right. It is only about thirty-five miles, mostly on gravel roads, and though there are only three junctions to negotiate, the road has perhaps another dozen turns. People who are not used to driving for miles without passing a house, or even another car, tend to lose faith and turn to technology. Our worst such experience was a father and his two daughters who discarded the printed directions in favor of their in-car navigation system. An hour past the time they were supposed to show up, I tried to talk them in by cell phone, but poor reception and their refusal to give up their strongly held belief in the mechanical voice from their On-Star navigator led to failure. At one point the man held his cell phone up to the in-car speaker so that I could hear what the automaton was telling him. At midnight I finally rose from bed and went out onto the gravel road, with a flashlight, to rescue them.

We had planned Carla and Vin's nomination-night visit tightly.

They were supposed to arrive at the airport a little before four o'clock in the afternoon. Figuring twenty minutes to get their car and bags, and a flawless trip to the ranch, they would be at our door a little after five o'clock. Even if they screwed up on the directions they would arrive before six o'clock. That would give us about three hours to have cocktails on the deck as the sun set and then a great buffalo dinner before Obama spoke. The table had been set since midafternoon with our best china and a row of Riedel wine glasses at each place. Jill had made a centerpiece from native grasses and wild chokecherry branches.

Then we learned that Carla and Vin's flight had been delayed. They called from Denver to say that the plane was having trouble. They didn't know how late they would be.

Six o'clock came and went with no sign of our guests. Jill stood at her cooking post, where she had been all afternoon. She was working on the main course—a deep dish buffalo pizza rustica—and already the kitchen smelled of serious herbs and spices. The ingredients were scattered around her in the final stages of preparation before the grand assembly just before baking. The Wild Idea Buffalo sausage had been seared and rested in a pan on the stove beside the sautéing red bell peppers. The baby spinach was resting its own pan, awaiting a touch of heat. Piles of grated Ricotta, parmesan, and fresh mozzarella sat on the butcher's block. Jill was rolling out the special pizza dough on a floured board near the springform pizza pan. Glitches did not usually faze her. But that night was different. She glanced at the clock as she worked the dough. Six-thirty. Seven p.m.

At seven-thirty the phone rang. They had just landed. Jill and I looked at each other. "Damn," she said, "they're going to get here at exactly the wrong time."

Then we began to hope that they would have trouble with the directions and not get to the house until after the speech. "If they get lost for two hours, this still might work." But I had no more than said that when we heard Hank begin to bark. We looked at each other and shrugged.

"They're here," I said.

"Yep." Dutifully I carried a tray of highball and wine glasses toward the deck and placed it beside the bar that had been set up for hours. As I walked through the kitchen area on my way to the front door, Jill was just sliding the pizza into the oven.

A large white-haired man was just emerging from a dark Chevy Suburban. His tall, elegant wife came around the back of the car, and together they moved toward us with no sign that they had just ended a difficult traveling day. We greeted each other and shook hands all around. It was hard not to notice how tall and robust they were, and it tickled me to imagine them in the Lilliputian O'Neill house. "Drink?" I asked.

"I could use one," Vin said. He turned genteelly to his wife. "Carla?"

"Sure, maybe a glass of wine."

We moved directly to the deck and I poured whiskey over a little ice in two glasses while Jill pulled the cork on a bottle of Malbec. We sat in chairs overlooking the Cheyenne River and it was clear that Carla and Vin were used to meeting new people. They talked easily with just the right amount of information about their day and questions about the ranch. Had it not been for the fact that Barak Obama was getting ready to talk to the nation, Jill and I would have been fascinated and anxious to engage more deeply. Under the circumstances, the conversation, forthright as it was, seemed to limp. Jill glanced at the clock when she went in to check the pizza rustica. I noticed Vin glance at his heavy watch a couple times as he quizzed me about the climate.

Jill couldn't stand it anymore. She reappeared on the deck. "Do you guys want to watch the Democratic Convention?"

There was only an instant of hesitation. "We thought you'd never ask," Carla said.

"Downstairs," Jill said. She turned and began collecting plates from the table. "We'll just eat this pizza in our laps."

Eleven

AFTER WE WATCHED OBAMA'S ACCEPTANCE SPEECH WE sat in our living room and talked easily about the dreams of Wild Idea. Carla and Vin had done their homework. They had been discreet customers for almost a year and knew our products better than I did. They had studied our website and picked up on the importance of conservation and social justice. They asked questions in a way that invited us to express the passions that drove us. Just below the surface of the conversation was curiosity about the profitability of it all. But that question was never asked.

The next day, Carla went on a sightseeing tour of the Black Hills and Jill went in to work at the Wild Idea office. Vin wanted to see the ranch and the buffalo, so we loaded into an ATV and drove up to the top of the ridge above the Cheyenne River. From that vantage point I was able to give him an overview of the entire place—the deeded land on the west side of the river and the leased land on the east side. We got out of the ATV and stood at the edge of the bluff in a light breeze. Below us and a mile off, the herd of buffalo grazed. Behind them, to the horizon, was the Pine Ridge Indian Reservation. The little town of Wounded Knee was just beyond the last purple buttes.

Showing the Cheyenne River Ranch to Wild Idea customers was something that I had begun to do more often. I was amazed at how a few hours out on the land affected people differently. Some people had a hard time getting used to the scale of the landscape. Some talked of freedom and the mythology of the American West. The most interesting people were those that knew something about ecosystems and wanted to understand the uniqueness of the Great Plains. The children wanted to be near the horses and the buffalo. Vin was interested in all of it.

He sat in the passenger's seat and encouraged me to rave on about plant communities, the birds, and the prairie dogs. He wanted to know about carbon sequestration, migration, and the part that the burrowing mammals played. He asked a question about hydrology that I could not answer. He compared what he was seeing to other places he had been and insisted that we drive through the old homestead farm fields that we were trying to restore to native prairie. On that part of the ranch there isn't much to see, just the rough land at the old field edges where the vegetation turned from the healthy native grasses that the early residents had not plowed up, to the weedy impoverished fields were they had exploited the fertility for decades. We stepped out of the ATV and, on hands and knees, I showed Vin the hair-like seedlings of western wheatgrass, green needle, little bluestem, sideoats grama, prairie clover, and purple coneflower. They were expensive native species that we had planted, and they were pitifully small and fragile. "But they're here again," I said.

"For the first time in how long?"

"Eighty or ninety years, at least."

"And the buffalo won't hurt them?"

I looked up at Vin and we both smiled. "If we do it right they won't."

"Well, then, let's go have a talk with the buffalo."

It took us some time to weave our way down the steep bluff to the flat ground where the buffalo grazed. When I could, I sneaked a glance at Vin, and found his pensive blue eyes taking everything in. We crossed the face of a small stock dam and a pair of mallards lifted off with an explosion of quacking. Before we reached the buffalo he offered this: "Carla and I would like to help with what you're doing."

I didn't say anything because I didn't know what I thought of that idea. But I did notice him nod in a way that said, "Fair enough." I gradually turned the ATV so that we would not be approaching the buffalo head-on. I slowed down and changed the tack so that we were proceeding toward the herd but not directly. A couple more angled turns and we were right in among them. Only a few buffalo bothered to raised their heads to appraise us. I turned off the engine and let the silence settle.

We didn't say a word and the buffalo moved around us. Slowly the tender grunting between the mothers and the calves became the central presence in the ocean of near silence. I watched Vin watching the buffalo and when a big, old bull ambled to within a few feet I readied the ATV to move—not because there was any real danger, but because I didn't want Vin to be frightened.

Vin surprised me in the very best way. Without raising his voice or taking his eyes off the old bull he told me of a time when he was a young man and came face to face with a similar bull. "It made a huge impression on me," he said. "I was hiking on a trail and we came face to face. Like this." There was a beat of prairie stillness with the twitter of birds and the rumbling of mother buffalo. "Since then," he said, "I've always sort of considered these guys my totem animal." It made me smile and I asked where that had happened. "Right near Jenny Lake," he said. "In the Tetons." That made my smile broaden. I could hardly wait to tell Erney.

A few days after Carla and Vin went home, Jill and I were in our kitchen talking over a possible expansion of Wild Idea Buffalo Company. It was clearly an opportunity to do some of the things that I had always wanted to do. It was a chance to bring many more acres of the Great Plains under the gentle grazing of the animal with which they had coevolved. It was a chance to show that buffalo did not need to be forced into feedlots and fed unnatural food. It was a chance to show that, for buffalo, a viable alternative to industrial slaughter plants existed. And it was a chance to employ a few more Lakota people and to bring them back into the loop of Great Plains life. But it was also a chance to work ourselves to death and lose everything we had worked so hard to gain.

We were convinced Carla and Vin had pure intentions. They had made it clear that Wild Idea was not the kind of investment their capital company would be interested in. Any involvement on their part would have to be personal. They talked about supplying business expertise and, although Jill and I knew that was an area in which we were definitely deficient, we also knew that meant we would have to cede some control. The increased business volume required to achieve the results we dreamed of would be huge. There would be additional meat inspection, workman's compensation, and auditing regulations, not to mention resistance from our neighbors in the cattle industry and resistance from the buffalo industry that was still modeled on the cattle industry.

After running down this list of hurdles, I turned to Jill and she shrugged. "It's another lifetime of work," she said. She had a point. All I really wanted to do was to have a place to fly my falcons and run my bird dogs. I wanted to eat red meat that wouldn't kill me. "It would be easier to get jobs in town and take up golf," she said.

"But where would all the native stuff live?" I joked. "Where would I find a piece of native pasture to walk over?"

She nodded and smiled. "The trouble is that that one piece of pasture is connected to everything else."

I had pulled on my dirty boots and stood on the doormat, ready to go outside, when the phone rang. I could see from Jill's face that it was Jilian calling from Wyoming. The last time she called she had told us that she was enrolled in a community college and we had been encouraged. But this was the first time she had called in a month and I was not going anywhere. I stood on the doormat and watched Jill.

The conversation began tentatively: "How's it going? What's going on?" And Jill started talking about Wild Idea.

I stood watching, frustrated that I could hear only one side of the conversation. Jill gave Jilian the highlights of our indecision about expanding Wild Idea. They talked about her college courses and it seemed to be a nearly normal mother-daughter conversation until Jill's face suddenly tensed with pain.

She nodded into the phone. "It's okay, Honey. You're not supposed to know what to do."

But it wasn't okay. I was frozen in place, trying to understand by reading Jill's face. But she only nodded and uttered a few words of comfort.

By the time she hung up I had moved off the doormat and stood beside her.

"What's wrong?"

"She wouldn't tell me," Jill said.

"Is she in some kind of trouble?"

"I don't think so. She's doing all right in her classes. She's just emotional. I suppose life with Cody Crawford isn't what she dreamed it would be."

"Probably thinking that being a full-time college student in Hawaii might be more fun than working at the Bath and Body Works and taking night classes in Gillette."

"I don't know," Jill said. "She seems to like the classes. Likes the job." She paused and looked at me. "I think she misses us."

I couldn't stand close to Jill any longer. I pushed out the door and took a big, deep gulp of cool air.

The conversation with Carla and Vin continued, and soon a young man by the name of Peter Binas joined in. He was the managing director of Vin's venture capital firm but was being lent to Wild Idea to explore possibilities. Through Google I learned that Peter was an expert in finance and strategy, with a focus on mergers and acquisitions. Google told me that he had a JD/MBA from Harvard Law and Harvard Business School, where he had been a Baker Scholar, whatever that is. He also had an AB with Honors from Harvard University, where he graduated Phi Beta Kappa in economics and social studies. I didn't know what to make of such a biography, so I printed it out and took it over to get Erney's opinion.

Erney was standing beside his hot plate, stirring a can of baked beans with a pencil. The television was tuned to the Nature Channel and blaring way too loud. I picked up the remote and turned it down before I even tried to talk. I held up the printout of Peter's bio. "Got something I want to show you."

He turned off the burner under the hot plate and dug around on his dusty fly-tying desk, which hadn't been used since his stroke. He came up with a filthy pair of bifocals, wiped them off on the sleeve of his blue union suit, and stuck them onto his face. The glasses were taped together but they stayed on as he took the printout from my hand and held it up to the light.

He read it slowly a couple of times. When he looked up at me the glasses hung crooked across his nose. "Well," he said, "he seems qualified."

"You think so?"

"Hell," he said as he waved the bio in the air. "Just reading this puts my high school diploma to the test."

"It's intimidating."

"Well, I don't know," Erney said. "He hasn't taken any agriculture courses." The idea seemed to tickle him, and he lowered himself down into his dilapidated chair with a smile.

"Yeah," I said. "And I haven't taken any business courses."

"He's got a leg up on you there."

"Seriously Ern, you think we ought to even get mixed up with these guys?"

"Why not?"

"'Cause they're going to take a huge chunk of Wild Idea. That's why not."

"So how's that work?"

"They put in a pile of money and take shares of stock."

"Livestock?"

"No. Shares in the company."

"Oh, securities. I wouldn't worry about that. That whole Wall Street deal is just funny business. You ever watch *Mad Money*?" He pointed at the television, where a pack of lions was chasing a baby warthog.

"No. This isn't like Wall Street. They just take a part of the company."

Erney sat in his chair, thinking. "Okay," he said. "They give you money and what do you do with it?"

"Well, we put it into the company to promote sales. The more pounds we sell the better things get." Erney was staring at me. He wanted more. "We have to encourage ranchers not to put their buffalo into feedlots. We need a new website, have to build our own processing plant, increase sales. Jesus, Erney."

"You'd have to hire more people?"

"Yeah, and people are a pain in the butt."

"True."

"But this partner would pay their salaries?"

"I guess. For awhile."

"So you and Jill might be able to push this buffalo idea and end up owning a real business?"

"We'd end up owning *part* of a real business."

He was standing over the hot plate again. He turned on the gas and fumbled with a kitchen match. By the time he got it lit there was a minor explosion under the can of beans. "So the choice is simple." He picked up the pencil and began stirring the beans. "It's either part of a real business that's getting something done or 100 percent of nothing. You want some beans?"

When I got back to the house, Jill was on the telephone. I could tell that she was again talking to Jilian, though she was mostly just listening. Her eyes did not come up to meet mine, but I could tell that the conversation was winding down.

"Yes. Of course, Honey. It's the right thing. Yes. Just get in your car and come on home." I was dumbfounded. "Sure. We'll have your room ready."

By the time Jill signed off, I was standing over her with my arms limp at my sides. "What?"

Jill shook her head. "We started off just talking. Then she burst into tears. Said she'd made a mistake and wants to come home."

"Is she all right?"

"Yeah. I think she's good." We stared at each other as silly grins spread across our faces. "She had a little speech all ready. She wants to get an apartment by herself in Rapid City and transfer her credits to Black Hills State. She wants to work for Wild Idea and she wants to have her own dog."

Jilian had already begun her transfer to Black Hills State University. To my surprise, she had an impressive number of credits. But there was a grayness around her that clouded her normally cheerful self. She had big plans to start her life over, which made her seem upbeat—at least on the surface. It took her longer to find an apartment than we thought because she insisted on a place with a fenced-in yard that would allow a dog. The only apartment like that in her price range was a terrible little place in the roughest part of town. It was tiny, with one smoky window and appliances that barely worked. Broken concrete steps led down to a solitary door. It, too, was broken, but fixable. The apartment and location were distressing, but it had a yard with a fence and Jilian could afford it on the nine dollars an hour that Wild Idea could pay her.

She started off as a full-time student working with Jill thirty hours a week—taking orders on the phone and running back and forth to the processor where the carcasses were cut and wrapped. They loaded up a pickup truck with packages of frozen meat and brought them back to a basement room, where an eight-foot-by-eight-foot walk-in freezer was installed. On Mondays and Tuesdays they packed the orders in Wild Idea boxes and had them ready for the FedEx truck that showed up at the end of the day.

On the weekends Jilian made the forty-mile drive that her mom made every day so that we could spend a few days together. Even though she was clearly saddened by her experience of the previous year, it was good to have her in the house again. Hank was thrilled to have his roommate back, if only for the weekends.

She searched online for a dog of her own. I was consulted as the search went forward, but from the beginning I knew that Jilian included me only as a tip of the hat to my years of dog ownership. She had grown up a great deal during the time she was away and she made it clear that this would be *her* dog and *her* search. I was afraid that she would want an English setter like Hank but Jilian had thought it over carefully. "A dog like Hank would be sad if he didn't get to hunt grouse," she said. "I just want an old mutt."

We were barraged with online photos of rescue dogs—a nearly pure white terrier-mix at a rescue center in Minneapolis, a collie-cross in Omaha, a cockapoo in Duluth. Jilian held her phone up for me to look at the cockapoo. "He's cute," she said.

"He's a long ways away," I said.

"Yeah. And he's not big enough."

"How big of a dog do you want?"

"*Big*," she said.

"You're living in an eighteen-by-twelve-foot apartment."

"But it has a big fenced-in yard and I'm close to the park."

"You're going to walk him?"

"Every morning. You bet."

She had never been one to shirk her duties and as she grinned and put her arm around me, I had to believe her. "Maybe a Great Dane or a Saint Bernard," I said.

"Yeah! But just part. I want a mutt." Then she looked down at Hank, who was looking up at her adoringly. "Oh, no offense, Hank." She tapped on her chest and Hank's paws were instantly on her shoulders. She hugged him as if he was a human and Hank glanced over at me, knowing that he was being naughty but also that, in this case, he would get away with it.

A week later I was on my way down to the Rosebud Reservation, following the SHA truck in my pickup. It was six o'clock in the morning. We had already covered a hundred miles and the sun was just beginning to peek over the eastern horizon when my cell phone rang. I assumed that it was Jerry or Shane in the semi truck ahead of me. They were co-coordinating our meeting place with Wayne Fredrick, the herd manager on the reservation, and Thad Stout, the meat inspector. But the call was from Jilian. "Hey," she said. Whatcha doing?"

"I'm driving."

She laughed. "That's what Mom said. Rosebud?"

"Yep, we're going to bring you a half-dozen buffalo carcasses."

"Keep those carcasses coming."

"What do you want?"

"Oh, I'm so glad you asked. Isn't Rosebud close to Valentine, Nebraska?"

"Yeah, kinda."

"Well, I'm looking at a Google maps."

"You're looking at what?"

"Never mind. I'm looking at a map and it looks like you're going to be about forty miles from Valentine."

"Yeah, about."

"Well," she said, "I was wondering if you could just swing down that-a-way and pick something up for me."

"What could you possibly want in Valentine?"

She squealed into the phone. "A *dog*!" Just then the road dipped down toward the White River and my phone lost the signal.

I tried to call her back, but there was no signal. I tried all day but the buffalo pasture where we were working had no service. Shane and Cliff were inside the trailer skinning and eviscerating and Jerry was shooting from my pickup. I dragged the guts out of the small side door of the trailer and into twenty-gallon plastic barrels. I pulled the barrels away from the truck and out of the way. It was a cool day and there were almost no flies, but still I covered the barrels with plastic so when the traditional people came to claim the ceremonial buffalo parts, the edible pieces were fit to eat. In most cases these parts of any animal are condemned for human use, but we had petitioned the authorities and they had eventually agreed that Lakota tradition was worth an exception and for religious reasons they could be consumed. All afternoon I helped load the heavy, bloody barrels into pickup beds and car trunks.

An old woman wearing a house dress like the one my own grandmother used to wear approached me shyly. I knew that she was after a buffalo stomach for making taniga. It is tripe soup and in the Lakota culture it is best made with the stomach walls of buffalo. I watched her pulling at the bucket of guts, separating the intestines from the paunch. She felt the delicacies with her weathered hands and studied every section with intense eyes. The organ meat—hearts, livers, kidneys—were prized by the younger women, and most of the hocks and hooves were carried off by artisans for making ceremonial rattles and talismans. They took all the buffalo skulls and most of the hides for Yuippe and Sun Dance ceremonies. The hides would be used for traditional drums and the skulls would be secured with rawhide straps and pinned to the Sun Dancers with chokecherry pegs driven through the skin of backs and breasts. They would be dragged in the dirt until the skin broke away in a sacrifice that was more than symbolic. The people were thrilled to have access to the sacred parts of Tatanka and I was a popular guy.

Near the end of the day my cell phone made a strange sound that I had never heard before. A pair of Native guys were standing very close and they looked at me, expectantly. "What's that noise?' I asked.

They looked at me incredulously. "You're getting a text, man." The one with the longest braids helped me punch the right buttons and a photograph came into clear focus. It was a pudgy black-and-brown puppy. The message said: "This is Gus. Call me when you get a better signal."

I showed the picture to the two young guys and one of them said something in Lakota that made them both crack up with laughter. "What did he say?" I asked. Neither of them could answer because they were still convulsing.

Jerry walked over to find out what was so funny. He held his hands out in a lazy shrug. "What?"

"I don't know," I said. "He said something about this." I held the puppy's picture up for Jerry to see.

"Cute!" he said. That set the young guys off again.

"What did he say?" I asked.

The long-haired guy spoke in Lakota again.

"Yeah, yeah," I said. "In English, please."

The long-haired guy got it together long enough to say, "If you'd pick up a six-pack you would have a seven-course meal." They collapsed in laughter again. Jerry and I looked at each other and grimaced.

Halfway to Valentine I finally got a good signal long enough to get directions to the veterinary clinic that had the rescue puppy. Jilian said that she had been in Internet contact with the vet's assistant, Ellen, for over a week and that they had sent a representative from the Rapid City Canine Rescue to Jilian's house the day before, to check that Gus was going to a good home. Jilian said that the representative didn't think much of the neighborhood but liked the backyard and the fact that the park was close.

Jilian seemed thrilled and relieved to have passed inspection. "Ellen says Gus is one of the best puppies that she has ever had come in."

"He's one of the luckiest," I said.

"I have a food and water dish and a bunch of toys. I'm going to be a good mom."

"I have no worries about that."

"Oh, my God," Jilian said. "I'm hyperventilating. When will you be here?"

"It's a good three hours."

"I'll be at the ranch. Hurry."

"I will."

"Oh, the vet is going to charge a fee for his shots and all that."

"You can owe me."

The veterinary clinic was on Valentine's main drag and I found it just before closing time. Ellen was expecting me. "Mr. O'Brien," she said. "You're here for Gus. He's a fortunate little guy, someone found him wandering around up on the reservation. I've got him all ready to go."

"Great."

She pulled a large paper bag from under the counter and began laying out the contents for me to inventory. "This is the puppy chow that we recommend, here are his medical records—he's had his shots for rabies, parvo, and distemper. He's been wormed and examined for ear mites and fleas. He came up negative but here is a bottle of mite medicine and some flea shampoo, just in case. Now," she looked at me very seriously, "where is your collar and leash?"

I stared at her. "He's just a puppy."

"We think he's about twelve weeks old. Maybe thirteen. But he still needs a collar and leash."

"I didn't bring one."

"Oh, my." She looked truly flummoxed. "Well, I suppose we could sell you a collar and leash." I nodded and smiled. She smiled back. "Is this your first puppy?"

"No," I said, "I've had a few."

"Oh, good. Then you have a travel kennel? Something that can be restrained with the seat belt?"

I had a half dozen of them at the ranch but I didn't bother to tell her that. "No," I said. "You just go ahead. We'll buy one of those too."

"Oh. Well. Jilian led me to believe that you'd be prepared."

"I am prepared, Ellen. I'm prepared to buy all this stuff."

She giggled as she pecked away at the cash register. "Oh, you're going to just love little Gus. He's a sweetheart." When she handed me the bill I almost said that he sure as hell better be. But I kept my mouth shut.

When they brought Gus out, I completely forgot about the bill. Another young woman was holding him like a baby and he looked at me with a serious yet curious expression that won me over instantly. He was much bigger than he looked in the picture. He must have weighed twenty pounds and was meatier than any twelve-week-old puppy I had ever seen. His feet were the size of teacups. He was the color of a Doberman Pincher—all black except for his paws and eyebrows—but he had none of the fine features of a Doberman. His body was more like a Labrador retriever's. In reality, he was 100 percent full-blooded mutt. Jilian was going to be ecstatic.

The woman put him into my arms as if I were a new father. They came out to the pickup with me to secure the travel kennel with the dusty seat belt that I had to dig out from under the passenger's seat. I held the kennel door open and the woman placed Gus gently inside.

On the floor was a horn from one of the buffalo we had slaughtered that day and she looked at it but didn't comment. They squeezed a chew toy shaped like a donut into the kennel and said their goodbyes to Gus. As soon as I pulled out onto the highway and turned for South Dakota, I opened the door of the travel kennel and gave Gus the run of the cab. He went right for the buffalo horn and dragged it up to my lap, where he chewed on it until we were through the Rosebud Reservation and halfway to Pine Ridge.

I let my right hand rest on the back of his neck as he chewed. Occasionally I would rub his ears gently, and before we turned north toward Wounded Knee, I could feel that he was asleep. By then the light was nearly out of the rolling hills where Big Foot's band of two hundred Lakota men, women, and children had been surrounded, partially disarmed, and slaughtered by Hotchkiss repeating rifles. There was enough light to make out the wide flat where the Seventh Cavalry held the men until the shooting began. I could make out the ravine where the women and children tried unsuccessfully to take cover. There was no traffic and the lights of my pickup cruised ahead of me like twin white snakes, hunting the cedar-streaked hills along the highway.

Soon it was dark and fifty miles had vanished without me noticing. Suddenly I was at the tiny ghost town of Scene. I was out of the reservation, and I realized I had made a decision about Wild Idea. The logic was simple: our little family business was not only a wild idea, it was a good idea. It deserved to grow.

Gus slept until I pulled up at the side of our ranch house. It was after nine o'clock and normally Jill and Jilian would be sound asleep. But that night the light still burned in the downstairs rooms where Jilian stayed when she was at the ranch. I saw the blue light from the television and knew that they were in their sweatpants, snuggled on the couch with Hank. I barely had time to set Gus on the ground before they came bubbling through the door. The girls squealed with delight when they saw Gus just finishing his pee. Hank sat down with an indignant expression that betrayed his French origins.

Jilian scooped Gus up and hugged him as if he was an old companion who had been lost at sea. Jill moved in and they actually had a small tug of war before she got a few minutes to hold him. By then the cool evening air had forced us inside. I sat down on the couch beside Jill and was instantly exhausted. Hank lay beside us, and we all watched as Gus was introduced to his food and water dishes. They inspected the bag of puppy tack I had been sold and Jilian laughed gaily when she found out about the expensive travel kennel I'd been forced to buy. "He's going to outgrow that in about a month."

"More like a week."

We watched Gus climb over Jilian as she lay on the floor. He was intent on licking her face and she closed her eyes and snuggled into the lavish tongue bath. I had my arm around Jill and, after a half-hour, I felt her slump with fatigue. "Come on," I said. "Bedtime."

Hank seemed glad to get away from the disgusting display of affection between Jilian and Gus. He followed us up the stairs and went to his bed in the corner of our bedroom. Jill barely made it. She crawled under the covers and lay on her back with her eyes shut and her hands folded as if she was dead. "I love my bed," she whispered.

I lay down beside her and switched off the night light. I was tired, too, but had to say one last thing. "We have to let Wild Idea grow," I mumbled.

For several seconds Jill did not speak and I thought she was asleep. But then she spoke low and slowly. "I know," she said. There was a long pause and I was certain that she was asleep. But there was one more mumble. "We don't have a choice."

Twelve

ONE OF THE FIRST QUESTIONS PETER BINAS ASKED ME was a hard one: "What's Wild Idea's EBITA for the last couple quarters?" Luckily the question came in an email and I had time to look up the meaning of EBITA: Earnings Before Interest, Taxes And something else. Until that point in the life of Wild Idea Buffalo Company, Jill had been doing the books with the occasional help of an accountant; I was able to turn Peter's questions over to them after I'd Googled the terms I did not understand.

Jilian explained to me what metrics and dashboards were and tried to show me how to operate Peter's spreadsheets. She had to install a new program on my computer before I could even open them. We tried to do what Peter asked us to do. "Just play with the inputs, and get a feel for how the business would operate under each configuration." Jilian looked at me and laughed. "Jeeese, I'm just a sophomore. I don't think my accounting professor could do this."

Jill understood Peter better than I did, but often, when she tried to explain it to me, we ended up in a fight. The tension between us rose as we tried to calculate the value of the business that we thought we already knew. Every night we talked about the future of Wild Idea and most nights we had trouble sleeping. We lay in bed, knowing that the other was not asleep yet afraid to say a word. By silent consent we took to listening to the BBC from midnight until five in the morning when we rose for work. The stories of child soldiers in Africa and the hopelessness of the Great Recession lulled us in and out of sleep. Our lives had changed even before we closed the deal to sell a percentage of Wild Idea. Just trying to figure out what that share might be worth had put our whole world on edge.

I know that I am being wheeled into an intensive care room at Rapid City Regional Hospital, but the morphine makes it feel like I am in the pasture where our buffalo spend the winter. Gervase is pointing at the top of a remote, eroding butte. He claims to have climbed up there the year before and that he found a few old planks and some rusty barbed wire. He says that someone lived up there in the "dirty thirties." He chews at his cheek and squints to the grassy horizon from under his stained Stetson.

"Used to be able to ride a horse up there," he says. It's easy to see that in another hundred years the butte top will be completely inaccessible above sheer cliffs. "They called him Crazy Johnson." Gervase laughs and the landscape sucks up the sound. "Crazy tried raising peanuts up there before the weather drove him out."

"How long did he last?" I ask.

He laughs again and looks at me like I am the crazy one. "Not very God-damned long," he says.

I am riding Camo, the same horse that landed me in the hospital. We are taking a last long swing through a thirty-five-square-mile pasture. We're checking to see that all the summer cattle are out before we turn the buffalo in for the winter. I wonder if Crazy Johnson loved this difficult land the way we do or if he came to this spot by happenstance. Maybe the sandy soil reminded him of his childhood home in Tennessee or Georgia, where his family had raised peanuts. But how could he have thought that peanuts could survive in such a hostile landscape?

Gervase and I hypothesize about how Crazy Johnson may have traveled to and from his homestead. He was likely too poor to own more than a single horse and there was no sign of a wagon road crawling along the ridges, so he either rode that single horse or walked. He probably didn't go back and forth much. The closest town would have been Scenic, and that was fifteen miles away over rough country.

What was Crazy thinking about? What sort of dream would drive a man that far from civilization?

The morphine dream takes me deeper into an area that is not dark, only slow as winter days waiting for spring. I feel no depression or pain, but no exhilaration either. In a corner of my mind I remember parts of the accident. This was no dream. We were just heading out to gather a neighbor's cattle. A cold day, a young horse. I should have known better. Too much confidence, not enough caution. I wore too much clothing to get my foot into the stirrup easily. I remember jumping up at the stirrup, then swinging up and on. But I don't remember getting off. They say I only stayed on for a couple jumps.

I do remember gasping for breath and staggering back up onto my feet. I remember Gervase putting his hand on my shoulder and telling me not to try getting back on. Camo's reins are somehow back in my hand and I look up to the saddle, then back to Gervase. He shakes his head and I have to agree. I lead Camo back to the corral where the neighbor stares at me and says, "You don't look too good."

"You should see it from in here," I say.

It was still early in the morning but the beer cooler in the back of a pickup truck attracted my attention. I wanted whiskey, but this was not my roundup and so there was only beer. I fished out a can of Bud and popped the top. The rancher was still staring at me. "Maybe you ought to go on into town and get things checked out." He looked concerned. "No foolin', Dan. Go get things checked out."

From the road I called Jill and asked her to meet me at the hospital. I didn't feel that bad when I left the corrals, but twenty miles down the gravel, about halfway to town, I felt myself sliding down in the pickup seat. By the time I got to the hospital I was looking through the steering wheel and driving on autopilot. Jill met me outside the emergency room and helped me inside and up to the reception window. The nurse took one look and called for a gurney.

After the x-ray and the MRI, the emergency room doctor popped his head through the curtains of my room. He was smiling. "Saw the x-rays. Three broken ribs and a fractured scapular." I remember wondering what a scapular was and I would have asked, but he was already gone. Jill took my hand and squeezed. Hospitals make her a little queasy but she was hanging in there. She held my hand tight and shook her head. It was only a few years before that she had nursed me through a similar incident. We were both experiencing déjà vu, remembering the long period of convalescence. We were worrying about the money when the doctor stuck his head back through the curtains. His smile was gone. "MRI says you have a collapsed lung. We called a trauma surgeon."

From that point until I woke up in the morphine haze, things were numb. I remember fingers tight in mine and I remember meeting the trauma surgeon. He was a good-looking young guy who told us that he had had a speaking part in the movie *Hidalgo*. He said he had played the part of the cavalry officer and that his lines consisted of a swearing tirade at the beginning of the movie. The surgeon laughed. He was obviously trying extra hard to put me at ease as he explained that he would have to put in a chest tube. I hadn't seen the movie but imagined it beginning with a cavalry lieutenant in a dusty campaign hat saying, "God-damn. Son-of-a-bitch."

But I was also thinking "chest tube" and wondering exactly what that was until he withdrew an eighteen-inch-long stainless steel pipe from a box as though it was a saber. "*God-damn. Son-of-a-bitch,*" I thought.

Jill's hand went limp in mine and she was ushered out of the room just as a group of nursing students was ushered in. I opted for my first round of morphine.

The cavalry lieutenant–trauma surgeon had made an incision in my side. The nurse's eyes went wide as he pushed on the foot and half long chest tube. I really didn't feel much, but I did hear a pop as the tip of the tube—about the size of truck driver's thumb—entered my body and started up toward my left lung. All I could see were the eyes of a nurse. They grew wide as I felt the weight of the trauma surgeon bearing down on me. This was a high-tech room in a high-tech hospital but inserting a chest tube is a low-tech procedure.

I could feel a lot of pressure along the inside of my rib cage and people were talking about monitoring this and that. Lines waved and lights blinked on the monitors. The several nurses and everyone else seemed to be doing their jobs, including the morphine. I was kind of looking down on the room, the nurses, the students, and the trauma surgeon. I was even looking down on myself like in one of those out-of-body experiences. It was actually somewhat pleasant until I heard someone say that my pulse rate had fallen to twenty. Even then, when people started moving faster, things seemed okay with me. They must have got my pulse rate up because the next thing I knew I was in my dark hospital room and the morphine dream had taken over.

Jill was sitting near the bed. For some reason I thought she was Crazy Johnson. She saw that my eyes were open and she reached out and took the hand with no needles stitched into it. That seemed like a strange thing for Crazy Johnson to do, but somehow it was all right. Or maybe I was Crazy Johnson and I wasn't trying to raise peanuts at all. No. It wasn't peanuts. It was buffalo. Jill and I were living on an eroding butte and we were trying to raise buffalo. We were both Crazy Johnson and we were in danger of starvation.

The broken bones and collapsed lung hurt like hell for a long time. I slept sitting upright in a chair for months and I'll probably never be quite the same. The most painful part was thinking that Camo would do something like that to me.

We put a price on 45 percent of Wild Idea Buffalo Company and made the deal. Though we believed that our new partners had been more than fair, there would be no grand upgrade of lifestyle. The first shot of new money would go into constructing a Wild Idea processing plant, to give us total control over quality. We would remodel an old warehouse and build a walk-in freezer bigger than Jilian's apartment. We would buy stainless steel tables, grinders, band saws, office furniture—all used. We would buy a few new computers. Soon we would hire butchers, salespeople, shippers, and an in-house accountant. Many more spreadsheets lay ahead, as well as package designers and internet consultants who knew all about website utilization, conversion rates, and tracking. We hoped there would be more free-ranging buffalo on the Great Plains because a market would now exist for their meat. Yet, no great economic windfall was in store for us unless the company could grow enough to pay all those other people. If it didn't grow, we could end up with nothing. As I sat in my convalescent's chair, the enormity of the task haunted me. In effect, we had bought ourselves even more demanding jobs and paid for it with part of all we really had: Wild Idea Buffalo Company.

I liked our new partners a great deal. I trusted that they would stick with us if things got tough. But sitting motionless in that chair, for months taking tiny breaths so the chest pain would not cripple me, I couldn't help thinking about how I had trusted Camo. Of course, Camo was a horse—maybe just feeling frisky on a cold day. Nevertheless, collateral damage was still damage and I was only a human. I was out weighed by ten times. My strength was insignificant. Trust was all I had.

I have always believed in the ability of government to assist people. From time to time I've been disgusted with the people who complained about bureaucrats. That was in the days before I began working with half a dozen such agencies at a time.

Although Sustainable Harvest Alliance had worked with meat inspection for several years by that time, the slaughter portion of meat inspection is a small part of the overall tome of regulations. The city-county planning department said it was simply impossible to build our own meat-processing plant, but they apparently begin all conversations that way. When building a processing plant you must first install a special sewage system. Pure, tested water must come in and separate sewage lines for human waste and conditioned processing waste must go out. Several kinds of traps and reverse-flow traps were required by the city building inspector and the South Dakota Animal Industry Board. We were halfway through the design portion of the new plant when the fire marshal appeared to inform us that we also needed an overhead sprinkler system. I pointed out that frozen meat, concrete, and stainless steel could not be made to burn if your life depended on it. But I was rebuffed like a sixteen-year-old-boy at a strip club door. The price of the system was twenty thousand dollars, which wasn't in the budget. The budget also did not include the cost of tearing up the street and replacing the old city water main with a new one large enough to handle the increased volume that we would never need.

We flew to Ohio to bid on a refrigeration system that was being auctioned off as part of a supermarket liquidation. I bought a hundred eight-by-four-foot insulated freezer panels and a few heavy freezer doors for a tiny fraction of what they would cost new. We were the high bidder on one of a dozen two-ton compressor units that were bolted to the roof of the supermarket. I tried to understand the local refrigeration expert when he explained that our whole plant could be cooled and heated by that single unit. We needed 120-, 220-, and 440-volt power, which took an electrical engineer to design. The electricians required a month to wire our little one-hundred-by-thirty-foot building.

Another month was consumed with writing the meat inspection plan. The idea is that every step of the processing that takes place in a plant must be analyzed and procedures must be put in place to ensure that food safety is never compromised. Like a lot of the regulations that made my life miserable for most of the next year, a government meat inspection plan is a good and necessary idea. But the regulations were designed with huge packing plants in mind and include procedures that are not appropriate for small-scale operations. The relative costs seemed grossly unfair to plants whose volume of production is not the only goal.

The cost overrun was about 35 percent. Had it not been for Carla and Vin, it would have ruined us. The whole project took the entire year, and in that time the bird dogs and Gyrfalcon that had given me recreation and calm every autumn for forty years stood stagnant in their kennels and mews. Their only real use during that time was to give Erney something to do. I didn't even try to ride Camo after the accident, and I neglected Erney in a way I am sure he didn't understand. During that time, Jill and Jilian sold buffalo meat, packed boxes, managed a website, and searched for employees who shared our vision. By the spring of 2010 Wild Idea had control of its production, three people in the front office, two butchers in the back, and one guy to watch the inventory and pack the FedEx and UPS boxes.

Even with the inspection plant finished, enough money spent to set my provincial mind reeling, and the construction completed, our production plant was microscopic when held up against the industry of corn-fed, feedlot buffalo meat processors. They represented over 90 percent of the industry and we represented only about 5 percent. And the entire buffalo industry is a speck compared to the beef and pork industries.

When I stood outside the newly completed Wild Idea Buffalo Company processing plant, with the Buffalo Girl parked out back, I did not fool myself into thinking that this business was going to change the world. The brick and mortar portion was nearly insignificant. What might prove to be important was the configuration of respect that supported this building's receiving dock and the corridor of health that began where the FedEx and UPS trucks were loaded and headed out. There was purity to the flow of what would happen here. None of industrial agriculture's gray fog hung over any part of the process. No unpaid expenses in the form of needless healthcare bills or environmental damage left for the next generation. There would be no imperiling of Earth's other species in the process, no moral nightmare for society to wrestle with down the road. But we had to do it right. Wild Idea had grown and must continue to grow. The new processing plant was completed, but the work stretched on forever.

Part Five

Thirteen

THERE IS A PICTURE OF JILIAN AT ABOUT TEN YEARS OLD. She holds a hamster in her cupped hands and her face is inches away from the hamster's head. Her smile is as bright as any flower. It was her trademark glow, but by the time she was twenty-one Jill and I wondered if we would ever see it again. After Gus came into her life the smile began to make a comeback, like a prairie sunflower after a summer thunderstorm.

With each passing week it seemed like Gus gained ten pounds. He was with Jilly 24/7 and, as dogs often do, he understood her perfectly. "Sit," "Stay," "Shake hands," "Roll over" were child's play. Gus could retrieve select toys on command. He was house-trained in no time. He walked without a leash in the park, even when full of other dogs, ducks, and the occasional cat, without leaving Jilian's side. "Go to sleep," "Get in the car," and "Wait at the traffic light" were performed better than most fourth graders could do. Only when they came out to the ranch on the weekends and he got together with our band of setters and springers did he backslide into puppiness. Sometimes Hank would take him on his security rounds of the ranch and they would end up exercising the rabbits, which was not allowed. We suspect that Hank was trying to get Gus into trouble.

He weighed a hundred pounds before he was a year old, and every visitor made a guess at his origins: Labrador crossed with a Doberman?; Mastiff crossed with a German Shepherd?; Rottweiler crossed with a Ridgeback?; Newfoundland crossed with a Clydesdale? I'm pretty sure that he was the result of more than a single cross. I knew the reservation where he was born and figured there was a good chance he was an inadvertent creation that had never existed before. He was certainly singular in Jilian's mind.

Early one Monday morning when Jilian and Jill were packing their respective cars for the trip to Rapid City, I stood in the driveway watching Jilian organizing her school books, freshly done laundry, and Gus. She drove an old silver Nissan that we bought cheap because it had been hit by a Great Plains hailstorm. I had a cup of coffee in my hand as I leaned against the split rail fence that encircled the patch of lawn. As Jilian stacked her books in the backseat beside the laundry basket she spoke to Gus as if he was human. He sat upright in the passenger seat and looked over at Jilian, clearly listening to what she had to say. I felt Jill step up beside me as Jilian slid into her car and started the engine. The power steering pump squeaked as she turned the steering wheel and I thought about stopping her to check the fluid. But we were too intent on watching her heading off to work with her little family. "That's quite a rescue dog," I said to Jill.

She nodded her head but took a moment to respond. "Yeah," she said. "I'm not sure who rescued who."

Jill and I met Rocke Afraid of Hawk and his wife, Pam, at the cafe in the iconic tourist trap known as Wall Drug. It is a huge indoor shopping center built around a cowboy theme. It began as an early twentieth-century drugstore in the dying town of Wall, South Dakota, and grew to its present seventy-thousand-square-feet configuration. It has a good bookstore, a first-rate collection of western art, a decent cafe, and the best donuts we've ever eaten.

We were there to talk about how Rocke might be able to establish some buffalo on his land. He wanted to do it more than anything, and we had discussed it many times before. I wanted to do everything I could to help him but it was nearly hopeless. On the reservations, control of land is a major source of contention. The land is owned and overseen mostly by the tribal government but the land that was allotted to individuals is administered by the Bureau of Indian

Affairs. There is also privately owned land, and the combination of ownership creates a patchwork that is divided into grazing units. Often grazing units are leased out to nontribal members and Native leaseholders get taken advantage of in the shuffle. The Afraid of Hawks had a nice grazing unit that would have made a wonderful buffalo pasture. But they were not able to borrow the money for either buying the buffalo or building the fence that would be needed to hold them in because they did not own their grazing unit and could not use it for collateral, as Jill and I were doing. They could only sub-lease it for a reduced rate to a man who ran cattle. That arrangement gave them neither a sense of pride nor enough money to live on. Because there was never enough money to pay the bills, the grazing unit was constantly in jeopardy. Other tribal members were always ready to weasel it away. The land situation on the reservation is structured so that Rocke's dream was almost certainly impossible.

Even so, I still love to hear Rocke talk about it. His speech is inflected with the Lakota language that he learned before he learned English. Rocke Afraid of Hawk thinks in Lakota. Metaphors come easily for him, symbols are everywhere, everything means something, and everything is connected. His dreamworld and his waking world run concurrently, like the braiding of a prairie river.

Jill, Pam, and I were chatting and eating donuts when Rocke leaned forward. "I had a *dream*," he said. "I had a *dream*," he said again. "We were all there." He a made an inclusive gesture by waving his hand in a circle. He nodded his head to dispel all doubt. Without pointing, he drew attention to Jill and Pam and me. "All of us. And the *buffalo*," he said.

Jill and I let our donuts settle back down to our plates. "There was a whirlwind." His arm rotated once above his head. "And it surrounded the buffalo. Dust and leaves. A *whirlwind*. And we all *ran* to help them."

I am sure that he could see the debris circling the buffalo because his eyes were focused somewhere beyond the walls of the cafe. "We had to *help* them, and we *ran*! We had to get to them and free them from the *leaves*." He fell silent. His eyes were still distant and his smile went crooked. "But it wasn't leaves. It was *money*."

Something unusual was afoot because Jill and Jilian never left the Wild Idea office at the same time. Jilian had gone to the post office and was going to meet Jill for lunch. They had left Cyd, a trusted friend and employ, in charge. But I sensed something was up because when I told her that I had to talk to Jill, Cyd smiled and shrugged like the kid who took the cookies. "I don't know where they are," she said. "I think maybe Jill had a little surprise for Jilian."

"What?"

She shrugged again. "I have no idea." But she couldn't stand not telling me. "Maybe they're meeting Kim."

"Oh no." Kim was a friend and also the mother of young man who had just moved to town. He'd been going to college at Chadron State College in Nebraska. He'd been playing football and tore up his shoulder. He was transferring to Black Hills State, where Jilian was going. None of us had ever met him, but we knew Kim. She was a very proud mother. "They're trapping Jilian," I said.

Cyd smiled broadly. "I think they're trapping Colton, too."

"Colton?"

"Colton Jones," Cyd said. "His Facebook picture sure is cute."

"Jilian isn't expecting this?"

Another shrug. "Maybe a little."

"Jill wanted me to take the deposit to the bank," I said. "She must have turned off her phone."

Cyd looked around her desk and shrugged. "I know she made it out. Must have it with her."

"Where are they meeting?"

"I'm sworn to secrecy."

"Where, Cyd?"

"Well, you might try Botticelli's. I hear they have nice lunches. Say hi to Colton for me."

I saw Jilian's beat-up Nissan parked on Main Street. The hailstone pattern was unique and no other car on the street had an enormous black dog in it sitting shotgun. Gus recognized me as I walked past and jumped back and forth between the passenger's seat and the driver's seat until I came over and rubbed his ears through the partially open window. For being so big and fierce-looking he sure was playful and friendly. He moaned with delight while I held his slightly drooly head as if I was contemplating shooting a free throw. "Is she in there, boy?"

"Mumm, mumm."

"Gotta go. Sit cool." He knew exactly what I was saying and sat back down to wait.

Botticelli's was not busy. A couple booths held businessmen in dark suits and a few other couples were scattered about. Jill, Kim, and Jilian held down a round table near the window and were just getting their water poured by a flamboyant waiter. He held the pitcher high and the water cascaded a couple feet into the crystal. There was some sort of symphonic Italian music playing in the background. By the time I got to the table Jill was ordering appetizers.

". . . and an order of the fennel mussels. Hi, Honey."

"Ladies." I tipped my hat to Kim and Jilian. The whole table was dressed smartly and the scene could have passed for a luncheon in Chicago or New York. I couldn't help noticing how pretty Jilian looked. Her blonde hair was pulled fashionably back and her country smile emitted light like a quasar.

"Do you want to join us?" Jill said.

The background music had changed to flowery show tunes with lots of violins. It was tempting but I held my hand up and declined. "Just heading for the bank."

"Oh, I forgot," Jill said. She was already digging into her purse for the deposit.

When I took the envelope from her, our eyes met and I tried to communicate something like, What's going on here?

She understood but evaded the question with an expression that said something like, Who? Me?

I was just saying my good-byes to Kim and Jilian when everyone's attention shifted to someone behind me. When I tried to catch Jilian's eyes I was too late. She was staring over my shoulder and I swear her eyes went to six fathoms.

I turned to introduce myself to Colton Jones and found the same distant look on his face. I held out my hand but I might as well have been the waiter for the attention he paid. I whispered to myself, Aw, for Christ's sake.

I managed to get Colton to shake my hand and tell me that he was studying sports medicine, though he had some interest in biology and agronomy. As he spoke, it was hard not to notice that he was tall and handsome and had a deep gentle voice and piercing blue eyes.

No one noticed my exit and, for some reason, it felt good to get outside and away from that music and the smell of mussels in fennel sauce. I headed back toward my pickup. When I got to Jilian's car, Gus was standing in the passenger's seat but focused intently to his right. When I looked, I saw a monster of a white German Shepherd standing in the driver's seat of the black Xterra parked in the next spot. He was happily panting and his heavy white tail was pounding the rearview mirror. There was a Chadron State sticker on the bumper. I shook my head and grumbled. Aw, for Christ's sake.

In years past, Erney and I would begin conditioning the dogs and falcons on the first of August. That date had been a special day for decades and we looked forward to it with more anticipation than any holiday on the calendar. During the last couple days of July we would dig out the dogs' roading harnesses and oil the leashes and jesses for the falcons. On August first we arose early to catch the morning coolness so there was no chance of overheating the dogs or stressing the falcons.

We had rigged a ten-foot-long piece of ridged plastic pipe across the front of an ATV in a way that allowed it to flex at both ends, where short chains connected the pipe to the harnesses. When the dogs saw that gear come out they always went crazy with joy. Soon we would be idling down the driveway with dogs pulling on both sides—but only for a half-mile at the beginning. In two weeks we would be going three miles at a lunging gallop. By early September they would pull like sled dogs for five or six miles in the heat of the day. But on the first of August we would get a very early start and be finished by 5:30 in the morning. The day would continue normally until that evening when it cooled down again. Then we brought the falcons out of their molting chambers, hood them, and begin the process of re-taming them for the hunting season that was still a month away.

After Erney's stroke, Gervase had helped me for a season or two but, since the increase in Wild Idea responsibilities and Gervase's decampment, the dogs and falcons had been practically deserted. We had only one falcon for a couple years. The pageantry that we associated with the first of August had been neglected. Since the retooling of Wild Idea, the first of August had been just another day and I had done nothing for two years but walk the dogs a few times and feed the falcon on the fist inside the mews.

My mother had told me fifty years before, "You can't do everything. You have to choose." I had chosen to try to bring more buffalo back to the Great Plains, so I was not surprised that at the beginning of the second summer's growth spurt of Wild Idea I found myself sitting in front of the kennel on the rough-hewn bench Erney had constructed just before his stroke, with three English Setters and one Springer Spaniel staring sadly into my eyes.

I was aware of the irony: my lifelong passion had been to watch dogs and falcons hunt sharp-tailed grouse over healthy grasslands. Encouraging ranchers to sensibly run buffalo would supply the biodiversity needed for good grouse habitat, but every day I spent encouraging the grassland management shift was a day I could not be in the field with the dogs and the birds.

Hank ambled up to where I sat mournful on the bench. He put his head in my hands and exhaled loudly. The two young setters inside the kennel sat bright-eyed and poker straight. Tootsie's stubby tail wagged at top speed. I thought they were simply trying to work on my emotions, but they had heard Erney struggling to come through the screen door. "Dan'l?" he said when he untangled himself from the door, "What's doing?"

"Just sitting."

"That's good. Just sitting is good."

"I don't know, Ern. Do you know what month it is?"

He was standing with his cane at his side. He moved it forward a foot and leaned ahead so he could see out from under the roof of the weathering yard. He squinted at the sky. "June?"

"Yeah, it's late June. The first of August is a month away. We missed it last year."

"Mmmm." Erney moved to a broken lawn chair that we had used in years past as a place to sit when the falcons were bathing—just to be near them. "I should get off my butt." He settled into the chair and we sat together in the glorious summer sunshine.

"No, I'm the one that should get things in shape to start working these dogs. You know what I was doing this morning?"

"Nope."

"I was Twittering!"

"You were what?"

"Twittering. The marketers that we hired told us we should be Twittering." Erney didn't bother to ask me again. He just looked at me. "It's a deal where you talk to people on the Internet."

"I thought that was email."

"It's like that, but shorter. A hundred and twenty characters."

He was still looking at me, trying to tell if I was serious or not. "What's it for?"

He had me stumped for a second, but when I thought about it the answer was easy. "It's to sell stuff."

"Twitter?"

"They call it a Tweet."

"You were Tweeting?"

"I'm going to quit tweeting," I said. "I'm going to ease off, and, in place of that, I'm going to work with Al, Trixy, and Tootsie." I pointed to the mews. "And Oscar." Hank pushed his head harder into my hands. "And Hank."

Erney let his head hang and I knew that he was feeling guilty. "Hell, Ern, it's not your fault."

"I don't know. Maybe I could get these guys going. Not like we used to but we could do it on a small scale."

"No." I was sorry that I'd drug him down.

"We don't have to catch every grouse on the place," he said.

"We'd be lucky to catch one."

"Well, that's not the point, is it?"

"No," I said, "that's not the point."

"Well, there you are. We could do it. I can drive an ATV. I could set Oscar on my fist and feed him a chicken. He likes to watch television. I'd get him back into shape."

"You have one good hand and it's missing the thumb. You drag a leg like a fifty-pound sack of feed."

"Now, Dan'l, it ain't that bad. It's more like a twenty-pound bag." He laughed at us both. "I might not have a thumb but I can pinch like a damn lobster." He made a lobster face and pinched with his index and middle fingers.

"But you can't snap a dog to a harness or hood a falcon."

"Not good," he said. "But you could help me." That stopped the banter and we looked at each other.

Several seconds passed before I said anything. "Yeah," I said, "I could help you."

He smiled with satisfaction. "Then that's what we'll do. We'll keep the expectations reasonable and that will give you more time for Tweetin'."

"If you had more than just four fingers on one hand I'd get you a computer and we could Tweet back and forth."

"All the Tweetin' I need comes from a bird's beak."

Fourteen

EVEN SMALL CITIES HAVE A ROUGH SIDE OF TOWN, AND Rapid City is no exception. On the poorer north side of town the houses are small, the yards have little grass, and maintenance is lax. The area is populated by a few airmen from Ellsworth Air Force Base, a smattering of students, and most of Rapid's displaced Lakota people. They cluster around a few poorly built churches and the Mother Butler Center, a sort of Lakota community center where kids can find a relatively safe place to hang out after school and where the beating of powwow drums can be heard many nights.

Jilian's basement apartment was located there. It is not the sort of place that a father wants for his daughter, but she and Gus had made a home in an apartment whose only door opened to an alley and the people upstairs fought to the point that the woman would come down to hide from a man who Jilian seldom saw but could hear raving and breaking things late into the night. She told me that when things got tense in the apartment above, Gus—who was big but still young—would jump onto her bed and emit a low growl until the racket stopped. I seldom went to town when Jilian was not at work, so I visited her apartment only a few times. But every time I pulled up in the alley I was glad to see Gus bound from the apartment steps to the back gate. I knew that there was no meanness in him, but for those who didn't know him, he could possibly re-ignite the primal fear of wolves.

It was a neighborhood with plenty of drunks and crazies, many of whom were capable of robbery, assault, and even the occasional murder. Jill and I worried about Jilian's safety and gently tried to convince her that she needed a change of residence. We offered to pay the difference in rent for a better place, but she wanted to make it on her own. Well, not quite on her own.

One Saturday morning I was in Rapid City to get new tires put on my pickup. After the tires were balanced and mounted, I drove to her place for a surprise visit. There had been a shooting in her neighborhood earlier that week, and when we questioned her about it, she said that it was not uncommon to hear shots at night. Since then I had been more worried than usual and I wanted to let her know that I was thinking of her. In reality I wanted the impossible. I wanted her under our roof where I could at least bask in the illusion that I could protect her.

As I snaked down the alley to her yard, I caught a glimpse of the rear of a black automobile in the spot where I had hoped to park. A flush of dread rose in my gut and I sped up to where I could see into the backyard. It was clear that something was different. Because I was primed for the worst, it took a moment to sort it out. I was still moving and could suddenly see Gus running hard then turning and going up onto his back legs to meet an attack. I inched forward until I realized that the attacker was a mammoth white German Shepard. They wrestled in Jilian's backyard like two baby NFL linebackers. By then I could see that the ominous black vehicle was Colton's Xterra.

Gus stopped his play and turned his head in recognition of my pickup, but I accelerated just enough to pull down the alley and out of sight. He must have wondered what I was doing, and I admit, I wasn't sure myself. All I knew was that I should keep going. No one would be needing the frail protection that I could offer.

The new Wild Idea Buffalo Company held its first in-person board of directors meeting in downtown Boston at a four-storey private home on the edge of Boston Commons. Jill and I still had some difficulty finding it in our rented car. We came from Logan Airport, through a tunnel and into the maze of winding narrow streets that had existed long before South Dakota was a state—since the existence of fifty million buffalo roaming the interior of the continent was little more than a rumor.

The distance between the airport and the home was only a fraction of the distance between Rapid City and our ranch, but it took almost as long to negotiate and, for an uninitiated city driver, it was a much more perilous journey. I was unnerved by the traffic and the sheer novelty of driving through the city. It was a relief to find the underground parking lot, grab the bags, and get walking.

The city felt old and, even in the short two-block walk, a million tidbits of history swirled around my head: Paul Revere, John Adams, religious freedom, whaling ships, and Yankee clippers. From the works of Emerson and Thoreau I knew something of the native state of New England. The steely resilience of the harsh land is as legendary as the fragility of the Great Plains. It's the sort of land that fosters enterprise. The streets of Cambridge had witnessed more human history than all the millions of Great Plains acres put together. Just getting to the site of our meeting was humbling for Jill and me. But the meeting itself showed a cold white light on our inadequacies as modern-day businesspeople.

The board of directors was made up of experienced businesspeople selected for their expertise in visualizing the path to a company's success. They had all sat on other boards, and though they realized that Wild Idea was unique, they knew quite well that the essential objective of any company was to make a profit. This was the course of the discussion for the next two days.

There were a half-dozen spreadsheets comparing Wild Idea's modest past performance with the performance of similar companies. How that information was collected was a puzzle to me. We talked about mail-order companies, meat companies, Whole Foods, the Internet, Google, electronic shopping carts, and business models of every sort. Experts were brought in to speak with us, and Jill and I struggled to keep up. We broke for meals, but never for very long.

By the afternoon of the second day we were lost in statistics. At one point when I looked at Jill, she crossed her eyes as if she had been in a serious pillow fight. I discreetly stuck out my tongue like a battered boxer. She didn't acknowledge me and I got the message that time for joking was over. Peter Binas was talking about EBTA again, but for the life of me I could not remember what the letters stood for. I let my mind wander back to the ranch. I thought about grouse and falcons careening over the grama grass flats, along the high benches, and on above the cottonwoods along the river. I thought of Erney, Oscar, and the dogs. I pictured Jilian working at her desk and studying accounting principles at night. I saw Colton fixing the barbed wire fence that I had not had time to repair myself. I saw him surrounded by those thousands of acres of grass and I saw him bend to pick a unique seed head he would take to his biology professor. Pulling away and upward, I saw the hundreds of buffalo that moved across those acres and then the thousands more that could be there if we could make board meetings like this work for them. It was difficult to connect the two worlds, but I was trying.

After Boston I began to see a connection between the power of business and the power of the Great Plains. I began to understand that the old dynamic of bending the land to work for business might work better in reverse. I came to think that in the short term—a hundred or so years—the only possible savior of wildness might necessarily be its old nemesis, capitalism.

Within a year Jilian and Colton had moved in together and Jill and I had no objections—what could we say anyway? Gus and Ace were inseparable. The kids lived the working student life in that cramped basement apartment but they spent every spare moment at the Cheyenne River Ranch. Jill and I looked forward to the weekends when Jilian and Colton could get away for a couple of days in a row. On Friday nights we waited impatiently for them to appear while one of Jill's special meals simmered on the stove. Their arrival was heralded by 250 pounds of nearly grown dog crashing onto the upper-level deck.

Their appearance would set off the kennel dogs like a pack of baritone coyotes and Hank would withdraw and look disgusted by the crudeness of these overgrown puppies. The girls would talk about the buffalo meat business and Colton and I would talk about the herd, the fences, the condition of the grass. In the daytime we tried to give the kids their space to ride horses or walk the dogs, but sometimes the four of us would take the whole pack of dogs to the river, on an hour-long tour of the pastures by horseback, or drive up to the O'Neill place to do maintenance.

We always hoped that the O'Neill place could be a source of income for us. People signed up on our website for tours and sundown dinners overlooking the Cheyenne River and they were invariably interesting, sincere, and concerned about the conservation of the Great Plains. Most visitors were well informed about food and the kind of people we wanted to spend time with. But the economics proved difficult. As Wild Idea got busier and busier, there was less and less time to spend keeping the lawns mowed, the windows clean, and the skunks away from under the buildings. Jill had high standards for the flower beds, the housekeeping, and every meal she served. We hoped to find people to help us with our micro-hospitality business, but no such people existed within driving distance, and even if there had been, any income that came in would go out in their wages. We ended up doing all the work ourselves at an effective hourly wage of just a few dollars.

Jilian and Colton knew the O'Neill place wasn't working as a revenue source and pestered us to let them move in. There were obvious advantages to their idea but there were also disadvantages that kids in their mid-twenties can seldom see. Sure, we could rent it to them for less than they were paying for their tenement in town, but it would put them an extra fifty miles from school and work. Though the romance of living on the ranch was attractive, the O'Neill place had been set up for occasional summer use only. The hard realities of winter and bringing the place up to truly livable standards were visible only to Jill and me. We knew about the week-long windstorms, the freezing pipes, the clogged septic systems, and the snow-packed roads that had to be traversed. In addition to all of that, we were unsure if we wanted to encourage the kids' dream of ranching life. Jilian and Colton were capable of more affluent, secure, and cosmopolitan lives in friendlier landscapes, and I wanted them to have that chance. It wouldn't be fair to saddle them with the responsibility of hundreds of living things, thousands of acres of breathing grasslands, and an enormous mortgage. I thought back to myself at their age and wondered how my life might have been different had someone held a restraining hand in my face.

In my darker hours I told myself that the kids had only known each other for a year. Their relationship might not survive the hardship and disappointment that I knew was this land's most consistent crop. I barely knew Colton, and a surprisingly paternal protectiveness told me to reserve judgment. The dilemma was this: any man rough enough to thrive on a ranch might well be rougher than I wanted for Jilian.

Jill and I avoided discussing the kids' move to the ranch, until one Sunday afternoon when we happened upon them standing in front of the O'Neill house. Gus and Ace were chasing each other around the homestead and the kids were laughing. They did not see us until our pickup shot past them on the gravel road. When they did, they raised their hands in friendly waves, and we did the same. We covered the quarter-mile to our turn without a word, then turned left and headed down the road toward the river.

We remained silent until I pulled to a stop in front of the house. "I know what you're thinking," I said.

"And I know what you're thinking, too."

"It would be nice to have them around all the time."

"They'd be gone all the time. They have lives—school, work. They have friends in town. They play on softball teams, for crying out loud."

"Look at the bright side. We'd get to take care of Gus and Ace." That thought made Jill smile.

"I love those dogs," she said.

"Of course Jilly wants goats and chickens, too."

"Fresh eggs and goat's milk."

"You ever milk a goat?"

"No, but we milked lots of cows when we were kids."

I laughed. "Then you remember what a pain in the ass it is."

"Yep."

We were still sitting in the pickup when Hank came barking from Erney's apartment. When he saw who it was, he trotted the rest of the way and sat down, waiting for us to get out. "You know they're up there concocting another way to pitch their idea," I said.

"I know. Every time they figure it, they increase their cars' gas mileage."

"They're going to have to get about two hundred miles per gallon for it to make real sense."

"Does any of it make sense?"

I shook my head, and suddenly there was a thump on the driver's side window. When I looked, I came face to face with Hank. His paws were wide against the glass and his face was quite serious. "He's casting his ballot for the kids," Jill said. "That's two against one."

"No," I said. "It's unanimous."

The best definition of success on the Great Plains is the ability to move from one disappointment to the next without losing your enthusiasm. It is not a definition that Peter Binas embraces. He saw the first stage of success as doubling our business that first year and he didn't plan to be disappointed. Jill and I went along, buoyed by enthusiasm more than true belief. I'd sometimes lay in bed, fuzzily thinking about exactly what "doubling the business" meant. Even if we sold twice as much buffalo meat as the year before, what if our expenses went up by three times? What if they rose by four or five times? Is it possible to double your business and lose even more money than you did the year before?

Our expenses were going up like crazy. The rent and utilities had shot up with the advent of the processing plant. We had a line of credit at the bank for buying other people's buffalo. Diesel fuel for the SHA truck was at an all-time high. But the column on Peter's spread sheet labeled Labor was the most sobering. By Christmas of that first year we had nine people working for us—three in the front office, four in the processing plant, and two who worked mostly with SHA. We wanted to pay everyone a fair wage, so paid more than comparable jobs in our area. Jill worked out a bonus system that was supposed to encourage efficiency and stimulate more production.

Jill and I thought the bonus system was a great idea because, had it been offered to us, it would have encouraged us to be more productive. But many of our employees did not seem to be motivated by money. Some of the guys in the plant would be gone for two days after they were paid. If we gave them a dollar raise in the hope that their attendance would improve, they instead took three days off after payday. There seemed to be more deaths in their families than I had family members. Cars failed to start. Childcare was sketchy. Drinking and substance abuse was common. Jill had experience with kitchen help, but during this first exposure to the world of meat cutters we went through half a dozen employees quickly. Many of them were transient and had worked in many plants over the years. We found out quickly that some were skilled and dependable and others were dangerous and couldn't be counted on. Many of the applicants had worked with our employees at other plants in South Dakota, Iowa, or Nebraska. Each one had a reputation in the industry and we would ask around about them. Sometimes family connections or jealousies would color an employee's recommendations. We learned that the only way to be sure about a particular person was to give him or her a try, so there was always a position or two in rotation.

That put pressure on Jill and Jilian. There were a lot of days when they were shorthanded and found themselves in the back room, helping to cut meat or pack boxes. This meant their work in the office was left until all the meat was cut and packaged, the plant was scrubbed down and disinfected, and every FedEx box was safely on the truck and heading for the airport. It made for very long days and, as the Christmas season approached, the days got even longer.

The orders came in at an increasing pace, and November of that year shattered the all-time monthly record by a percentage that impressed even Peter. In December, Colton and I were pressed into service as builders of boxes and packers of meat. Luckily, Colton was on Christmas break from college and I could let my work slide.

By the last week of shipping before Christmas, everyone was working overtime and we were calling out for pizzas and Chinese food.

The last day of shipping orders that can be guaranteed to arrive by Christmas Day has always been the craziest day in the Wild Idea year. In those early years, Jill would manage to pack and ship fifty boxes. But that year we shipped 102 orders and darn near met Peter's sales goals.

After the last FedEx truck had pulled away from the dock, everyone sat around the shipping room, collapsing into chairs or onto the floor, while I mixed a monster batch of rum punch. "Damn," Jilian said. "I thought we were going to make Peter's year-end goal."

Jill was sampling the punch and adding more rum. She was smiling and I thought it was because the rum was perfect. But she was thinking about those sales goals. "We can do it," she said. When we looked, she smiled even more broadly. "We still have four days before New Year's. Everyone needs to be here bright and early on the twenty-sixth. We can make it!"

Jilian and Colton moved to the O'Neill house early in the spring and immediately went to work making it their own. Even though the furniture and decorative touches had come from second-hand stores, it was better stuff than they had had in their basement apartment, so move-in day mostly involved moving their clothes, books, and personal things. The bulk of the work went into fencing the yard for Gus and Ace, establishing a new garden plot, and cleaning up the two outbuildings. Colton put together a little workshop in one and Jilian built a chicken coop in the other. She planned to go into the farm-fresh egg business and bought a dozen chicks that she turned over to Erney to raise up while they worked on the hen house.

I helped Erney set up a small wire enclosure in the corner of the barn. We hung a heat lamp from the ceiling, spread some straw on the floor, and filled a feeder and a small red water trough that screwed onto a quart jar. When we turned the chicks loose they ran around like nitwits, reveling in what must have seemed like incredible freedom after spending the first week of their lives in a cardboard box indoors at Jilian and Colton's apartment.

The kids were at work or school and Erney and I were watching Gus and Ace. They sat between us, and we all watched the chicks running around, exploring their new digs. "I'm surprised those dogs don't try to get them chickens," Erney said.

"They've known those chickens since the day after they hatched. Besides, those are the two mellowest dogs I've ever known."

Erney was skeptical. "They're still dogs," he said. "And a chicken is a chicken. Natural prey for a dog."

"Not these two." I reached out and petted them both on the head. "They're just like people."

Erney shook his head. "I've taken care of chickens ever since I was old enough to walk, and there are a thousand different varmints that eat chickens. Hawks and owls and skunks and raccoon and weasels and snakes. They all live around here."

"Yeah, but not these guys." Erney looked at Gus and Ace as they sat there between us like total equals.

"They're big enough to eat buffalo," Erney said.

"They're pacifist."

Erney nodded and stretched his good hand out to give them both a scratch behind the ears. "I got to admit," he said, "they're easygoing. But I learned a long time ago that it doesn't pay to bet on a chicken. Guess that's something that the kids are going to have to learn."

"They're going to learn a lot by living up in that shack. It's going to be hot in the summer and cold in the winter."

Erney shrugged. "That's the way it is."

"Yeah, but there's no insulation in that house. They have an electric space heater in the bathroom and a wood-burning stove for the rest of the house. They're going to freeze their butts off."

"Oh hell, Dan'l, kids are tough. That'll be good for them." We both smiled, remembering the first place that we ever lived together. "That's all *we* had. Remember those mornings we'd wake up and the dirty dishes would be frozen in the sink? Mice floatin' around in the cistern? Falcons perched on the bookcases? God-damn, those were good times."

I couldn't disagree. That house was rougher than the O'Neill place. There wasn't even an indoor toilet when we moved in. We had jobs, books, and total access to the out-of-doors. I slept a straight eight hours every night—then woke up quick and jumped out of bed every morning.

There is something about the outside of a horse that is good for the inside of a man. Nobody knows who first said that, but it has been repeated thousands of times by people who have understood the truth in it. That feeling comes upon me strongly in the spring of the year when the horses come in from their winter pastures and stand close to the house like visiting gods with winter hair beginning to shed and wild, winter-deep eyes staring straight into mine.

That spring there was a strange nuance in the feeling I got from the horses. It was the first time I had seen Camo up close since he bucked me off in November. The limp in my gait had lessened but the ribs still bothered me at night. He stood with his pasture mates—Roany, Brown, Blacky, and Colton's horse, Bade. Camo was the youngest of the bunch and had buddied up with Bade. Roany and Brown were older but still had some fire in them. Old Blacky had barely made it through the winter. I rubbed his ancient, graying head and then all the others in order of age. When I came to Camo, I hesitated. He was just three years old. If he were human he would be a teenager—the kind that stays up all night, drives cars too fast, and attracts us in spite of ourselves. I would have to get back on him eventually and I was scared stiff. He, too, must have felt that our relationship had changed. Perhaps he didn't trust me either. His eyes rolled with uncertainty as I ran my hands over his back, withers, rump, legs, and finally neck and face. He'd put on a hundred pounds over the winter. He had scabs and was missing hair from where he had battled his pasturemates. Over the winter he had fought his way to the top of the pecking order. After he had been tied to the corral fence for a half-hour I picked up his feet. The tension was draining out of him as he stood tied to the fence but I was not ready to hop aboard. I chased the other horses into another pen and snapped a twenty-foot-long line to Camo's halter. I stood in the center of the corral, and when I clucked to him, he began to circle me in a high-headed trot. I was still sacred of him, but being at the center of his circles, I began to feel better

For a week I had been gathering buffalo from their huge winter pasture on the east side of the Cheyenne River. That time of year brings thousands of migrating cranes overhead and small bands of buffalo back to the west side of the river from miles away. Like the horses, all winter the buffalo had been scattered to rough country, where they had found good grazing in the hills and canyons along Big Corral Draw and Indian Creek. Some of them had not seen or been seen by a human for five months. In years past, Gervase had helped me bring them in, but that year Colton was my right-hand man. He was learning the lay of the land, how to get home from six miles out in the badlands, and how best to steer a group of twenty buffalo the entire distance.

During the last week in March, Colton had a couple days off from school and we found two dozen buffalo in almost the same place I had found a group the day before. Jill's son, Lucas, drove us the twenty-five miles to unload our ATV on the edge of Badlands National Park, where we could make a sweep back to the ranch house. We located the buffalo on a rugged hillside miles from the nearest road or building, and pointed them toward the west. There was no racing around, hollering, or waving of arms. We idled back and forth on the opposite side of the buffalo from where we wanted them to go. After awhile they moved away and we followed. When the buffalo went into country too rough for the ATV, Colton got off and walked behind them while I swung around the rough spots to where I could pick him up behind the herd. For three miles we moved like that, through nearly impossible crumbling cliffs relieved by charming basins of grass where the buffalo would stop to graze. We turned the ATV off. The sun was warm and we could hear the buffalo chewing as they have done for thousands of years. All day long we experienced scenes and sensations that have seldom been witnessed since before white men came into that country.

The day before, it had taken eight hours to bring a small herd back to the ranch, and this group followed a similar path. We saw antelope mixing in and out of the herd, eagles flying overhead, prairie dogs barking at us from the lips of their mounds, and burrowing owls bobbing their heads. Hour upon hour we watched the buffalo, and all the while I watched Colton. He was under a lot of pressure. Finals week was drawing near, he and Jilian were barely into the O'Neill place, and he'd been doing double duty—landscaping and building a fence for Gus and Ace and helping me every spare moment. He looked tired, but the landscape and the moving buffalo drew his attention and his instincts seemed to sharpen.

I told him what I could about the buffalo and the land. I showed him how a herd of buffalo could be moved from a hundred yards away simply by moving slowly. We plucked grasses as we idled along and held the seed heads up between us to identify them. We saw no men and no sign of men. Most of the day we were within a few yards of the grazing buffalo and we came to know each one by its shape or personality. The oldest female, who we called Granny, was usually in the lead. I had known her since she was a calf and she knew where she was going. Behind her came a string of younger cows that could have been her daughters. There were a few yellow-tagged yearling bulls and heifers that we had bought from the Pine Ridge Reservation. Last year's calves ran around, playing with whoever was friendly and staying out of the way of those who were grumpy. The last buffalo in line we nicknamed Mud Face. Her forehead was covered with white crusted badlands mud that dried to a powder by the time we were three-quarters of the way home.

Colton's blue eyes grew sharp and piercing. He could light things up when he smiled. But sometimes his forehead wrinkled, he looked older than his years, and the internal tension was obvious. I watched from the corner of my eye. The wrinkles eased as we followed the buffalo to the last hill before the ranch house came into view. I had passed this way the day before, and on the slope a quarter-mile ahead

I had stumbled onto something that Colton might want to see. The buffalo seemed to read my mind and altered their path just enough to find the hillside where I had found grass that was grazed oddly short and the ground was strewn with bird droppings and feathers. It was a large mating ground for sharp-tailed grouse, a place where the males from miles around gather in the early mornings and late afternoons to attract a mate. Their little feet pound the prairie tens of thousands of times in a dance intense enough to flatten the vegetation. The sun was still high, so I didn't expect to find any grouse present, but as we passed over the dancing ground, I wanted to see if Colton would notice that this hilltop was a special place.

The buffalo went right to the spot. They lowered their heads and began to graze on the short grasses. We moved very slowly into the herd and Colton's eyes immediately cast to the ground below. "Feathers," he said. The world went silent when I stopped the ATV and turned to watched him. He knew that something was different, and I saw a look of understanding come over his face. As if on cue, a male sharp-tail fluttered in and settled between two buffalo. Colton did not look at me. He was looking out over the Cheyenne River. "This is a dancing ground," he said.

There was no reason for me to respond. I glanced sideways at his smooth young face, and then followed his gaze out through the buffalo to the horizon. The animals were beginning to lie down and roll on the dancing ground. The single grouse was not disturbed. He stretched out his wings and practiced a little two-step in preparation for the late afternoon, when the females would show up.

Jill and Jilian planned to grill steaks at the O'Neill place that evening. It was the first time the kids had entertained, and Jill and I were honored to be their first invited guests. It was late when Colton and I got the little herd of buffalo to the summer pasture and Colton was anxious to get home and help Jilian. The ATV had barely rolled to a stop when he jumped into his battered Dodge half-ton and roared up the hill. I was tired but had to turn the horses out of the corral before I could head over for dinner.

When I opened the gate the horses filed out: Roany first, then

Brown, and old Blacky. Bade and Camo followed. But Camo stopped at the gate and stared at me. The other horses were grazing just fifty feet into the pasture. I looked at the sun and found that I had plenty of time, so I pulled the halter off the corral rail and slipped it onto Camo's head. I led him to the tack room, exchanged the halter for a bridle, and saddled him up. I snapped the line onto the bit and clucked to him the same way I had earlier that morning. He started around me at a walk and when I clucked again he broke into a trot. We reversed direction and he moved out nicely from walk, to trot, to lope. When I asked him to whoa, he stopped dead in his tracks, and I walked to him and rubbed his face. A tiny trace of sweat showed behind his ears and when I petted his neck it also felt damp.

Then something came over me and I unsnapped the rope and tightened the girth. I led him out of the corral, raised my foot to the stirrup, and swung up into the saddle. We both stood still for a few seconds, then I touched his sides with my heels and we started up the hill for dinner at the O'Neill place.

Fifteen

THERE IS A 320-ACRE PORTION OF PASTURE THAT WAS A wheat field for a period of perhaps two decades before we moved to the Cheyenne River Ranch. In one of the first rounds of a government program to take wheat land out of production, this parcel had been plowed up and planted back to grass. Whoever owned that little piece of pasture at the time got paid for not growing wheat. The idea was to reduce the acres of land devoted to wheat in order to raise the price for everybody else. The secondary purpose of the program was to give wildlife—the ground nesting birds, deer, antelope, and other critters—a safe place to live and raise their young. The 320 acres on the Cheyenne River Ranch was retired from the government program years before we bought the place, but it is still the best place to find sharp-tailed grouse.

Erney conditioned the dogs at least three days a week during the month of August. I got up early enough to help him harness them to the roading chains. They set out with the joy of Malamutes and by the time Oscar was tamed down from his time in the molting chamber, the young dogs were pulling hard for five miles without a rest and even Hank and Tootsie were as fit as athletes. I watched Erney take them up the hill that leads to the flat ground on top. He moved slowly because he didn't trust himself to steer the ATV at a pace any faster than a crawl. It was the perfect speed for roading dogs, and as soon as he got to the first pasture he turned slowly into the open gate. I tried to be around when they returned so I could help him unharness the dogs but it wasn't long before Erney could unsnap the harnesses using a locking wrench without my help.

Some days he would swing through the O'Neill place and cause a commotion with Gus, Ace, and the growing flock of chickens. Erney would give the dogs a break in the thin shade of the elm trees. It was usually well before seven o'clock in the morning, so Jilian and Colton were often not at work yet. They would help Erney water the dogs and reassure the chickens that the strangers were not chicken eaters. Gus and Ace always wanted to go with the pack and occasionally they showed up at our house along with the rest. They were not in the shape of the professionals and their tongues lolled like wet laundry on a clothesline. All the dogs would jump into the stock tank and stand neck deep with silly, pleased-dog smiles on their faces. Gus and Ace were like high school freshmen who had been allowed to practice with the varsity.

By the first of September I was taking the setters out to the 320 acres and putting a polish on their training. I walked with them individually to make sure that they remembered to pay attention to where I was, to come when called, and to freeze in place when they smelled a grouse. Their job was to find the birds and stand stock still until I was able to get to them. In years gone by, Erney and I would both gently restrain the dog and praise him when he stood still and let the grouse fly away without chasing. But Erney did not want to come out with me. He still had trouble getting into a pickup, he couldn't walk over rough ground, and he probably couldn't hold a dog if it decided to chase the bird. "I'm just not much good, Dan'l."

We had pulled Oscar out of his molting chamber on August 1 as usual. The ancients called this taming process "reclaiming," which happens after the falcon has grown a new set of feathers. During the months of molting, falcons are fed high-quality food and left alone so that the new feathers grow in perfectly. The birds get wild when they are not around people, and it takes a week or two to get them back in the swing of things. We had not hunted with Oscar for almost two years and he was a bit of a handful when we brought him out.

After a couple of weeks of work, the year's first cold front slipped in from Canada and Oscar began to remember his role. The touch of frost was gone with first light, but it was enough to push both falcon and dogs into a different gear. Trixy and Al started running hard and slamming onto their points. Hank ran very big—a quarter-mile was nothing—hitting his points as though the air around him had turned to syrup. He pointed with a low tail, which gave away his European heritage, but he was almost never wrong and would hold birds for an hour. Oscar just kept going higher and higher. Without Erney to help watch, I had to choose to look at either the dog or the falcon and sometimes I ended up losing track of one or both. Sometimes I would give up and simply send Tootsie in to flush. Without someone to help watch, I missed at least half of every flight and could never be sure what had happened.

"Erney, you just have to come out with me."

"I'm useless."

"All you have to do is watch the dog or the falcon."

"I can't walk. No way I can keep up with you guys."

"We'll take the ATV. Follow the dogs with the ATV. You can just sit there."

"Well, I'm pretty good at sitting."

"There you go."

We waited until Oscar was at the perfect weight, which is light enough to really want to catch a grouse but strong enough to be independent and fly high. I didn't worry about the wind because it seldom blew strong in the mornings. I did worry a little about Erney. He kept saying that he couldn't do me any good and I kept telling him that just being out there would do us both good. We put a pair of dog boxes in the back of an ATV and chose Tootsie and Hank for old-time's sake. Just as we were setting out, Jill stepped out of the house to remind me that I had a conference call at nine o'clock. It was still before seven, so I waved away her concern.

A standard 320-acre piece of ground is a mile long and half a mile wide. To hunt it well takes a couple dogs and a good hour of walking. Usually I drive the pickup to the edge of the pasture, pick the bird up on my fist, and turn a setter loose. Erney and I like to hunt downwind. You may miss a few points doing so, but using good dogs that know the game, the grouse they find are between the hunter and the dog's nose. That way, when the flushing dog is sent in, there is a much better chance of the grouse flushing downwind, which makes the falcon's stoop even more spectacular. That was how we started off: Hank casting several hundred yards back and forth and a hundred yards ahead, and Toostie walking at heel. Oscar stood hooded and calm on my fist and Erney idled along behind us.

The grass was about a foot high and the land rolled so that Hank was not always in sight. When he disappeared to the right and did not return in a few minutes, we walked in that direction until he came into view. Once he saw us, he hustled to get to the front. Occasionally I would glance back at Erney to find him smiling as he looked around at the grass and the sky.

We watched Hank cast out to the south and caught a glimpse of him topping a small knoll before he disappeared. I walked slowly in that direction but expected him to show up in front of us and head north. After fifty yards of walking there was still no Hank and I waved Erney to drive up alongside. "Did you see where he went?"

"Just up that-a-way." He pointed to the little knoll that was still a hundred yards away.

"Run up there and see if you can see him. Tootsie and I will keep walking on line."

Erney gave me a little salute and took off after Hank. I was relaxed and had begun to concentrate on the warmth of the Autumn sun on my cheeks when I sensed something and looked up. Erney and the ATV were coming at me at breakneck speed. I jogged to meet him. When we got close enough I saw that he was driving with his good hand and waving the damaged one. His eyes were wild with excitement. "Point!" he yelled. "Point. Point!"

I hopped into the ATV and Tootsie hopped in as well. When we got to the knoll, Erney slowed to a crawl as we came over the crest. Hank stood like a tombstone a hundred yards ahead. What breeze there was came from our backs, and Hank's big square head stretched up into it. When Tootsie saw him she jumped out of the ATV but did not give into her desire to streak for the spot. "Heel, girl."

She came to my side and I started forward. "Can you see everything, Ern?"

"Way better than Animal Planet."

"Just sit there and watch," I said. "Those grouse will likely flush past us and head this way."

"I'm going to be right here."

I removed Oscar's hood. He scanned the field, saw Hank pointing, bobbed his head, and lifted off. As he rose he went ghost-like: a pure white streak familiar to sharp-tails. They see falcons every day and are professionals at escaping them. When they see a falcon on the wing they hunker down and become invisible. They will fly only when they see a chance to out-fly the falcon or when a dog gives them no alternative. The trick is to wait until the falcon is as high as he will get and then send the flusher in when the wind is at the falcon's back.

We took our time as Oscar pumped like a disembodied piston in wide circles that spiraled upward. It is hard to understand how a predator could evolve to be nearly neon white, until you see one flashing up through the thousand-foot level into a powder blue prairie sky with wispy clouds coming between it and the earth. I stood sixty yards upwind of Hank; the grouse were between us. Oscar continued upward. I took my eyes off of him for just a moment to be sure that Erney still saw him. Erney was squinting up in the right direction, and when I looked again it took me a few seconds to find the bird. A microscopic twinkle of silvery wings brought my eyes to the right place, and I knew that the time had arrived. I kept my eyes on Oscar's area of sky and tapped my leg with my right hand. I heard Tootsie come to a sitting position and touched her head with my hand. "Get 'em up," I said.

I heard her take off for Hank. There was a tiny flicker of silver far above and the chuckle of flushing grouse below. It was all I could do to keep my eyes pointed upward. Another few flicks of light and the anchor shape consolidated, accelerated, and began twisting in freefall. The sizzle of wings came to my ears. Then Oscar was coming right at me and I heard the grouse whirr overhead.

There was a puff of feathers and Oscar shot skyward as the grouse tumbled to the ground. He reached his zenith and flipped to spin downward and settle on the grouse halfway between my position and where Erney sat in the ATV. "God damn," I said. Then I turned to call the dogs to me. They came at a sprint and we tumbled into the grass in a pile of laughs and wagging tails.

When we got to Oscar, Erney had driven the ATV to within a few feet. He sat looking down at Oscar as the falcon ceremoniously plucked grouse feathers. Hank and Tootsie lay down, waiting for their cut of the spoils, and I smiled at Erney. "So, what did you think of that?"

He didn't answer right away, and when I looked, I noticed that he was choking up. "Probably the last really good flight I will ever see," he said.

I sat down in the grass with the dogs. The breeze was warm and the grouse feathers that Oscar had plucked drifted into a little wake. Whenever we would get a flight like that in the old days, we would let the bird eat its fill. Sometimes it would take hours. I decided to let all of us—Oscar, the dogs, Erney, and me—enjoy ourselves. I was going to miss the conference call, but it was worth it.

There was a message on our answering machine that had clocked in only minutes before I came into the house from adjusting a gate along the river. Jill and Jilian were at work and I thought that they might be checking to see if I needed anything from town. But when I pressed the button, Colton's excited voice came on. "Hey, we got a fire! If you get this, get up here!"

I was in my pickup and streaking up the hill in seconds, but it seemed to take forever to cover the two miles to the O'Neill place. As soon as I topped the hill I looked for smoke and when I didn't see any, I relaxed a notch. The prairie wasn't on fire and I could see no flames coming out of any of the buildings but I kept moving as fast as the driveway would allow. When I pulled to a halt beside his pickup, I looked up and saw Colton running from the toolshed with an axe in his hand.

Time stopped and I was awash with thoughts of Colton. Only weeks before, he had come down from the O'Neill house and caught me in my office at first light. By the way he fumbled with his work gloves I knew he had something to say. He stood before my desk and wrung the gloves as if they were wet. "Do you have a minute?" he asked.

"Sure." I waved him to a seat and closed the book I'd been reading. "What's up?"

He couldn't bring himself to sit back in the chair. He perched on the front edge and leaned forward. "I've been wanting to talk to you," he said. I had an inkling what this might be about but didn't want to make it easy for him. "I've got something real important to ask you," he said.

I looked at him over my reading glasses. "Yes?"

"I . . ." He tried to look me square in the eyes, but for an instant he flagged and looked down at his gloves. "I . . ." his eyes came back up. ". . . I want to marry Jilian."

It wasn't a surprise. Jill and I had talked it over. But still, it sobered me. "Oh?" I said. "How's Jilian feel about this?"

"She wants to. She knows I'm here. She's waiting to hear what you say."

I think he was hoping for an easy answer, but I disappointed him. "How are you guys going to make a living?"

He was a little scared, but my question firmed him up. "Jilly likes her job at Wild Idea. I'll graduate next year, thinking about graduate school."

I nodded my head that day in my office and I nodded my head when I saw Colton coming across the yard with the axe in his hand. I was out of my pickup before it stopped rolling. "It's starving for oxygen," he yelled. "It burst into flames when I opened the door, but choked down again when I shut it."

Smoke was seeping from every crack in the house, but Colton scaled the porch without a thought. There was a hose hooked up to the hydrant beside the house and I tossed a coil up to him. "Chop a little hole and let's get some water on it." He was through the roof in three whacks and I turned the hydrant to full blast.

In another minute I had a second hose hooked up and was on the roof and taking the axe from Colton. He knelt on the roof trying to direct the stream of water to the hottest spot. Smoke and steam were boiling through the hole. When he looked up, his face was streaked with soot. I had no idea how long he'd been fighting it alone.

In another minute I had my own hole chopped through the roof and lay on that hot metal roof ten feet from Colton. "You call the fire department?" I asked.

"Yeah,"

Then we lay there, feeling the silence of the prairie and the heat mounting below us. There was just the sizzle of water and the occasional spiral fluting of a meadowlark. We listened to hear the sound of the volunteer fire department but time drug on. Colton's eyes met mine. "They didn't make it," he said.

There was the ominous hissing of boiling water below us and I could not understand what Colton meant. "The dogs," he said. "They didn't make it."

"They're in there?"

He shook his head. "No. I got them out."

We didn't speak again until the fire truck pulled into the yard. A neighbor's wife was manning the outfit and with our help, she started to get some water into the house through the front door. The door belched steam and sizzling smoke. By the time the second truck arrived, the fire was nearly out. Colton and I did what we could to help put out the smoldering interior walls, the furniture, and everything that the kids owned. But it was hopeless. The fire had started in a faulty wall plug and the place was a total loss.

I watched him work with the neighbors. He was soaked through with sweat and his clothes were wet and grimy. He was exhausted but still going and, for the first time, I was absolutely sure that I had been right to say "yes" to his request for Jilian's hand. Hours later, as the fire trucks rolled up their hoses, we stood in the sooty, smoky yard and embraced the same way we had that day in my office. But this time there was no holding back. I squeezed him with all my might, and he nearly crushed me with his strong, steady arms.

Perhaps the worst thing about that day was the sound of Jill's wail when she found out that Gus and Ace were dead. It was a sound that I had never heard. It was ancient and primal and shot a shiver down my spine. Some would say that they were only dogs, but on the Great Plains the line between "two-leggeds" and "four-leggeds" is blurred.

The next day Jilian stood fragile as Colton and I lowered the two dogs into a grave beside their favorite waterhole. "Those dogs pulled her through," Jill whispered, as we lay in bed that night. We turned to look at each other and the moon lit our moistened cheeks.

"Colton, too," I said.

We lay staring at the ceiling until the moon moved its brightness north along the west wall of our bedroom. "Now they have each other," Jill said.

I wanted to say that was all any of us really had, but I stayed quiet. Life is tough and both Jill and I knew that we had chosen a particularly difficult place to live our life. But it isn't hard to find people on the Great Plains who have had it much tougher.

We live in the borderlands between fertility and dust, where everything struggles to survive, where progress is slow and civilization staggers a few steps behind. There are the usual effects of drought, blizzards, low wages, racism, and ignorance. We can count on one year in four being too dry to make a profit, winters that kill livestock, no good jobs when we're forced to work in town, condescension if you are Native, and mean spiritedness borne from fear of the future. The serendipity of our catastrophes is numbing—the rancher and his wife who stop to rest their horses in the shade of an over-hanging cliff that collapses and kills the wife, the pickup that goes out of control on a road traveled every day, the gentle old horse that slips at the wrong time, the random lightning strike, the price of beef in Argentina.

The Great Plains is like riding on the wheel well of a fast pickup traveling a rough road. If you don't hold on and sit down you are going to bounce out.If you do sit down, you find that there is no cushioned seat—just your own bony ass between your guts and the cold, hard steel. There are a lot of things that can go wrong and not much leeway for error. It has been that way out here since just after the glaciers receded and it is not likely to change. The people, organisms, and the cultures out here have had to be resilient to every twist of evolution.

In the early winter after the O'Neill house burned down I shot my favorite horse. Blacky was over thirty-five years old. He'd taught me a lot and he'd taught Jill a lot when she took him over fifteen years before that day. The summer had been good and he had gained a few pounds from the lush grass. But he would have never made it through another winter. When the days started to get cold he wouldn't have been able to eat enough to keep from freezing and it was my responsibility to see that he didn't suffer. No one to call, no help on the way. Give him a pan of good clean oats, pet his grizzled-gray head, hold the .357 in the perfect place, and pull the trigger. It is startling how hard a dead horse falls.

The kids stayed with us from October to May, and during that time we struggled to get a house built for them. The O'Neill place wasn't insured for enough to build a decent house because it wasn't worth much. Wild Idea wages allowed us to secure a loan for a modest modular home. Jilian and Colton wanted it on the same piece of ground as the O'Neill house but, from then on it would be called the Jones Place. The wedding was scheduled for June.

The Christmas season at Wild Idea was again record-breaking. Buffalo meat must make good Christmas presents. The income was more than I had dreamed it could be, but so were the expenses. We had to borrow more money, but I never lost heart that it would work out in the end. Things would turn around fast when Wild Idea became profitable. We had to believe that.

We needed to have Christmas-like sales numbers every month of the year. It sounded like a child's daydream, but Peter Binas set exactly that as our goal. We just had to make every month a reason to buy buffalo meat: President's Day, Valentine's Day, Saint Patrick's

Day, Easter, Mother's Day, Beginning of Barbecue Season Day, Fourth of July, Labor Day, End of Barbecue Season Day, Halloween, Thanksgiving. At first I rejected this strategy because it made me feel like how I thought Sam Walton probably felt. I poured my frustrations out to Erney. "It's just not a pleasant way to make a living."

"What? Work? I could have told you that." He smiled and wiggled those eyebrows. "You're just too sensitive. What the hell are you worried about? You're doing a good thing."

"The end doesn't justify the means."

"Failure doesn't justify the means either. Come on, Dan'l, you're not waterboarding people. You're trying to get them to eat good food and take care of the prairie."

In the depths of that winter, with the kids crowded in the basement of our house and the snow lashing down on us, I was able to sleep only sporadically. I dreamed of Sam Walton rolling buffalo carcasses into our cooler, Peter's spreadsheets with hundreds of columns and lines, and the alchemy of Google placement and analytics. I craved the physical work that winter made nearly impossible.

It was good to have the kids around, and we often ate together as we hadn't done for too long. But they longed for a place of their own, and sadness and memories hung in the corners of the rooms like cobwebs. Luckily there was not much time to dwell on the past, because by the end of February, with the first break in the weather, wedding preparations had to be made. I had no experience planning weddings. Though Jill and I had taken nearly ten years to pull the trigger on our own wedding, it was a very simple affair. We picked up the license at the courthouse in Rapid City and met a Unitarian minister at the public library. Jill joked that it had to be held in the nonfiction section. We settled for a beautiful reading room with winter sun filtering through tall windows. Lucas was best man, Jillian was the maid of honor, and Colton was the photographer. With the librarian and a homeless Native man serving as witnessess, we tied the knot in five minutes flat. Jillian's wedding would be different and, though June Ninth was still four months away, once Jill began laying out the tasks, it didn't seem like much time at all.

There is no question: a daughter's marriage marks a generational rebirth, a changing of the guard, the handing off of a baton. But with all the activities—the bridal showers, wedding invitations, dresses, and menus to consider—a lot of that meaning gets lost. We also had a ranch to run, though I suddenly had Colton to help out. Even so, it was a recklessly busy spring. We all pulled together to ready the place for the wedding, but still I was not convinced that the style of the event matched the landscape and our underlying philosophy.

I had trouble understanding what the wedding would be like. I had a picture in my head of people sitting on hay bales with paper plates in their laps, but that was not what Jill and Jilian envisioned. There would be rented silverware, china, and crystal. Jill knew what she wanted even if she could not make me understand. She saw a buffalo ranch wedding as somehow a continuation of the circle of life. She repeated what a Lakota friend had told us years before: "The buffalo and the people are the same. We emerged from the earth together. We depend on each other."

On our ranch we take care of the buffalo because they take care of us. In this sense it seems reasonable to consider us as one entity. I understand how people can come to believe that buffalo come from under the earth. It is a phenomenon of the Great Plains that buffalo herds seem to disappear into the folds of the prairie. I have ridden to a valley where I last saw them, only to find that they are gone. Sometimes they move out of an invisible depression and create the illusion of reappearing right before one's eyes. But I couldn't see how that idiosyncrasy of the Great Plains could help pull the disconnected parts of our wedding together.

My spirits rose when I saw where they planned to have the actual ceremony. They chose the flat top of a finger of land above the Cheyenne River that points off toward the south. It is one of the prettiest spots on the ranch, with a view of miles of untrammeled country that extends to the Pine Ridge Reservation on the south and Badlands National Park on the east. From there you can see the huge pasture where the buffalo spend the winter and a corner of the pasture where they would be on the day of the wedding. They planned a buffalo robe for an altar and both a Lakota Holy Man and an enlightened Christian Minister would officiate.

The day of the wedding was chaotic. We had rented trucks the day before and hauled chairs and tables. We made another run to the rental store that morning for tablecloths, candelabras, flatware, and china. The catering staff was set up both in the house and in an outdoor kitchen under the deck. The bridesmaids and the groomsmen had been out the night before, but they showed up and pitched in. The girls were put to making placecards and the boys joined me decorating the machine shop with green cottonwood boughs and strings of sparkling lights. They were all in their twenties, capable, and clear-eyed—despite the lingering effects of the bachelor party. With Colton and Lucas as their leaders, they were the kind of young people that it felt right to have on the ranch.

Jill and I were the last to get dressed. We retreated into our bedroom and jumped from sweatpants to the fitting attire of parents of the bride. I chose a classic black tuxedo and Jill wore a fitted, strapless, lacy brown dress. We smiled at each other but there was no time for more than a quick hug. The bridesmaids were waiting for me in the bed of a borrowed hotrod pickup and Jill rushed up the hill to where the head usher waited in the buffalo grass behind the guests. They all sat mesmerized by the view of the Cheyenne River. We pulled up behind Jill and I watched as she took the usher's arm and descended the grassy aisle as the music began. I stood in the rear with the bridesmaids and Jilian. Her golden hair and brilliant white dress glittered in the sun and she clung to my arm in a way that melted my heart.

Jill had been adamant that this part of the ceremony come off in a certain way. The groomsmen were somewhere off-stage but I had seen them earlier. They were dressed in beige western-cut suits that made them look even taller and bolder than they were. The first song was coming to an end and I was afraid that the guests might turn away from the river valley to look at the bridesmaids before the groomsmen were in their places. But, suddenly, in the far distance, buffalo appeared and all eyes went to them. A guitar and violin started up like apair of meadowlarks. The buffalo continued to come but suddenly they dipped out of sight—back into the earth. The music went bravely on without the buffalo. Appearing in their place came those tall, elegant boys. They rose up from below and into the sunlight as if for the first time. The music shifted and the bridesmaids moved to join with the boys.

Finally the music changed again and all eyes swung to Jilly and me. She squeezed my arm and I guided her down the aisle through our family and friends. I caught Jill's eyes as Jilian stopped to kiss her. She was teary but beautiful and I had to look away. My job was to deliver Jilian to Colton's side and I managed it. I shook Colton's hand and felt tears flood my eyes as Jilly stretched up to kiss my cheek. I had to look past her to maintain my composure. The guests were watching the kids but my eyes were fixed on the near horizon, so I was the only one to see the herd of buffalo reappear. They lined up solemnly on the rugged hillside. They were still shaggy with spring shedding and I could see their gentle black eyes and shiny horns. They had come with a purpose.

PREVIOUS WORKS BY THE AUTHOR

NOVELS

Brendan Prairie
Center of the Nation
The Contract Surgeon
The Indian Agent
Spirit of the Hills
Stolen Horses

SHORT STORIES

Eminent Domain

NONFICTION

Buffalo for the Broken Heart—Restoring Life to a Black Hills Ranch
Equinox—Life, Love, and Birds of Prey
Great Plains—America's Lingering Wild with Michael Forsberg
The Rites of Autumn—A Falconers Journey Across the American West